WISHING you much
ENGAGEMENT

Ruth Passweg

Praise for

Predicting Market Success

"Brand marketing is at a crossroads, and Robert Passikoff shows the way to the future—shattering conventional branding wisdom with one hand, and giving actionable advice with the other. *Predicting Market Success* delivers the key ingredients for breakthrough marketing strategies: a clear-headed understanding of brands, and a predictive approach to measuring them."

Marc E. Babej
President, Reason, Inc.

"In the newly created world of utility deregulation, companies like KeySpan need to be able to differentiate themselves from their competitors. *Predicting Market Success* provides an easy to understand manual for applying engagement metrics to the brand, and defining what values create differentiation to create a successful brand platform for success."

Bob Catell
Chairman & CEO, KeySpan Energy

"Managers who cannot accurately measure and predict the performance of their brands cannot succeed. They are doomed to failure. This book provides an excellent road map with proven measurement tools. If managers follow it, they will not just succeed, they will dominate their competition."

Larry Chiagouris, PhD
Associate Professor of Marketing,
Lubin School of Business, Pace University

"In a world where any marketer's most important skill is dealing with constant change, Robert Passikoff is consistently the best signpost for what will happen next. His book will help marketers be more nimble and more purposeful in our nimbleness. Robert Passikoff has a well-established reputation as the guru of loyalty. By sharing his methods and insights, he offers all marketers a chance for engagement enlightenment."

Scott Deaver
Executive VP Marketing, Cendant Car Rental Group

"Robert Passikoff comes as close to understanding how brands can profitably differentiate themselves in an increasingly commoditized world as anyone we've ever known. His data is clear, the measures concise, and his findings totally actionable. He is our resource of choice for the most complex branding assignments we undertake."

Joe Dell'Aquila
Managing Partner, Continental Consulting

"Think of customer loyalty as the air that viable brands must breathe in order to survive. Then think of Robert's customer loyalty metrics as a brand's life support system."

Leonard Eber
CEO, Karen Neuberger

"Robert Passikoff's single-minded approach to life and his amazing Brand Keys invention takes much of the uncertainty out of making tough marketing decisions. It's a predictive tool that works. Putting your money on a 95 percent sure thing as part of the process, is just common sense. Following Robert's advice is a staggeringly obvious 'no-brainer.' Reading *Predicting Market Success* will help all of us do what we do better."

Ray Hanks
Regional Business Advisor, Creative Industries, U.K.

"There is no more important category to understand a consumer's emotional bond than in the automotive segment. All decisions are emotional with a rational component, with each component rarely defined in proportion and perspective. Brand Keys does this with true insight and accuracy and quantifies this critical intelligence for actionable planning."

Kevin Kitagawa
SVP Dentsu, Latin America

"*Predicting Market Success* is a 'must read' for marketers who want their brands or their companies to survive—and thrive—in a cluttered and chaotic marketplace. Dr. Robert Passikoff, a pioneer in customer loyalty research, shows how to get beyond what consumers say to learn what is unsaid—the true, unspoken feelings that shape how people view brands, categories, and companies and ultimately make buying decisions. The insights contained in this book will help you improve the power and effectiveness of your communications, re-energize your brand, and build and maintain a bulletproof corporate reputation."

George McGrath
President, McGrath Matter Public Relations

"Robert Passikoff is one of the most thoughtful and practical researchers on the planet. His insights into how public relations builds brand engagement go well beyond the typical rear-view mirror research common today. These methods are predictive. He can tell you what's going to work before you spend the budget. If you want your brand to succeed, read this book."

Tom Nicholson
VP Public Affairs, HSBC North America

"Robert Passikoff not only successfully argues that twenty-first century consumers are much more savvy about their brand choices and identifies loyalty as the real battleground for brand marketers in the future, but provides the research weapons with which to arm yourself. For the first time, a truly predictive weapon with which to win the brand loyalty war. Read, learn, and be thankful!!"

Kerry O'Connor
Mirror Group Newspapers, U.K.

"Loyalty is the single most important factor in determining the depth and longevity of any customer relationship. Loyalty is the key determinant of profitability—nothing else even comes close. Yet for something so important, surprisingly few do it well. We have little control over risk and no way to manage it, until we measure it—and measure it accurately. The techniques and approaches in this book represent the leading edge of customer loyalty measurement—making this a must read."

Barry Sheehy
Founder, CPC Econometrics

"Success in this crowded and competitive consumer marketplace comes to those brands that understand what drives customer loyalty. These unspoken motivators are difficult to quantify which is why Brand Keys is so valuable. Passikoff's Brand Keys helped us develop metrics with which we can compare advertiser brand loyalty effectiveness across various cable networks. The results of this study proved the value of our networks in enhancing the brand image of our advertisers and resulted in new and increased share of business."

Charlene Weisler
SVP Research, Rainbow Media

"In a business landscape getting cluttered with watered-down product differentiation and commoditized brands, marketers are quickly realizing that fact-to-face events create a bond with customers that no media can break.

Robert Passikoff and Brand Keys have pulled the curtain back and showed us the power of developing loyalty metrics that brand marketers can take to the bank."

Dan Hanover
Editor & Publisher, *Event Marketer Magazine*

"In this postinformation age world, it is tragic that so many companies rely on old, dated preinformation age sources of brand tracking data. It's about time they learned about Robert Passikoff's Brand Keys approach to tracking consumer brand loyalty. Measuring brand loyalty, not just brand awareness and usage, is key for consumer product companies that want to get out ahead of the competition and take control of the future of their brands. Robert's new book provides essential insights for companies to manage their brands better."

Pam Danziger
President, Unity Marketing

"Loyalty is not about being complacent with the past; it's about being proactive and predictive about the future. This book shows the way forward."

Joseph Jaffe
President & Founder, jaffe, L.L.C.

"Internationally acclaimed, Dr. Robert Passikoff, pushes aside today's systematic malaise of data-heavy marketing methodologies to reveal a clear-cut path toward pinpoint accuracy in defining and building brand success. *Predicting Market Success,* is no book on theory, but an insider's look at the Brand Keys approach to measuring customer loyalty—very possibly the GPS of twenty-first century brand marketing navigation. Passikoff punches through the ponderous, carpet-bomb, marketing mantras that beleaguer corporate America today in one book with a shelf life that will most assuredly be measured in decades."

Timothy R. Laurence
CEO, Richards Laurence Communications Inc.,
Toronto, Canada

Predicting Market Success

New Ways to Measure Customer Loyalty and Engage Consumers with Your Brand

ROBERT PASSIKOFF, PHD

WILEY

John Wiley & Sons, Inc.

Published by John Wiley & Sons, Inc., Hoboken, New Jersey.
Published simultaneously in Canada.

For general information on our other products and services or for technical support, please contact our Customer Care Department within the United States at (800) 762-2974, outside the United States at (317) 572-3993 or fax (317) 572-4002.

Wiley also publishes its books in a variety of electronic formats. Some content that appears in print may not be available in electronic books. For more information about Wiley products, visit our web site at www.wiley.com.

'Have You Stopped Beating Your Wife' Extract from YES PRIME MINISTER © Antony Jay & Jonathan Lynn. Copyright agent: Alan Brodie Representation Ltd., 6th floor, Fairgate House, 78 New Oxford Street, London WC1A 1HB info@alanbrodie.com. Reprinted with permission.

Library of Congress Cataloging-in-Publication Data:

Passikoff, Robert, 1948–
  Predicting market success : new ways to measure customer loyalty and engage consumers with your brand / Robert Passikoff.
       p.   cm.
   Includes index.
   ISBN-13: 978-0-470-04022-5 (cloth)
   ISBN-10: 0-470-04022-X (cloth)
    1. Customer loyalty.   I. Title.
   HF5415.525.P37   2006
   658.8'343—dc22

                                                                              2006014656

Printed in the United States of America.

10 9 8 7 6 5 4 3 2 1

Dedicated to my why and wherefore,
my cause and effect—my family.
Who never, ever have to thank me
for coming home at night!

CONTENTS

Foreword   xi
  Jack Trout

Acknowledgments   xiii

**Introduction: Why the Four P's No Longer Work
and the Three Words (Including Loyalty) That Took
Their Place**   1

Chapter 1
Why Marketers Can't Predict Customer Behavior—
  Whoops, Now They Can   15

Chapter 2
From Brand Guessing to Brand Building: How to Profitably
  Engage Your Customer   28

Chapter 3
How to Measure Customer Values, Expectations, and Loyalty   58

Chapter 4
Loyalty Is 70 Percent Emotional: An Emotional Bond Engages
  Customers and Makes Money   88

Chapter 5
Easy-to-Implement Customer Loyalty Metrics: How to
  Supercharge Traditional Research and Marketing   111

Chapter 6
The Four Proven Drivers of Customer Loyalty:
  A Category-by-Category Exposé   152

Chapter 7
The Power of Human and Celebrity-Based Brands: When
　It Works, When It's Wasted　175

Chapter 8
The Future of Branding　207

Conclusion　228

Epilogue　232
　Don E. Schultz, PhD

Index　235

FOREWORD

by Jack Trout

They promise me miracles, magic, and hope, but somehow it always turns out to be soap.

> —*Allan Sherman (last line of "Chim Chim Cheree," parody on his album* My Son, the Greatest*)*

It's become a lot tougher for marketers to differentiate their brands and engage consumers. With smarter customers, and more competition, there is no shortage of companies slipping from glory days to grueling days. The truth is, it's going to get even tougher. My own books, *Positioning, The 22 Immutable Laws of Marketing,* and *Differentiate or Die,* were written to help marketers recognize the key issue they needed to address: creating the right differentiating strategy.

Robert Passikoff has pioneered a method for helping marketers create an effective differentiating strategy, based on customer loyalty research. Now it's captured in a book. If you read and apply *Predicting Market Success,* you will be able to measure the values and expectations of your customers, and more important, you will know whether your next marketing/branding campaign will succeed or fail, because you will be able to *predict* how customers will respond. There is an elegant, effective simplicity in Robert's method.

A good example of values-based differentiation is the tag line I created for Papa John's Pizza: *"Better ingredients, Better pizza"*® which acts as a powerful differentiator for a brand in a highly competitive category. Papa John's ongoing success with this strategy is substantiated year after year by winning the *Brandweek* magazine Customer Loyalty Award (which is powered by Robert's own Brand Keys measurement system). This is just one example of how, if you know which customer values really count, you can rally your whole team to create an extraordinarily successful brand platform. Take a look in this book at the results of Robert's Brand Keys *Customer Loyalty Index*® for your product category if you want proof that differentiated positioning and loyalty lead to increased market share and increased profits.

Many modern branding difficulties are the result of companies relying on legacy research tools that measure customer attitudes but are lousy at predicting customer behavior. The problem is that people talk one way in an interview and behave differently when it comes time to actually make a purchase. Mark Twain put it perfectly when he said you don't get the truth until people are dead—and dead a long time. The best marketing research combines the traditional, rational measures with customers' emotional perceptions of the category and the brand. This requires building customer loyalty metrics into any research and capturing real emotional perceptions and deep brand insights—techniques pioneered by Robert and described in this book. Miss that and you miss out on the perceived strengths and weaknesses, and what strategic opportunities exist in the mind of the target group of consumers. In short, you may miss out on the key customer insights that will lead you to make the soundest strategic brand decisions with the greatest measurable return.

In my book *Big Brands, Big Trouble,* I wrote that "big trouble isn't easy to fix." Customer loyalty metrics are a powerful navigational aid to keep your brand, and profits, off the rocks and out of big trouble in the first place. They are predictive, and they are preventative. If anyone still has any doubts, see how far out Robert was able to predict the rise, and fall, of brand titans the likes of Coke, AT&T, Kmart, Krispy Kreme, even the most famous of what he calls *human brands,* Martha Stewart. Understanding and applying a new generation of customer loyalty metrics will help you to successfully differentiate your brand. It's a pretty simple idea once you put your mind to it.

ACKNOWLEDGMENTS

This book is the result of a process that was developed and nurtured over a long period of time. Many people made significant contributions that got us to this point, and the book would be incomplete without such an admission. So my thanks to the following "collaborators," starting from our very earliest days:

Kerry O'Connor, who provided "Bundles from Britain" in the form of substantive support, stationery, and enthusiasm when we needed it most. Without him, there would be no Brand Keys. To Paul Kaplan who knew about computers and computer simulations when virtually nobody knew about computers and computer simulations. And to Len Stein of Visibility Public Relations, who made us more famous than we ought to have been so early on.

Peter Boyko and Bill Callahan who for the past 22 years have seamlessly allowed the statement "the research goes out, and the research comes back" to have been made in complete honesty.

The Brand Keys Brain Trust; Steve Hunter and Charles Karmiol, who knew all about creative, Jack Trout, who knew all about positioning, Lisette Berry, who knew all about statistics, George Javornik, who knew about TQM and strategic dashboards, and Tom McCann, who quite literally knew about everything else, whenever we needed it.

Our loyal clients, whose faith and trust allowed us to jump light-years in the development of the postmodern, customer-loyalty engagement model and its applications. But five in particular: Joe Dell'Aquila formerly of American General, Al Gerber of KeySpan, Manuel Gutierrez of Kohler, Bruce Leonard of Leonard/Monahan fame, and Charlene Weisler of Rainbow Media.

Michael Lefkowitz, our smart financial guy and the best unofficial clipping service in the world, my agent Nat Sobel (to whom I hope I kept my promise about not being a pain), and my editor, Richard Narramore, whose invaluable skill helped us to separate the loyalty wheat from the research chaff.

Dean Christopher, writer, essayist, word magician, and our Los Angeles General Manager—one of the most talented and insightful brand strategists of our time. Only he knows how much we owe him for our success.

Finally, to the Brand Keys team of Marilyn Davis, Pam Batalis, Gary A. Chalus, and Gabriella Warburton, who are living proof that *nothing* is impossible for the man who doesn't actually have to do it himself.

Introduction:
Why the Four P's No Longer Work and the Three Words (Including Loyalty) That Took Their Place

Three little words, oh what I'd give for that wonderful phrase.

—*Bert Kalmer ("Three Little Words")*

Understanding the customer loyalty metrics for your category and brand makes the difference between having an iron foundation and pillars of clay supporting your brand—no matter how clever, novel, popular, or cash positive you might be. The good news is that loyalty is understandable. The better news is it can be quantified and predicted, maybe even more easily modeled than interest rates or global warming. My goal is to teach you not just 20/20 hindsight but 20/20 foresight, so that you can predict both customers' loyalty to your brand and how customers will respond to your next marketing campaign.

Conventional wisdom teaches that wise men learn from their mistakes, and exceptional people learn from other people's mistakes. This book deals with an even higher order of learning: Learning how to avoid mistakes in the first place. My goal is to show that modern customer loyalty metrics are the most effective way to predict success, customer engagement, and profitability.

We desperately need customer loyalty metrics because so many brands are in crisis. Few brands have the luxury of hit-or-miss experimentation. Absolut is a typical example of a brand in crisis. Absolut is one of the most iconic brands in the world—yet it is feeling the loyalty pinch as new brands and flavors flood the market. With more than 100 vodkas recently launched in the United States alone, Absolut's share in the market is down from 58 percent to 36.5 percent. Clearly Absolut's problem is not a lack of awareness among vodka consumers, or any consumers, for that matter. It established its presence a long time ago. Neither is the problem an issue of a lack of established brand imagery. You don't become an icon with brand imagery that is unclear or disappoints. The problem is, however, an inability (or unwillingness) for the brand to engage consumers by addressing the vodka category driver for which consumers have the highest expectations: "smoothness and mouth-feel."

If you look at the category, you'll find that value has been co-opted by successful entries like Grey Goose, Rain, Ketel One, Skyy, Chopin, and others. All the image advertising in the world won't engage customers when the need is to believably address a functional benefit. But to do that you need to know where customer expectations are high and where your competition is doing a better job meeting them.

Mistakes like that are the result of one factor beyond all other market forces: *the failure of a business to measure, understand, and predict loyalty*—the preferences and expectations of the twenty-first-century, bionic customer. Add customer loyalty metrics to your marketing toolbox and you virtually ensure brand profitability. Ignore loyalty metrics and you'll find yourself in trouble—and more suddenly than gradually.

Part of the problem is that many marketers and brand managers are stuck on a model that no longer works very well: the four P's. You know, those letters from your old marketing texts that stood for *Product* (the stuff being sold), *Price* (the cost of stuff being sold), *Place* (where the stuff is available), and *Promotion* (marketing and advertising communications for the stuff).

Today, three C's have taken the place of the past century's four P's:

1. Customer engagement
2. Customer expectations
3. Customer loyalty

Engagement and expectations are both integral parts of customer loyalty.

This book is about customer loyalty—how to understand it today and tomorrow. We live in a world with more brands, more choice, and more information than ever before, and there is no turning back to the good old days. The four-P's marketing approach espoused the theory, that *if* you could manage one or more of the P's better than the competition, your product or service would actually be preferred by more consumers and, therefore, more profitable. That was then. A number of widespread initiatives conspired to come together to dramatically change that playing field making the four P's moot.

Some companies realized that if they just tried a little bit harder—if they actually *satisfied* the customer—it would give them a market advantage. So, they tried harder. It turned out that consumers were actually willing to pay for service. Then, marketers realized that if their products were demonstrably better than the competition, they would have something to advertise that would differentiate them from the competition. That ushered in the Total Quality Movement. But if you *were* going to provide quality products and services you had to be able to create them in a high-quality and a time- and cost-effective-fashion. Enter Process Re-Engineering. Finally, as things seemed to be humming along pretty well, the companies rightsized (or downsized) their workforce—the name of the initiative dependent on which side of the desk you were sitting when it was introduced.

THE FOUR BIG REALIZATIONS

This convergence of marketing, production, and satisfaction initiatives produced a large set of companies all of whom were doing it right. Not different or differentiating, just doing it right. Customers eventually realized that:

- The *Products* (i.e., services) were all basically the same.
- The *Places* (i.e., distribution) were ubiquitous—for virtually everything. The Internet has a lot more to answer for than just readily available pornography.
- The *Prices* were competitive (and are becoming more and more so, forcing brands to turn themselves into more commodity-like "stuff").
- The power and control of *Promotion* (i.e., advertising and marketing programs) migrated away from the advertisers and into the hands, hearts, minds, and pocketbooks of the consumers.

So, if the products are the same, and the distribution outlets are the same, and the pricing is extraordinarily competitive, and the consumers have control over the information and persuasion that they allow into their lives—what's a brand to do?

Follow the three C's. First, a brand is going to recognize that today a brand's marketing efforts must *engage* the customer. That means that *any* marketing effort must reinforce the brand's equity and contribute to making the brand stronger—the degree to which the brand is seen (i.e., is judged) as being able to *meet or exceed the expectations that customers hold for the category in which the brand competes.*

Which brings us to *expectations.* That means understanding what consumers *really* want. You need to have expectations that are not constrained by reality but have the kind of sky's-the-limit expectations that identify where the best opportunities lie for your brand. In the past 10 years, customer expectations have increased an average of 27 percent, while brands have only kept up on average by 8 percent. That's an awfully large gap. But the good news is that unfulfilled expectations present an equally large opportunity for a marketer who is positioned to meet those expectations.

And that brings us to the final word of the new marketing triumvirate: *customer loyalty.* In the absence of any significant four-P's competitive advantage, the *only* model available is customer loyalty because it is the only model that identifies expectations and measures engagement. And it has the advantage of being *predictive.* I know because I created a company, Brand Keys, which measures customer loyalty for leading brands. Based on these measures, we can predict customer behavior.

Loyal customers purchase products and services again and again over time and increase the volume of their purchases. Loyal customers will buy beyond traditional purchases, across available product lines, and will refer a company's products and services to others. Loyal customers become immune to the pull of the competition and pricing strategies and are more likely to give a company the benefit of the doubt—six times more likely to do so.

Take a look at companies who have recognized that customer loyalty is a profitable path to follow:

- *Google:* Who among you doesn't have this Internet site bookmarked on your computer or available on virtually every other site? In August 2004, when it went public, Google's stock was at $85. In early 2006, its value had increased by 4.5 times to nearly $400.
- *Toyota:* It earned $11 billion in 2005 and expect to earn more in 2006. It didn't have to cut the price of its cars, as much as most U.S. manufacturers did.
- *Starbucks:* From a single store in the Pike Place Market in Seattle, the brand now has over 6,000 locations in 30 countries. In first quarter 2006, its net revenues were up 22 percent to $1.9 billion. There are 181 locations within five miles of the Brand Keys offices in New York City. You have to have a lot of loyal customers to maintain that kind of growth.

- *Apple:* How many of those white iPod earbuds do you see people on the street wearing every day? The iPod shuffle sold 1.8 million units in the first three months of its introduction. Figure an average retail price of $99. You do the math. Is there anything I can offer you to get you to buy another MP3 player? Is there even another MP3 available?
- *Lambertville Trading Company:* It introduced a customer loyalty program, increased customer engagement, and category sales moved upwards of 25 percent.

And the success stories of companies relying on customer loyalty and higher levels of engagement go on and on.

"Wait," you cry, "Who is the Lambertville Trading Company? I've never heard of it. How did it get on a list of multinational juggernaut brands?"

Lambertville Trading Company is a family-owned, single-location store selling coffee and gourmet baked goods. For holidays, it offers really nice gift baskets. It is located in Lambertville, New Jersey, on the Delaware River. It is proof that you don't have to be an enormous multinational company to engage loyal customers successfully and profitably.

Anyone can leverage the insights in this book to measure customer loyalty, build your brand, and better engage customers even if you are a small business, or a business that's starting out. You don't have to have a Fortune 500 budget to get the insights you need to succeed.

I do have one caveat emptor about the book. Most of the examples I give *will* relate to larger companies. The reason for that is they don't have an excuse for not measuring loyalty, not engaging their customers, or not meeting or exceeding customer expectations. They can't turn around and say, "We didn't have any money to do the research." They can't say, "We didn't advertise enough"; or "we didn't know the right media to use." These days, most companies can't blame the product or their ability to distribute it.

So, read carefully for the principles we outline. These rules, applications, and advice apply to big, medium, and small businesses. Any product, any service can benefit from a booster shot of real loyalty metrics. An ounce of loyalty is worth a pound of newspaper ads, whether it's the *Boston Globe* or the *Pennysaver.* Customer loyalty and customer engagement is, ultimately, the great equalizer.

Customer loyalty was always desirable, but it was not as critical in the past as it is today. Loyalty is an economic and engagement model for *predicting* consumer behavior and boosting profits and future revenue streams, since today:

- It costs 7 to 10 times more to recruit a new customer than to keep an existing one.
- An increase in customer loyalty of only 5 percent can lift lifetime profits per customer by as much as 95 percent.
- An increase in loyalty of just 2 percent, in some sectors, is the equivalent of a 10 percent across-the-board cost reduction.

If you acknowledge that consumers are more sophisticated, you also have to acknowledge that you need more sophisticated tools to understand them.

The traditional marketing research questions were "Would you buy us again?" and "Would you recommend us to friends?" Answers to these questions may be positive indicators about the brand, but this approach is also simplistic, and simple is not always good.

Such simplicity does not help you understand customer expectations or what's working for you to attain real levels of engagement. You can't only rely on those kinds of questions and expect to understand what's really *going* to happen.

Modern customer loyalty assessment techniques—the ones we discuss in this book—provide *predictive* measures of the direction and velocity of category and customer values. By understanding what really keeps your customers loyal, you can:

- Rely on a leading indicator of profitability when planning your marketing.
- Know what consumers expect, 12 to 18 months ahead of the competition.
- Know how to sequence marketing initiatives most efficiently.
- Fight commoditization.
- Leverage competitive strategies to your advantage.
- Enhance your brand's equity and better engage customers.

Most people understand the need to address those issues, but we've done something about it, and that's the reason for this book. Now, you can pick a brand, any brand, learn what's important to know, and be able to predict customer reactions to harvest the most loyalty, the highest engagement levels, and the most profit along the way. You just have to keep your eyes on the right ball—in this case, customer loyalty.

Here's an example. A number of years ago we noticed that consumers in the Discount Retailer category—the Wal-Marts, Kmarts, Targets, and JCPenneys of the world—weren't exhibiting the same loyalty values as they had in years past. Value best expressed as what they got for the money they paid had become *less* important to them. Value still played a part in the loyalty-purchase decision, it was just less of an influence on their decision to shop (again and again) at one chain versus another.

What had become more important to these consumers that it was changing their shopping patterns? The answer was style. People wanted better-designed things. What has now become known as cheap chic. But who among that group provided that? Each of the chains had lots of cheap stuff, but back then very little chic stuff.

Target mounted a concerted effort (over a number of years) to own design. Over the years, the store and the designers became joined at the brand, as it were. It was very nearly impossible to mention Isaac Mizrahi, Michael Graves, or Mossimo and *not* think of Target. (Go ahead. Name a designer from Wal-Wart. Do you see what I mean?)

Cheap had become the price of entry to the category—not a big loyalty or engagement generator. Penny-quibbling aside, all of the competitors were cheap. Chic, on the other hand, was an uncommon value to come across in these stores. As a differentiator, chic was a winner. Consumers were just waiting for someone to step up and fulfill their expectations.

And along came Target, with Liz Lange, amy coe, and Thomas O'Brien. Before you know it, 1,397 stores with same-store sales year after year. That's keeping your eye on the right ball. This was not so for those selling strictly on price. So, building customer loyalty values was the key to success.

What happens when you keep your eyes on the wrong ball? Remember Kmart? It is a classic example of a brand that wouldn't listen or look away from four-P's data. Kmart executives simply looked at what they had, what they thought was going wrong, and asked themselves: What are we? Answer: A discount store. What do we sell? Answer: What everyone else sells. We sell commodities. So, a blue light-bulb went off over their collective heads and they arrived at the solution to their sagging profits: *We'll compete on price.* They adopted a fire-sale strategy by reducing prices as low as they could, laying people off, and slashing inventory.

This move was misguided because Kmart executives did not base it on how it would affect customer expectations, engage the customer, or move the loyalty needle. Essentially, Kmart was aggravating the problem that was killing its sales in the first place: the shopping experience (i.e., actual inventory and items you want on well-stocked shelves, with a salesperson within 500 yards). It's not particularly effective to claim you can undercut anyone's price when you don't have the product in the store.

Call it brand hubris or brand ignorance. When you don't have data that sheds light on customer buying behavior, expectations, and loyalty, you are swimming upstream in handcuffs: It's just a matter of time until either your energy runs out, or the steam runs out, and you get pushed out to a deep, indifferent sea.

Two books have recently received much attention in the marketing world (and elsewhere): *The Tipping Point* and *Blink,* both by Malcolm Gladwell (New York: Little Brown and Company, 2005). The "tipping point" is "the name given to that one dramatic moment . . . when everything can change at once." *Blink* is about how we think without thinking—a skill Mr. Gladwell calls "rapid cognition." The system is essentially based on knowing which information to keep and which to discard.

You can see how marketers would be attracted by these concepts. What if you knew when everything *was* going to change? What if you knew *which* information about a product, service, or brand consumers were going to keep? Even if they can't (or won't) articulate the rational or emotional reasons for doing what they do. I mean, if you had answers to those questions, you'd really have an edge over the competition.

Because the premise was so compelling, for each book, marketers have asked, "How? How do you know when everything is gong to change? What information will people rely on to make purchase decisions?"

Well the fact is that loyalty measures *can* provide those answers. Everything in a category changes when the things that drive loyalty shift and consumer expectations about the things that drive loyalty increase. For example, after 56 years of faithful service, Dunkin' Donuts has taken on a new aura. The category changed—reached a tipping point, if you will—and customer values and expectations changed, and the company has responded admirably. Admit it. All of a sudden, you think about the brand in a slightly different, probably better, way. You can't quite tell when it happened, or articulate it, but the change is there. Loyalty measures predicted this change.

There is the temptation to feel, maybe even convey, a hint of conceit when you know you have the answer to what ails a flagging brand when loyalty is in crisis. When you have the numbers in front of you, when you know with almost 100 percent accuracy the direction and the velocity of the customer's loyalty, it's hard not to feel like the smartest person in the room, or at least the one with the information that will have the biggest positive impact on the business strategy. It's a nice feeling to be in that position, to have the kind of confidence that goes with having really valuable, reliable information with which to steer your brand.

We are indeed in a brand crisis. *But we are in a brand crisis mainly because we are in a loyalty crisis.* They are, in effect, two faces of the same crisis. Where there is no loyalty, there are no brands. And with no brands, we have only commodities acting like well-heeled generics, competing largely on the basis of price, hoping that massively increased above-the-line advertising media budgets and *anything* new in below-the-line promotion will somehow give the appearance of differentiation, engage consumers, and earn real profitability. It's gotten so bad that products and services *everyone* knows have lost so much brand equity, meaning, and the ability to even meet expectations that a recent study of 1,700 brands had to create a new segment for such products: Category Placeholders.

Brand equity, for many people, can be the same as brand personality, brand essence, brand DNA, or brand image. It isn't brand awareness. The confusion is wreaking havoc on those responsible for defining strategies, designing programs, and, ultimately, improving the sales and profit lines. Brand equity, when properly measured as customer loyalty, using reliable, predictive research, yields the pay dirt of strategic insights, market information, and brand differentiation, as well as an ability to craft and sequence your marketing communication. Put simply, it provides the details behind everything that you already do every day but wish you knew more about what was working and why.

Every ad agency and local market research supplier has its own customer research method. It's all going to sound good, with golden promises of working for the client. That's okay. But never forget that, like anything in the ad world, they are in the business of selling things. Research (i.e., planning) is a profit center, too. To get a substantial loyalty education that leaves old-fashioned satisfaction metrics in the dust, you must ask the right questions. Require the right output. Be willing to argue from a place of understanding, not desperation. Toughest of all, you need to be able to walk away from the table if you can't get what your brand needs.

If the research you have developed, inherited, or bought seems fine to you, here's a test: show *how* it is predictive. How it measures emotional bonds with your customers. How it correlates to customer buying behavior and profitability. How it identifies *what* consumers expect and shows how your efforts engage consumers. If you can demonstrate this list, you should not bother reading this book. You should be lolling on a yacht in the Mediterranean or sprawled on some Polynesian beach.

This is the challenge: Talk the talk or deliver against it.

A Brand Gone Wrong: General Motors

I'm a career-long participant in the Madison Avenue circuit, and a card-carrying member of the Baby-Boomer generation. So, I remember when there was a certain infallibility, even glamour, being involved with a great big brand that did well, sometimes even at times in spite of itself. It was like watching the dull-witted son inherit his daddy's $150 million, and not run the family business into the ground—at least, not suddenly.

In first quarter 2005, General Motors (GM) reported a $1.1 billion loss; it's worst quarterly performance since 1992. We note for the record that that's an awful lot of money even by twenty-first-century standards, and it managed to top that loss in 2006.

The surprise was not the sudden loss (loyalty metrics had predicted that a long time ago), but the remedy that management suggested: Put the GM badge on all recently introduced and 2006 models, in an effort to link the corporation to its divisions. This was deemed a good idea, presumably because, as the company pointed out (with tremendous mid-twentieth-century confidence, clarity, and resolve that should have made present stockholders uncomfortable), "*everyone* was familiar with the GM brand."

Given that customer loyalty was down in virtually all their divisions, it was, to phrase it kindly, an interesting marketing proposition: *Link automobiles that stand for very little in the consumer's mind with a manufacturer who stands for even less.* Consumers all know who GM is and that it makes cars and trucks. Not necessarily cars and trucks that people want to buy, perhaps, but when you base your marketing on awareness and not on loyalty, this approach makes a twisted kind of sense, despite years of proof that general awareness and an ability to recall your name are *not* pathways to profitability.

High levels of general awareness and consumers' ability to recall your name combined with low levels of loyalty make you a "category placeholder," a classification only a few steps away from being a commodity—the Acme car of the twenty-first century.

And rather than do the kind of research that might identify the values and expectations on which GM could engage consumers and profitably capitalize, they relied on the "same-old, same-old" approach of the last century. First, they thought, "if we only had more attention paid to the cars, that would solve all our problems." So, they gave away cars to everyone in the audience at an Oprah show. Here's a test to the efficacy of the promotion: Call up 10 of your friends and ask, "Do you remember when Oprah gave everyone in the audience a car?" Ninety percent will say "yes." Then ask, "What was the car she gave away?" Be happy if you get one correct answer. (By the way, it was a Pontiac G-6 midsize sports sedan.)

Second, they lowered their prices. They called it *GM Employee Discount,* which, I have to admit, was a really creative way of positioning a price cut, so kudos to the agency. (Shortly thereafter, Ford and Chrysler made the same offer, thus turning delight into price-of-entry consumer expectations.)

Finally, GM ran ads lauding 16 J.D. Power satisfaction awards: for things like "Gold (and Silver and Bronze) Plant Quality Awards,"—which may actually mean something to the gear heads in Detroit, but are extraordinarily unlikely to show up on an actual list of things that are important to consumers, and a litany of "most dependable midsize, full-size, premium midsize, compact, and sport utility" vehicles. All this was oblivious to the fact that consumers did not think badly of GM cars in the first place. They just didn't think of them when it came time to buy a car.

Show me a brand—any size, any place—that has a firm grasp on its loyalty metrics and I'll show you a brand whose profits you can bet on. Remember the Lambertville Trading Company? This book is a means to understanding and executing that kind of performance. It is part how to think, part how to ask questions, and all how to use customer loyalty research. The information allows you to reverse-engineer valuable loyalty measurements you need, by starting with a checklist of the questions you want answered about your brand and your customers. All before you spend one dollar.

The book's explanations and examples are taken from today's brands in every major consumer category.

Here are 13 of the crucial questions that you will be able to comfortably ask—and intelligently answer—about your brand after you master the lessons in this book:

1. What are the leading-indicator (predictive) drivers of loyalty and profitability for your category?
2. What individual attributes, benefits, values, and communication elements (e.g., image, essence, personality, or even DNA) make up the drivers?
3. What is the order of importance of the category drivers? How do consumers view your category? How do they compare brands, and how, ultimately, do they buy (and remain loyal)?
4. What percent of contribution does each driver make to loyalty and profitability?
5. What expectations do consumers hold for each of the drivers?
6. How does this vary by service offering? By user segment? By region/ country?
7. On which drivers is your brand strong and weak?
8. How does your brand compare to the competition?
9. In which driver(s) does your brand's equity reside (i.e., where does your brand meet or exceed consumer expectations)?
10. Brand Credibility: What are consumers *willing* to believe about your brand?

11. What market strategies and opportunities can the brand sustain?
12. Which above- and below-the-line media, advertising, communication, and sponsorship opportunities will optimize your marketing efforts?
13. How are you going to quantify the impact of your marketing efforts, and can you correlate your activities with sales or fiscal return on investment (ROI)?

CUSTOMER LOYALTY RESEARCH AND TRADITIONAL MARKETING RESEARCH

Any researcher can spew impenetrable and silver-tongued jargon about marketing and loyalty measures. But keeping the secrets of brand research shrouded in quasi-impenetrable mystery ultimately does no one any good, especially not the secret keeper. *The jig is up.* People behind good brands need new methods and reliable answers to the loyalty mystery now, so we're open-sourcing our approach to reenergize the brand loyalty development process for the twenty-first century.

We're not suggesting that you jettison your traditional tools. But, even done well, they still provide only 30 percent of the insights and direction you need to succeed in today's marketplace. We talk more about that later. However, a customer loyalty metrics overlay lets you optimize the effectiveness of your traditional tools. Loyalty measures can help you design more tightly targeted questionnaires, making them more time- and cost-effective. They can improve your integrated marketing efforts (whether you are talking about cross-department efforts, or just integrating sales with marketing and communications).

Loyalty measures can also help optimize the engagement effectiveness of your media plan (both above *and* below the line) via a customer loyalty application we call *Brand-to-Media Engagement* that produces increased results of upwards of 20 percent in most cases. Customer loyalty measures can help you to figure out a real ROI for virtually any advertising, public relations, Internet, sponsorship, and product placement effort. I'll show you how.

To help put all this into a real world framework, throughout the book you find "Loyalty Tales from the Real World" which offer broader examples of how loyalty affects our lives, and how it may affect your business.

Finally, remembering Eugène Ionesco's comment that, "it is not the answer that enlightens, but the question," you'll also find, in this book, question-and-answer sessions with media, advertising, and business press journalists. This is because some of the most interesting, progressive, and challenging questions I get come not just from clients but also from journalists and analysts who have the time (and the obligation) to ask the "what ifs" and report unflinchingly what they find.

Those are probably the same kinds of questions that keep you—and other concerned, aware business people—awake at night. We hope that our answers and ongoing work in the area of loyalty metrics provide some marketplace insight, and help you get a little more sleep.

Q & A

Defining Loyalty

Jon Fine, *BusinessWeek:* How can you come up with a metric for something as nebulous as loyalty?

Robert Passikoff: Loyalty isn't as nebulous as one might think. First, we need to agree that loyalty is defined as the consumer-to-brand bond that ensures future purchase. Second, we need to agree that the traditional research methods have major limitations when it comes to measuring loyalty. For example, the traditional "Would you buy this brand again?" and "How likely are you to recommend this product to friends?" type of questions lack one key element: the ability to predict what consumers *will actually do* in the marketplace. They tell you what they *say* they will do, but not what they will really do. The best example is when a brand wins national satisfaction awards while at the same time loses market share.

You can't make direct inquiries and get to the emotional pay dirt of loyalty and expectations. You need to get below consumers' 30 percent conscious radar of what they say they think and tap the 70 percent of what they really think and feel on an emotional level. I discuss how to do this.

CHAPTER 1

WHY MARKETERS CAN'T PREDICT CUSTOMER BEHAVIOR—WHOOPS, NOW THEY CAN

If you want to do something new, you have to stop doing something old.

—Peter Drucker

Most twentieth-century marketing research, no matter how updated, is basically a superb rearview mirror. The problem with rearview mirrors is that they make for very crummy windshields. They don't help you see what's about to hit you in the face. Data mining and Customer Relationship Management have made it possible to be excellent at knowing the past, and even get up-to-the-minute feedback on the present. But as a trend predictor, the bulk of the research I see (and am asked to salvage) usually produces what we call "excellent answers to meaningless questions"—analysis that may be impressive, may be phrased brilliantly, and may even be true but is totally valueless as a leading indicator.

Yet that is what you need your marketing research to do: help get you where you want to go, by the most direct, cost-effective route possible.

Despite all the rhetoric, hype, and promises, there seems to be a robust market for *lagging* indicators dressed up in new clothes. It's no wonder researchers are increasingly uninvited to, and even banished from, the table where the decisions are made, given what many of them offer as answers and insights.

To a limited extent, traditional research can help inform brands about what's going on "out there," externally, in the market, and in the words of the consumer. But there is much more to the story, and it is now a much more knowable story. Given the way the world works today, present-tense thinking is no longer enough. It's essential to predict not only what customers want but also what they *will* want.

Some marketers are blessed with what can only be called a gut feeling for the market at any given time. But few can really see the future so clearly that you would be willing to bet your money, your career, or your brand's future on their vision. And few researchers do a remarkably good job of measuring the *direction and velocity of customer values*—and identifying the values for which customers have the highest expectations.

A while ago, we received a mailer from a major research trade association advertising a market research conference entitled, "Earning a Place at the Table." The blurb asked, chillingly we thought, whether researchers have a place at the table where marketing decisions are made, whether they have *earned* that place—and whether they would even know what to do if they had. Wow.

This is scary stuff regardless of the way you feel about research. Research is at the very root of all intelligent, directed action in business. Did something happen to this premise while we were out grabbing coffee? What sensible person or organization acts without understanding context, alternatives, and probable consequences? Who in their right mind would dive into a business, social, or military program without due diligence—in other words, without good intelligence or proper research?

The problem lies squarely with what currently constitutes "proper research." At another organization's conference, the Advertising Research Foundation anointed the consumer as the "new marketing compass," assuring attendees that acknowledging this idea would lead the way to profitability and, one assumes, a place at the decision-making table. This was echoed on the January 15, 2006, cover of *Marketing News,* which announced this year's marketing outlook to be: "Under My Thumb: The Consumers Take Control." Well, the consumer has been in control for a while now. Proper research isn't always the old model stuff, no matter how it gets dressed up for the new millennium.

The problem, and the trick, is to identify research that gives you the best chance of always measuring *how* to meet or exceed customer expectations. The best research constantly updates understanding of *customer values and how they impact expectations.* Understanding that concept, and acting on it, is what will bring research back to the table where key decisions are made. We need research techniques that slip behind respondents' unconscious defenses and other right-brained shenanigans. Methods that can show where customers' loyalty drivers lie, and where not just present satisfaction but also future happiness lurk—for the brand as well as for the customer.

If good research is not influencing corporate decision making as much as it should, there are reasons. Repeated attempts to bundle telecommunication services, create concepts like Pets.com, or produce *Martha Stewart-The Apprentice* type of advertising strategies did not occur in a vacuum—without some sort of research on which to base those magnificently failed plans. Most companies like these realized how little they understood only after their "compass readings" misled them and the brands tanked.

So, what is to be done? What's the solution? How do we get research back into the boardroom, back to the decision-making table? A good first step is for researchers to recognize, even admit aloud, the limitations of traditional research and the benefits of updated methodologies.

To illustrate the power of loyalty metrics, we're going to start with some "real example True Tales" that my firm has collected on some leading brands.

The loyalty metrics are expressed in easy-to-read bar charts. Each product category is described in four bars representing the *category drivers* that are listed (from left to right) in order of their importance to the customer in the engagement-purchase-loyalty process. (Despite the simple labels on the category drivers, each is made up of multiple components—attributes, benefits, category values, and consumer values.)

The order of importance of the drivers reflects how the consumer views the category, compares offerings in the category, and, ultimately, will buy in the category (and if you do your job right, buy again and again). That is, when thinking about which brand to buy, consumers will naturally give greater emphasis to the more important loyalty drivers.

The height of the bars—the indices—indicates the level of expectation that consumers hold for each of the drivers (see Figure 1.1). It is possible for a consumer to have higher expectations for a less important category driver, as is usually the case for category values like "Price"—where it is not, except for commodities, the most important driver, but rather the driver for which consumers hold very high expectations—they want to pay as little as possible.

The benchmark is 100, so a 112 means that the expectation for the driver is 12 percent higher than the norm. The higher the index, the higher the level of expectations a consumer has for a particular driver.

A higher index for your brand is better than a lower index (some things in research *never* change), and a brand's equity (i.e., its strength in the category) is judged by its capability to *meet* or *exceed* the expectations that the consumers' hold for the drivers that define the category Ideal (i.e., the theoretical yardstick against which all offerings are ultimately judged). Examining the brand on a driver-by-driver basis allows you to diagnostically measure your strengths (and weaknesses) against an ideal or competitive set.

Because marketers sometimes want to discuss or compare a brand on an overall basis, a single-index number representing the weighted average of all

Figure 1.1
An Example of Category Drivers

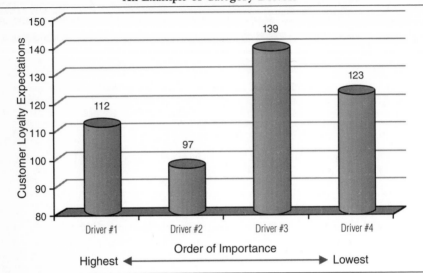

four drivers provides this overall brand equity measure, which we call the *Overall Brand Equity Score*. Higher is better here, too. The true value of these metrics is that they are predictive, with shifts in category values and brand assessments that show up 6 to 18 months before they do in traditional research efforts or in the marketplace itself (and, shortly thereafter, the balance sheet).

TRUE TALES

Krispy Kreme

In the first quarter of 2003, when the entire world was riding the Krispy Kreme stock-price high, our Brand Keys metrics accurately predicted that the brand was heading for a fall due to unmet consumer needs and expectations. By the third quarter of 2003, new store sales were below expectations. By the second quarter of 2004, the average weekly retail customer counts had declined severely, leading to a stock price decline of nearly 60 percent (see Figure 1.2).

Miller

The Miller Brewing Company reported declining sales for the Miller Genuine Draft brand in 2003 and 2004. But as early as 2000, when sales appeared sta-

Figure 1.2
Krispy Kreme Brand Keys' Assessments and Stock Prices

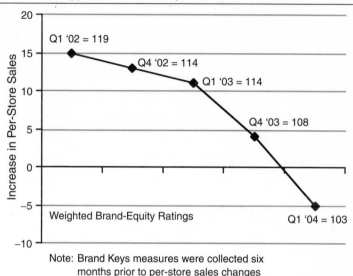

Note: Brand Keys measures were collected six
months prior to per-store sales changes

ble, our Brand Keys metrics documented that Miller was losing ground with
respect to its delivery to the consumer of the key brand loyalty drivers. We
predicted that the brand would lose previously loyal customers, which it eventually did, to brands such as Corona and the microbrews. It has come back
since, but keep your eyes on those microbrews (see Figure 1.3).

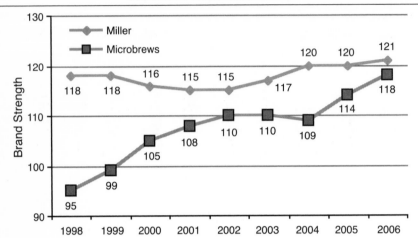

Figure 1.3
Miller Beer versus Microbrews

Coke

Coca-Cola experienced booming sales and earnings in the mid-1990s. Since then, all major soft drink makers have been challenged, with Coke's retail sales performance lagging behind its top competitor, Pepsi-Cola. Since the first quarter of 1998, the Brand Keys metrics accurately predicted an annual decline in Coke's brand equity and customer loyalty—predictions that correlated highly with actual Coke sales and Pepsi's gains (see Figure 1.4).

Martha Stewart Omnimedia

The Brand Keys metrics accurately predicted the directional rise-fall-try again of Martha Stewart Omnimedia profits across 27 separate points in time between May 20, 2002 (before the stock sale scandal) and to date. The loyalty metrics correlate perfectly with Martha Stewart Omnimedia profitability, or lack thereof (see Figure 1.5 on page 22).

PROBLEMS WITH MOST
LOYALTY RESEARCH

I'm haunted by a scene in the movie *Monty Python and the Holy Grail*. A scraggly band of Pythonesque crusaders approach a castle. "I'm Arthur, King of the Britons," shouts the leader to a soldier atop the parapet. "Come and join us in the quest for the Holy Grail." The soldier leans over the edge and shouts, "Go away, we already have one!"

Figure 1.4
Coke versus Pepsi

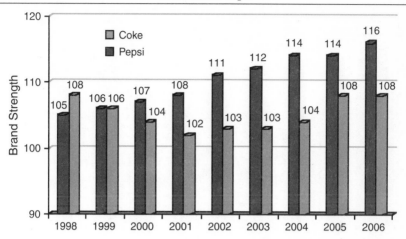

Coke		Pepsi
↑ 2.3%	Sales in Past 5 Years	7.5% ↑
↓ 2%	Quarterly Profits	13% ↑
↓ 13.5%	Stock Price Over Previous Year	5.6% ↑

Why does this haunt me? Because my company, Brand Keys, realized more than a decade ago that for companies the Holy Grail was going to be customer loyalty. More often than I care to recount—most recently at the headquarters of one of the largest telecommunications companies on earth—as I am describing our process, the client will interrupt to tell me: "We already have loyalty measures." Invariably (as was the case at the telecommunications company), the client is an intelligent and seasoned top-ranking executive. And, invariably, the intelligent and seasoned executive was dead wrong.

There's a simple reason why most top executives don't know what they're talking about when it comes to brand customer loyalty measures: their *research departments are misleading them.* Not intentionally, but misleading them nonetheless. And they have been for years. It's not that research directors are consciously lying—not exactly. The real problem is that the brand loyalty data cited by research directors does not have much to do with actual customer loyalty. That's

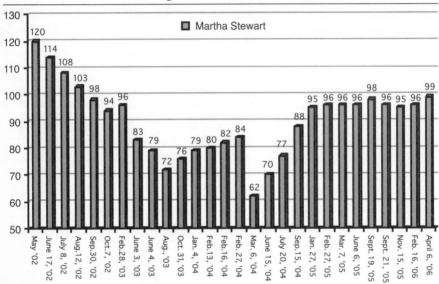

Figure 1.5
Tracking the Martha Stewart Brand

because *there is no way to measure customer loyalty using traditional methodologies.* Why can't these methodologies measure customer loyalty? Because traditional research uses the direct question-and-answer approach—direct answers to direct questions. And there is no way on earth—and probably not on any other planet—to determine through direct questioning, with a reasonable degree of statistical accuracy, whether customers are and will remain loyal to a brand.

In light of today's commoditization of virtually everything, the consumer decision process is driven more and more by *emotional* elements and values than by *rational* ones. We calculate that 70 percent of decision making is emotional. Rational elements do factor into product and service usage, so to accurately measure real loyalty (and expectations and engagement) you need to fuse the two. The traditional textbooks and approaches don't take that into account.

It's not a methodology issue. I have faith that all legitimate researchers ask their questions properly, collect data accurately, and crunch the numbers according to all the rules. The problem is that *the questions themselves are wrong.* Answers to direct questions are not predictive of future behavior. They do not correlate to any notable extent with real marketplace activity. In other words, the traditional research methodologies yield statistically reliable and valid answers, but to meaningless questions. If you doubt me, ask yourself this: If

AT&T had answers to questions that were really reflective of customers' values, predictive of profitable activities in the marketplace, and ultimately provided insights that helped to increase shareholder value, it would have stopped the bleeding long before it was taken over by SBC and Cingular and relegated to the "Brands That Used to Exist on Their Own" file. Instead, AT&T bled for two decades, a slow death indeed, without ever getting it. Makes you wonder about all the research that got fielded!

There are two reasons why top executives won't be hearing this from their research directors. First, most research directors don't know any other way to obtain loyalty data, nor do they pay attention to the lack of correlation between their data and the actual purchasing behavior of their customers. Their conscience is clear when they say that they have loyalty measures, because that's what they believe. As the psychologist Abraham Maslow said, "When your only tool is a hammer, the whole world starts to look like a nail."

The second reason is slightly more sinister. Imagine yourself in the position of a research director who does understand that the loyalty data he or she has been serving up for the past two decades is, in fact, incapable of doing the one thing you would expect a true loyalty measure to do: predict future customer behavior. Would you be willing to admit it? Or would you tend to hunker down and insist to the higher-ups that everything's just fine on the loyalty front? This dilemma is compounded by the fact that most high-ranking executives look only at research results, paying no attention to the methodologies that produced those results. Even the most hands-on executives generally keep their hands off the research department, the theory being that such secret rites are best left to the experts.

Well, guess what? The experts in your research and planning departments still rely on methodologies that were developed during the Eisenhower administration. What is the capability of these methodologies to track the direction and velocity of fast-changing customer values? It is somewhere between zero and nil. What about the capability to predict whether your customer will remain loyal or be peeled off by the competition? Don't ask.

What's the solution? You can start by calling your research people or research suppliers and grilling them about how well their current customer and brand loyalty numbers match up with bottom-line profits and stock prices. They'll protest. They'll howl. But, ultimately, they'll roll over and admit that they don't have the goods.

You'll also want to be very, very careful when researchers and marketers use the phrase *ethnographic research* as a surrogate for the research you really need to do to produce real loyalty metrics. Ethnographical research is usually a written description of a particular segment of consumers, typically based on some past purchase behavior, based on information collected through interviews, observations, and documents.

Ethnography literally means a portrait of a people, and when in an attempt to describe the observed behavior as it is related to brand choice, interpretation rears its ugly head. Researchers take their particular observational data and, to use their popular and comforting phrase, "paint a picture of what is actually going on." The problem here is that results inevitably differ from observer to observer. What is ultimately produced is open to multiple interpretations that are consistent with multiple—and inconsistent—personal points of view. There's the added disadvantage that this approach is a rearview technique. It's based on what folks did in the past and doesn't provide the diagnostics to explain how customers weré originally engaged.

BE INFORMED BEFORE YOU GO TO MARKET (AS WELL AS DURING AND AFTER)

Instead of measuring what went wrong after a campaign or new product launch, wouldn't a proactive approach make more sense—before you hit the market, blew through the budget, maybe even eroded the loyalty bond between the brand and its customers?

Measure and anticipate values and expectations so that you position your brands ahead of shifts in customer sentiment. Value shifts show up ahead of what the marketing world calls *trends*. Trend forecasting and measuring of customer values and expectations are both methods that seek predictive information, but they do not produce the same insights. Only methods that use the appropriate design, execution, and analysis can reliably focus on the future customer landscape. When you know what the market is anticipating, what it is willing to believe or stay loyal to, you have the ultimate competitive advantage. Combine this forward-reaching insight with knowledge of what the most effective ad drivers and media outlets are to resonate with targeted customer segments and you have a brand jackpot.

Volumes—indeed, entire shelves—of new or revised brand and marketing strategic advice are constantly coming out. But ask yourself: What specifically in the proliferation of the business press really equates to new insights or methods? Is the burgeoning collection coming any closer to answering pressing, contemporary questions on how to know your customer base, how to best engage them, and how to keep them loyal? Best practices and case studies are interesting, insightful, and entertaining. The inside story usually is.

But how often do we learn that what spurred a spell of brand success was as much a product of chance, situation, and unintended consequences as it was a deliberate, informed strategy? Such a phenomenon makes a good story or is fun to talk about, but it is hard to apply or replicate. We already know that the plan always changes. The question is in response to what?

The most impressive attribute any of us can ever deliver on is the one absent from most brand calculus. I'm talking about the *accountability*—that nagging, scary thought that just will not go away. More people in higher places are asking for it, requiring it as a prerequisite to any successful brand strategy, and talking about it without specifics. What is to be done? Sophisticated shareholders, CEOs, brand managers, and small business owners all want to know why something is working as much as why it is not. We need brand accountability.

Have you been looking backward at market and consumer history to devise a strategy for facing your competition in the future? Are you attempting to protect your turf from invasion without using predictive research to project how the marketplace might shift in the next year?

Following a customer loyalty approach helps to ingrain the habit of constant updating—regularly focusing on new values and new ideas; deliberately violating your own comfort zone, and refreshing and challenging your imagination. It also keeps you from being ambushed by the old the-way-it's-always-been-done stratagem.

Q & A
Measuring Loyalty

Roderick White, *Admap* magazine: *Is there really any way by which we can measure loyalty, except by actual in-market behavior?*

Robert Passikoff: Yes, by understanding the consumers' behavior at a deeper level than what product they just purchased. By "actual in-market behavior," I assume you mean "last/past purchase." If past purchase was a true measure of loyalty, then all the transaction data that brands capture would actually provide the caliber of strategic guidance needed to differentiate those brands. But it doesn't.

While measurement of actual transactions has become common, measuring loyalty via past-purchase behavior is not feasible for most categories because of a purchase-switching consideration period. This time lag is what makes the measurement of the direct effects of advertising, marketing, and promotional activities so difficult.

However, nontransactional behavior data is available that does not reflect the final action, but rather is related to the *potential for a purchase*. This behavioral data is not adversely affected by the lag factor associated with actual transactions because it is based on customer values, which do not change quickly.

New, measurable patterns will enable brands to grow customer loyalty in ways hardly imaginable just a short while ago—blends of psychological and higher-order statistical analyses that provide clear identification of the drivers of loyalty and profitability. Our particular model identifies four such loyalty *drivers*, which let us understand precisely how consumers view a given category and how they will compare brand offerings and buy. This is because well-designed drivers highly correlate with sales. The customer-brand analysis also identifies the expectations that consumers hold for each driver. And herein lies the key to true measurements of loyalty: A brand's ability to meet or exceed those expectations will identify an actual loyalty metric and potential for sales success.

Advertising and Loyalty: Actions and Effects

Theresa Howard, *USA Today*: *Does liking an ad on television, or interacting with an ad on the Web, necessarily engage consumers and build brand loyalty?*

Robert Passikoff: Not necessarily. Welcome to the twenty-first-century "media ecology." It all comes down to whether the interaction positively reinforces the consumer's perception of the brand. More TV and cable network options mean that the consumer has increased power to self-select the ad message to which he or she will be exposed. People now spend 10 percent of their time online, and advertisers seeking the Holy Grail are willing to try virtually anything to get attention—but that does not necessarily equate with loyalty or engagement.

"Let's face it, Fred. You and I are not exactly apostles of change."

CHAPTER 2

FROM BRAND GUESSING TO BRAND BUILDING: HOW TO PROFITABLY ENGAGE YOUR CUSTOMER

Errans saepe, dubius numqan ("Often wrong, never uncertain")

—*Latin proverb*

About 86 percent of all new product launches fail. Or 92 percent of all new product launches fail. The numbers are not consistent but they are mind-bogglingly high. We hear frightening numbers like these all the time. Less heard is the why. The surprising aspect of this fact is not the rate of new product failure. It is that marketing and strategic-planning professionals have resigned themselves to the overwhelming odds of failure. It's almost as if failure rates this high are an axiom of life, far beyond anyone's control.

Why can't marketers successfully launch a new product or service *most of the time*? They employ competent people who enjoy virtually bottomless research coffers. Yet, the odds are in favor of them failing in their mission. The failure is caused primarily by the absence of a proven marketing procedure to improve a new product's chances.

To a certain extent, we can rationalize this failure by claiming that consumers in the major markets have become increasingly more knowledgeable and sophisticated. We can say those new products that are genuinely desired by consumers will be manufactured and then, weeks later, competing manufacturers will be offering the same product or features. Depending on the category, if an innovative manufacturer enjoys two months of market domination before his product begins to disappear into the commodity crevasse, he may be doing better than most. Sanyo was the first mobile phone manufacturer to put

28

a camera in a cell phone. The technology was there and it could do it—so it did. It differentiated Sanyo from the competition, and it engaged a segment of the cell phone-user population. Forty-two days later, Samsung had a camera phone in stores.

Whatever the cause, the success rate of new product launches (from the point of view of product configuration, customer engagement, and advertising support) has never been encouraging—even before the advent of the bionic consumer and hypersaturated markets.

But we have an opportunity to get better by more clearly understanding target audiences. We must also realize that identifying the target group, developing a new product, creating advertising, and ultimately getting the consumer to buy the product is dependent not only on the *content* of the product itself but also on the *placement* of the product in the consumer's life—the meaning it holds for the consumer.

We postulate that *consumer bonding* (i.e., the theoretical framework for customer loyalty and engagement) is the key to a successful new product launch and brand success, generally. *Immediate* consumer bonding is a prerequisite to a successful product introduction. But how do you induce consumers to bond immediately to a product or service—especially if they have never heard of it before? For a truly new product, innovation can do it for you. Think Apple iPod. For most other categories, only new research and planning techniques can answer that question, and they do so by crossing the line between research and human psychology.

FIND THE FIT BEFORE YOU LAUNCH THE BRAND

Loyalty metrics actually measure the degree to which a consumer will engage with a new product, concept, or campaign on the basis of how well the system bridges the gap between traditional research and human psychology. Loyalty metrics provide strategic insights into brands and categories and allow for the development of new product concepts that are most likely to engage consumers, thus giving the product a higher chance of success.

Customer loyalty metrics reveal the position a brand *could* occupy in consumers' minds. Traditional research measures only the position *currently* occupied by the brand. Loyalty metrics determine what consumers are *willing to believe* about a brand. Well-designed metrics can be used as *input* to marketing and brand-strategy development rather than a *checking mechanism*.

Loyalty-based research reveals the real, motivating forces of the consumer rather than the considered and amended opinions of the rational research guinea pig. The best loyalty measures are *not* direct questions and answers but a system that fuses the emotional and rational elements that define how a consumer views a category, compares offerings, and buys a product. It is able to capture and identify new brand values, products, and services that meet or exceed consumers' ever-expanding expectations.

These are values that often go well beyond the practical issues of product performance or rational benefits and further than the emotional and psychological aspects of brand personality and image. These deeper values factor into any definition and measurement of brand equity and consumer insights, especially if we are to use these measures as a means of assessing engagement and return on investment (ROI). This is real *brand equity.*

CONSUMER INSIGHT-DRIVEN DEFINITION OF BRAND EQUITY

The concept of *brand equity* has been defined in different ways for different purposes. The highest-profile definitions have generally been provided by advertising agencies looking to differentiate products and services with layers of discriminators. Some of the coined terms that are sometimes interchangeably used as surrogates for brand equity include *brand image, brand personality, brand assets, added values,* and *brand DNA.*

Most of these definitions refer to imagery and positioning—they attempt to create manifestations of a brand's equity—but they are not a definition of brand equity itself. Talking about brand equity in those terms is easy. But if we define the central goal of strategic marketing and planning as the creation of an expanding pool of engaged, loyal customers and profits for the company, then talk is cheap. If each *conception* of brand equity yielded customers, there would be a lot more loyal and engaged customers in the world.

A real definition of brand equity required consumer insights that:

- Took account of the rational and emotional values that help define the purchase drivers of the category
- Captured the direction and velocity of customer values and meaning in the category
- Provided real levels of customer expectation
- Correlated closely with in-market behavior

In the end, this was our definition:

Brand equity is the status or strength of the brand and its ability to meet or exceed the expectations consumers use to define the *Category Ideal.* This identifies how consumers view the category, compare offerings in the category, and, ultimately, buy in the category. It's what they really expect from a brand.

Correctly measured, real customer insights identify how customer values and category values come together to form the dimensions of purchase, loyalty, and profitability.

Correctly measured, real customer expectations identify precisely "how high is up" to the customer.

And, correctly measured, real customer expectations provide a yardstick against which the brand, communications, and attendant brand loyalty and engagement efforts can be measured.

To accomplish this, you need statistically reliable customer perceptions of customer *expectations*. Most research systems have certainly *not* kept pace with the changing dynamics of customer values. This is not meant to suggest that we should ignore traditional, reliable, and valid marketing research techniques. Such techniques are generally quite helpful in identifying marketing opportunity, but they are *not* leading indicators of success.

Here are two big failures where companies did not utilize correctly defined brand equity: McDonald's introduction of the Arch Deluxe, and AT&T's leap into the computer marketplace with the acquisition of NCR.

We can reasonably assume these companies did research before they threw their money away. We can also assume that they did the *wrong* kind of research—research that measured *market opportunities*. But they did not correctly measure and utilize their brands' equities to determine the actual likelihood of success in these ventures. A correctly defined, brand equity-based assessment system would have tipped them off that most adults were *not* willing to believe that McDonald's is qualified (by product formulation *or* venue) to make an adult hamburger. Customers were *not* likely to accept an AT&T logo on a computer. Knowing that ahead of time might have convinced both companies that no amount of image advertising, graphic design, or promotions was going to change their customers' minds.

If these fiascoes teach us anything, it is that there is a need to understand the difference between (1) what appears to be a really good marketing opportunity and (2) a really inferior brand strategy, especially if they rely on an erroneous definition of brand equity.

PROVIDING CONSUMER INSIGHTS

My company, Brand Keys, has adapted the loyalty model to meet twenty-first-century marketing requirements. The theoretical framework of the system was shown to be the most highly correlated with sales in the seminal 1990 Advertising Research Foundation Copy Research Validity Project, and it is based on a widely accepted psychological theory—each consumer has psychologically based tendencies and expectations that determine his or her behavior in the marketplace. This tendency has been termed *liking, bonding,* or *engagement,* but whatever term you use, it translates as the consumer acting favorably toward your brand.

In the marketing context, *acting favorably* toward something means preferring it and actually buying it, and buying it again, even in the face of tempting competitive price points. This all sounds like customer loyalty.

As the True Tales in Chapter 1 showed, the loyalty approach enables marketers to measure (and replicate) in a clear and consistent way the level of engagement that consumers exhibit for product categories, brands in these categories, and communications from above- and below-the-line disciplines.

For the statisticians among you, our research uses a psychological questionnaire that has a test/retest reliability of 93 percent (from national probability samples in the United States and United Kingdom). The questionnaire has been tested in 26 countries around the world, with similar results in Business-to-Consumer (B2C) and Business-to-Business (B2B) categories. Twenty questions are used, employing personification as a device for gaining consumer insights into the bonding or liking for a category and a brand.

The questionnaire asks the respondent to ascribe various attitudes and behaviors to the brand; it also asks how he or she would feel or behave if he or she were the brand itself. In the respondent's assessments of a brand, he or she is encouraged to move beyond familiar dictated, sometimes-learned perceptions—like product attributes and benefits—and into an arena of higher-order, brand-based, emotional values.

Answers to the questionnaire generate scores that yield a picture in four category-driver dimensions that describe how the consumer views a category, compares brands in a category and, ultimately, *makes purchases in a category.* In addition, the answers provide a measure of customer expectations for each of the four identified category drivers.

We review the technical aspects of measuring loyalty in Chapter 3, but the following example will give you an understanding of how you have to reconfigure your thinking about your category and how to measure customer loyalty.

Think about your own product, service, or category and try to answer the following questions:

- What are the drivers for the category?
- Which specific key attributes, benefits, and values get placed (i.e., bucketed) in each of the drivers?

- What's the order of importance of the drivers? How do you think consumers view the category? Hint: Think about the Ideal for your category.
- What expectations do consumers have for each of the drivers? (Ours are indices, but you can use a 1 to 20 scale. Just keep in mind that "importance" does not equal "expectation," and try not to be constrained by what you know to be reality. The consumer won't.)
- How does your brand—or your competitor's—stand up to the Ideal?

If you want a real acid test, then ask a customer the same questions. You'll be surprised at the discrepancies!

Barnesandnoble.com and Amazon.com

Now, look at how this approach worked for evaluating customer expectations for online books. The four category drivers for the Online Books category were identified as:

1. Product Range
2. Easy-to-Use, Secure Site
3. Good Prices/Added Value
4. Useful Content: Reviews, Recommendations, and Ability to Personalize

Each driver is made up of a number of attributes, benefits, and values (ABVs) that are used to define and make buying decisions in the category. The order of importance of the category drivers (read left to right) and customer expectations (expressed as a driver index or height of the bars) appear in Figure 2.1.

For evaluations of brand strength and weakness, a difference of five points is required for a significant difference at the 95 percent confidence level. The status of the two top brands is shown in Figure 2.2 on page 35.

Interviews were conducted (50:50) with Barnesandnoble.com and Amazon.com customers. Respondents qualified for the survey by having used one of the sites three-plus times in the past quarter, thus establishing them as customers. The respondents were unaware of the program that was being assessed.

They rated:

- The category Ideal
- The web site (Amazon.com or Barnesandnoble.com)
- One site-specific program (for the site they assessed)

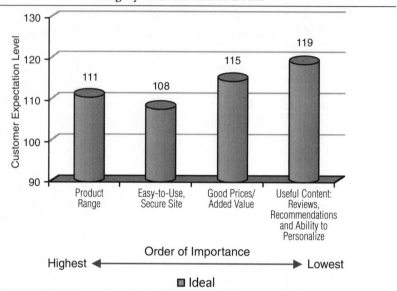

Figure 2.1
Category Ideal for Online Books

The Amazon.com loyalty program was called *New For You,* and provided customers with the ability to create a personalized section of the web site, and was a vehicle for getting subscribers to Amazon.com's semimonthly e-mail of new recommendations (see Figure 2.3 on page 36). This e-loyalty program directly reinforced e-values like "Useful Content" and "Product Range."

Barnesandnoble.com's program was called *Barnes & Noble MasterCard® Credit Card Reward Certificates* (see Figure 2.4 on page 37). When customers used the credit card, they earned points that could be redeemed for reward certificates that were good at Barnes & Noble brick-and-mortar locations or on B&N.com.

The Barnes & Noble program was a vestige of the past century's version of utilizing consumer insights to create a loyalty program. If it resonated with any e-values at all, they were found in the "Good Prices/Added Value" driver—the one driver where Barnesandnoble.com was actually competitive with Amazon.com—which was only the third most important driver.

VALUABLE VALUE CONCLUSIONS

In June 2001, after conducting a major survey of e-commerce customers for the Brand Keys *Customer Loyalty Index®*, we published a definitive list of the consumer insight-based value drivers that were most important in stimulating e-commerce loyalty.

Figure 2.2
Amazon.com versus Barnesandnoble.com

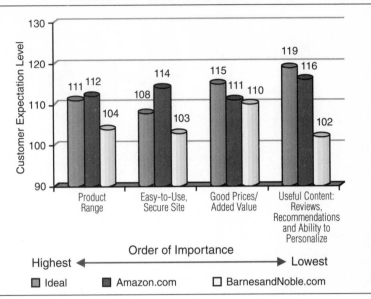

According to our research, e-companies that were perceived as embracing the consumer values represented by these value drivers were well positioned to better engage customers and build a loyal franchise and therefore would tend to be more profitable.

We also noted that the values to which people responded in Internet retailers were *quite different from those they sought in traditional retailers.* This was true even for those traditional retailers who, with newly built web sites, were in the early stages of a click-and-mortar strategy.

In 2003, our pronouncements smashed into their expiration date, and we discovered that the two sets of values had officially become one. Customer values in the retail category had become a mélange of both e-values *and* traditional retail values.

Many of the values people once associated exclusively with brick-and-mortar stores were now being sought online, while online values were permeating the nonvirtual world. Retailers who missed or ignored this major tectonic shift in customer values did so at their own peril.

Barnes & Noble, despite its poor showing in the dot-com arena, has recently started advertising that customers who place an online order by 11:00 A.M. can have their books delivered anywhere in Manhattan that same day. This is an example of the integration of some of the best values of both

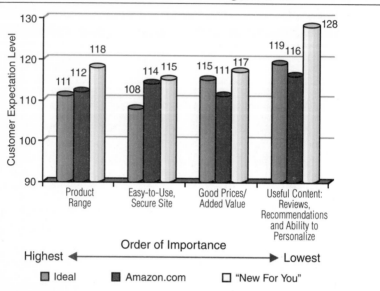

Figure 2.3
How Well Did Amazon.com's Program Work?

worlds—the speed and convenience of the Web coupled with the ability to hold the merchandise in your hand on the day of purchase.

What is clear is that as the number of choices available to customers continues to proliferate, and the values that customers embrace continue to evolve, insights will become increasingly difficult to capture by traditional methods.

What also is clear is that retailers—all marketers, for that matter—have an ever-growing need for a customer-loyalty strategy that includes a means of tracking and understanding consumer values.

How do you stay on top of this changing world? Hint: *Ask your customers.*

But not with the rearview-mirror approach of satisfaction studies or static marketing research. The real world isn't a snapshot; it's a movie. The world is no longer a 10-inch diagonal black-and-white TV, but a wide-screen, plasma-vision, high-definition, 3-D TV, with consumers who have 24/7 access to video (and virtually everything else) on demand.

EMOTIONAL MEASURES: IMPLEMENT THROUGH RESEARCH BEFORE OPTIMIZING THROUGH ADVERTISING

Do you want to own your research output and be able to extend it in a meaningful fashion into marketing programs that will help differentiate your brand?

Figure 2.4
How Well Did Barnesandnoble.com's Program Work?

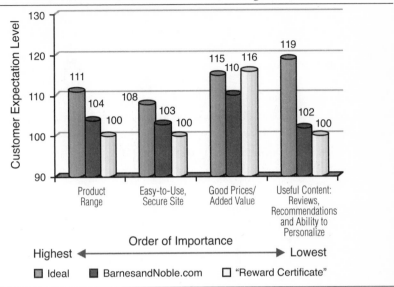

Getting emotional information for your category is a start, but most of the time, you cannot get emotional information by slicing and dicing the demographics. Segmentation may identify some interesting consumer subdivisions, but more often than not, it identifies segments that can't actually be marketed to very efficiently or effectively. By the very statistical nature of classic market segmentation, you end up with stuff, but not always stuff you can use. What good is it to identify five audiences that you cannot reach in a meaningful way? Segmentation is *not* just about demographics, psychographics, and lifestyle activities—it's about where people live, what they love and fear. But, mostly, it's about how they view a category and what they expect.

It is *you* who needs to know better. Ask your ad agency or your local research supplier a question, any question at all; they'll answer it. After all, when was the last time you heard them say that they could not give you what you asked for? So, make sure you ask them the right question. If the answer comes back in such a way that you could substitute *any* brand for your brand, you've been ripped off.

If you haven't heard it yet, you'll be hearing more and more about *emotional* foundations for branding and strategy development and engagement. This is a good thing. *Emotional bonding* is the best framework for managing brands and creating strategies and messages that effectively engage customers and that actually correlate with sales.

Providing emotional measures and insights has generally been the purview of advertising agencies. After all, they're the ones who are *supposed* to be creative. Write yourself a mental Post-it® note to remind you that most of the time when advertising agencies talk about "emotion" and "bonding with or engaging the consumer," their reference points are image items, personality nomenclatures, and interesting positionings and layouts. For example, given the newly recognized importance of the Baby Boomer, emotion is more often than not dredging up a rock-and-roll song from the 1960s and slugging it into a commercial over a visual of a lava lamp. These are usually creative expressions—entertaining, eye-catching, and visually differentiating—but they don't have an emotional underpinning that moves the brand closer to its strategic goal—creating brand effects that help the brand better meet or exceed consumer expectations.

We've noted that many companies have processes with really cool names like "Brand IQ," and "Brand Culturing," and "Brand DNA," and "BrandScape," and "EBAI aka Emotional Brand Asset Identifier." Although the outputs of those coolly named processes are rigorously derived (usually a process involving focus groups and importance ratings of image and personality terms, and sometimes, if they are really trying, ethnographic research), they are *not* emotionally based and cannot provide generalizable, predictive, below-the-radar, emotional insights. No matter how hard you try, you can't use the phrases "emotionally connecting with the consumer" and "derived importance" in the same sentence without some sense of the oxymoronic!

So, the next time the agency, planner, or consultant tells you that you are actually going to get emotional measures, imagine yourself in a car dealership where the salesperson has just proclaimed that this hot, new model has "warp-o-matic drive." Stop him right there. Insist that he pop the hood and show you precisely *how* that's going to happen. Just what is "warp" and how is it "matic"?

You have to actually execute emotional measures through predictive research *before* you can translate them into creative and engaging advertising and promotion. Brands that last—and more important, those that lead—are brands that benefit from deliberate integration of value-based customer loyalty research into their strategy, marketing, creative, and communication development.

TRUST CONSUMER VALUES—BUT DON'T LINGER

Some values change faster than others. But they all change, morphing with people's views of the world and the brand environments in which they live. After looking at Table 2.1, think about what the next then-and-now comparison will

Table 2.1
Shifting Consumer Values

Then	*Value Shift*	*Now*
Cigarettes were cool	Health	Cigarettes evil
No seatbelts/Air bags	Safety	Cars rated for safety
Water from a hydrant	Image	Bottled water
Had a GP	Health	Have specialists
Used public transport		Owns 1+ cars
Robby the Robot (1956)		Sony SDR–4RX robot (2003)
Record stores		Download music
LPs	Technology	8–Track
8–Tracks	Personal space	iPods
Audio cassettes		CDs
CDs		iPods
Eyeglasses		Contact lenses
Contact lenses		Laser surgery
Cupcakes, bread, butter	Diet/Health	No carbs, sugar, fat
Went to the market	Convenience	Ordered on Internet
Sent away for stuff advertised in the back of comic books	Technology/Speed	E-tail
Call home with a dime	Technology	Cell phones
Cell phones	Connection	Internet chatrooms
Played ball with a stick and Spaldeen	Technology	Computer games
Pong	Technology	PS/Nintendo/X–Box
Went to the movies	Entertainment/Social inter-action	Rented/"On-Demanded" a movie
Rented a movie	Entertainment/Social inter-action	Dialed up a movie/VOD
Family vacation trips	Technology	Virtual reality
Major metros: 4 TV networks	Media ecology	Cable/Satellite TV
Doors weren't locked	Security	Photo/Electronic key cards
People hitchhiked	Trust	Laws against hitchhiking

look like five years from now—or even sooner. What took a decade to shift in the past century may take only a year or two to move in this one. In some categories, a 30-day lead will make or break you.

GROWING LOYALTY THROUGH CLOSING THE EXPECTATION GAP

Can you remember the first time you were on a business trip and you returned to your hotel to find a small, wrapped chocolate on your pillow? Can you remember thinking, "What a nice thing to do"? Or when you checked into a hotel and, as the desk clerk gave you your room key, he said, "There's complimentary coffee and juice in the lobby each morning"? Think back to the very first time you saw someone use a wireless lock opener on his car. Remember how he reached into his pocket, took out this little square of plastic, and pushed the button. Can you hear the thunk as the doors opened, while you thought, "That's pretty neat. I wish my car had one of those!" Or in the movie *Wall Street,* when Michael Douglas makes a call from the beach using a shoebox-sized cell phone, admit it, you thought, "Cool, I wish I had one of those." You probably didn't use the phrase *added-value,* but a value infusion is what you were feeling.

Now, think about what you expect today. Chocolates on the pillow have become warm chocolate cookies with cold milk or a split of good champagne. Juice and coffee have become a full, complimentary breakfast. And which cars today don't have some form of electronic fob to open the door? Or the trunk? As for cell phones, British scientists created one small enough to fit in a tooth.

In the first instance, in each example, the emotion was "delight."

In the second, your most current state of mind was "expectation."

And when delight turns to expectation, brands generally find themselves in trouble.

Think about this: When you buy a brand, you are reacting to the built-up demand that comes from all of the advertising, PR, promotion, news coverage, word-of-mouth, clutter, product placement, and general buzz surrounding the brand. This amalgam of communications creates a certain level of expectation in you as a consumer—and if the brand doesn't make the grade vis-à-vis that expectation, heaven help the marketer. You will not only avoid buying it again, but you will tell your friends how bad it is, maybe even write a letter of complaint, and generally raise a fuss. Now, multiply your reaction by several million similar reactions, and you begin to see the power of expectations.

In 2006, customer loyalty expectations have increased dramatically in each of the 35 categories tracked in the Brand Keys *Customer Loyalty Index.* Consumer expectations are growing 3.5 times faster than brands are able to keep up.

The significance of the growing gap between expectations and brand delivery in these categories is profound, even shocking. *The growing gap between expectation and reality is living proof that marketers are increasingly incapable of identifying and leveraging rapidly changing customer values to their brands' advantage.* They are living in a brand ecosystem that produces a less loyal customer base (see Table 2.2).

Table 2.2
Percent Increase in Category Expectations and Brand Gap (Highest to Lowest)

Category	Increase in Expectations (%)	Brand Ratings (%)	Brand Gap (%)
Mobile Phones	12	−18	30
Online Books and Music	10	−15	25
Parcel Delivery	9	−7	16
Long Distance Provider	8	−22	30
Computers	8	−10	18
Gasoline	8	−17	25
Online Travel Sites	7	−12	19
Pizza	7	−10	17
Office Copiers	7	−17	24
Quick-Serve Restaurants	7	−13	20
Bottled Water	6	−9	15
Wireless Provider	6	−19	25
Car Rental Companies	6	−18	24
Mutual Funds	6	−15	21
Retail Stores	6	−14	20
Search Engines	5	−14	19
Diet Soft Drinks	5	−13	18
Regular Beer	5	−10	15
Online Brokerage	5	−9	14
AM News Shows	5	−8	13
Coffee & Doughnuts	5	−7	12
Major League Sports	4	−18	22
Airlines	4	−17	21
Hotels	4	−16	20
Insurance Companies	4	−12	16
Banks	4	−11	15
Athletic Footwear	4	−10	14
Clothing Catalogs	3	−12	15
Regular Soft Drinks	3	−11	14
Credit Cards	3	−10	13
Light Beers	2	−12	14
Energy Providers	1	−14	15

The range of expectation increases runs from the smallest for Energy Providers (+1 percent) to the highest increase of 12 percent for Mobile Phone manufacturers. The average increase in consumer brand expectations for the 239 brands surveyed was nearly 6 percent. The average ability of brands to keep up with consumers' rising expectations was −13 percent.

These are incredibly revealing statistics. At a time when most brands are struggling to differentiate themselves from the competition and remain profitable, it is essential that they know what consumers really expect of their brand. Clearly, they don't.

The highest absolute expectation levels were found for Long Distance Providers, Mobile Telephones, Wireless Providers, Car Rental Companies, and Search Engines. Leading brands in those categories included Verizon, Samsung, Treo, BlackBerry, Cingular, Avis, and Google.

Lowest expectation levels were in the categories of Coffee and Doughnut stores, Satellite Radio, Pizza, Overnight Parcel Delivery, AM News Shows, and Major League Sports, where the most successful brands were Starbucks, XM, Domino's and Papa John's, UPS, the *Today* show, and *Good Morning America*.

The top-10 largest gaps—the difference between what consumers want and what brands actually deliver—appeared in the following categories:

1. Long Distance Providers (30 percent)
2. Mobile Phones (30 percent)
3. Online Books and Music (26 percent)
4. Gasoline (25 percent)
5. Wireless Providers (25 percent)
6. Office Copiers (25 percent)
7. Car Rental Companies (24 percent)
8. Major League Sports (23 percent)
9. Quick-Serve Restaurants (21 percent)
10. Airlines (21 percent)

The bottom-line is that the speed at which consumer expectations are growing and the brands' inability to keep up makes for a very dangerous situation for brands to find themselves. Loyalty, engagement, and profitability will be governed by a brand's ability to meet or exceed customer expectations, and an inability to do so results in products turning into something less than actual brands—what we call *Category Placeholders*. These products are one step closer to becoming a commodity. That's not where you want your company to wind up.

The key to avoiding that is to close the expectations gap between your brand and the consumer's ideal of what your brand should be—and to do it faster than the competition can do it.

EXPERIENTIAL EXPECTATIONS

Experiential marketing is essentially setting out a process map for the environment in which you are going to place the brand. Just as companies study process engineering to best meet the physical and delivery demands of the consumer, experiential marketers should do the same for their customers—meet expectations in a particular experience-engendered brand environment.

A brand as a store experience is a great and popular example of this. Going into Diesel or Apple stores is a rich, fun, and wonderful experience, when it's done right. The key to right is not trial and error. Right means retrofitting the experience to match up to customer expectations. *Retrofit for the future,* based on what people want and value, and how they give their loyalty.

Remember the half-life of delight? There are always specific things you know you can do as an informed brand that people will love and value. The problems start when this delight turns into expectation. Honeymoons last only so long. Without measuring and changing the right stuff, soon all you will have done is satisfied the price of entry—if that.

So, once again the question resurfaces: Where to best invest in building brand equity? Which experiences pay off best in terms of reinforcing values and loyalty? There is no way to know anything except vague impressions unless you measure values and expectations first. Very few of us have an infallible sense of timing: A product's life cycle begins when it's invented. It hits the market when it's valued and affordable enough to sell and make a profit. How long the effectiveness of new tactics engage customers, or how fast expectations change, cannot be known unless you measure. Only then, can you differentiate and evaluate values within and between experiential programs.

There are always different creative tactics for responding to the same need. Study and prioritize your needs based on what drives purchases by delivering on expectations. Then, design tactics as efficiently and effectively as you can around the objectives that information suggests.

A significant number of people may say in an exit poll that you need to improve the user friendliness of your retail environment. Whether that will make people buy more or just like the shopping experience better is still unknown.

Whether to move on that data should depend on concrete knowledge of the loyalty lift you can expect. A much higher percentage of contribution to loyalty may come from rotating your stock more often rather than retrofitting your store.

THE BRAND OR THE LOGO: WHICH CAME FIRST AND HOW DOES IT AFFECT THE CUSTOMER EXPERIENCE?

Today, logos represent many things. They are part art form, part fabric of modern consciousness, and part popular brand culture, but logos are also part of experiencing the brand. And although art lovers we may all be, value in the form of recognition tops most executives' consideration list when it comes to making informed spending decisions on logos and brand identity. We all agree that brand logos are a requirement, the price of entry into any market, and an integral part of the public's common visual lexicon. It's right about here where many companies get stuck. How much does the fact that we recognize a logo, even *like* a logo, change our behavior toward using or purchasing the brand that logo represents? I raise that question because logo is very nearly the first thing that is mentioned when companies are looking to address brand equity or rebranding issues.

That's because conversations about creative elements like logo and imagery are the easiest ones to have. Yet, a great disconnect between modern branding and customer loyalty programs is distinguishing between making a logo everyone recognizes and making something that strategically returns value in the form of customer loyalty and brand recognition directly linked to sales.

Logos are visual touch points. Everyone, corporate and public alike, has a fascination with semiotics (i.e., public symbols not spelled out in letters). And everyone has an opinion on them. Like flags to nations, logos give people something in common to identify with, something to rally around, share, and talk about. Where the process gets blurry is when companies mistake the development or revamping of their logos for actions that significantly contribute to customers' brand loyalty and, therefore, brand value.

Just to be clear, I am no Philistine. I appreciate great design and recognize the creative challenges involved in capturing a brand's visual essence and personality through an icon. Our goal here is to better measure and contextualize a logo's role and value in an organization, and, ultimately, with the customer. The assessments here, represented in simple percentages, are the words and feelings of the customer. The numbers do not lie. All logos have their place. The questions should always include where, to what end, and for how much.

It really got us going when yet another of our clients, heavily attuned to ROI, commented on the high price of having his corporate logo "revitalized and iconicized," to quote the strategic-corporate-brand-identity-design-branding firm he worked with. He said:

> I'm not exactly sure what we got for our money. Everybody already knows our company. You had to have been living in a cave in Nepal for the past 50 years *not* to know our company. So why did we spend the money to "revitalize" the company logo? The "iconicization" added 20 percent to the development costs alone!

It was a reasonable question.

This is a process companies generally go though when they have reached a point where traditional marketing options have ceased to effectively address problems associated with flagging brand share and increased levels of consumer ennui. It's a kind of corporate midlife crisis when you supplant a brand logo overhaul for the greater good of marketing reconnaissance and revised strategy, even though there are virtually no substantive changes that can be attributed to the exercise—beyond increased levels of consumer perceptions that the company has a new logo. Fair is fair.

At Brand Keys, we track over 500 brands, most of which have logos of one sort or another. Our client's question about logo moved us to measure to what extent—and more precisely, with what percent of contribution—a brand or corporate logo, emblem, sign, symbol, icon, or avatar actually makes to consumer engagement, brand loyalty, and company profitability.

We included a component in our survey designed to reveal whose logo was actively contributing to loyalty and profitability, and whose logo was sitting there like a prom beauty that never gets asked to dance. Given that different companies have different nomenclatures for their visual elements, we use *logo* to represent any graphic or visual ID a brand uses consistently in its marketing.

Knowing You, Even Loving You, Is Not the Same as Using You

As you look at the figures, remember what we are investigating: the percentage of contribution made by the logos that we tested, judged by how they correlate to customer attitudes, engagement, and behaviors that reinforce brand loyalty and affect sales.

If you look at the findings in Table 2.3 and hear yourself say, "I didn't remember that they even had a logo," it says a lot about how hard a logo is working from a communication, engagement, *and* loyalty level, regardless

Table 2.3
Is Your Logo a Leader or a Loser?

	(%)		(%)
Apple	33	The Hartford	12
Polo	26	Wachovia	12
CBS	25	Shell Gasoline	11
Nike	25	Citibank	10
Verizon	25	Chase	10
MetLife	24	Gateway	9
Starbucks	24	NBA	9
NBC	23	Wal-Mart	9
La Coste	23	AT&T	8
MasterCard	20	Coke	8
Merrill Lynch	20	Expedia	8
Brand Keys	19	Pepsi	8
Cingular	19	MLB	8
NFL	19	Minolta	8
McDonald's	18	Marriott	7
Motorola	16	Fidelity	7
Little Caesar's	15	Kmart	7
American Express	15	Taco Bell	6
Target	14	United	6
Dunkin' Donuts	13	Janus	6
White Castle	13	UBS Financial	5

what the annual spend may be to keep the logo alive, polished, and not shaken from the consumer's top-of-mind Etch-A-Sketch®.

Interpreting Logo

A logo, it turns out, 99 percent of the time is a component of the driver that deals with "Corporate Reputation/Brand Status," which makes perfect sense. The measures in Table 2.3 represent the percent of contribution they make to that driver. We understand that many other components make greater contributions, but this gives you a real sense of how one logo performs compared to another, and how they contribute to engaging customers and their decisions to purchase. We figure that many business folks out there are wondering the same thing as our clients. Well, now you know. Equipped with this kind of information, the allocation of dollars on logo development can be wisely and directly correlated to the value it brings to a brand in terms of the ultimate consumer metric: profitability.

Of all the logos we measured, Apple Computer's apple made the highest percent of contribution at 30 percent, which translates to serious levels of engagement and loyalty and profits. How serious? Early in 2006, the record label Apple Corps, founded by the Beatles in 1968, sued Apple Computers, insisting that Apple Computer drop the apple from the iTunes Music Store. Apple Corps lawyer acknowledged that Apple Computer is entitled to produce programs such as iTunes, but it should stay out of the music business if it uses the Apple logo. "We were the people supplying the music. And they crossed the dividing line," he said. A monetary figure for damages has not yet been named, but you can bet they're talking serious dollars.

But here's something you don't have to go to court to settle: If a logo isn't increasing public awareness of the company, and isn't (implicitly or explicitly) differentiating or reinforcing corporate imagery, and isn't contributing to brand experience, and isn't ripping through marketplace clutter, it should, at least, be reinforcing customer engagement, loyalty, and profitability. *Problem is, engagement, loyalty, and profitability may not involve fonts, color pallets, and design elements as much as we think or would like.* My inner art director is not dead yet. I like to talk about logos, too. Loyalty and profitability, however, do provide a very steely basis for understanding your logo's ROI and its impact on your brand.

The cyclical primacy of logo in brand identity may very well be a combination of many factors. However, our habitual conditioning and feel-good practices belie traditional marketing's current limitations to identify more significant brand differentiation strategies. There's also the possibility that we're approaching a domain where the possibility for originality is nearing extinction. *It could be that there just aren't any really good names left to call yourself or your product.* Not that a name contributes any more to people's willingness to desire, believe in, or buy you as an icon. Whatever the reason is, to know you is not necessarily to like you, use you, or to buy what you're saying.

Whether you call it logo, symbol, icon, or avatar, no matter if it's a swoosh on your feet, a piece of fruit on your desk (or elsewhere), or even an alligator or a polo player on your chest, a company's visual identity *can* materially influence public perception of the brand. What we are able to do now is unflinchingly answer precisely how much the face of your brand's personality is indeed something that customers value and, ultimately, are willing to pay to be a part of.

Barbie: Redux or Retirement?

What's more experiential than a toy? As a toy marketer, you should be looking at product development from a kid's point of view, which is what drives and maintains toy loyalty. Unless you understand the values of your real audience, what makes them buy and continue to buy, you will be in trouble. The greatest ideas based on the most socially and educationally sound principles flop unless they resonate with real-life values and meet or exceed expectations in the category.

Furthermore, even if you are only marketing dolls, you are not just competing in the category of dolls . . . you're competing against all kid entertainment brands. And in that broad category, what makes a very high contribution to loyalty for the ideal toy is fun and excitement. What do kids expect? Look at the values shown in Figure 2.5.

Put a Barbie, with or without a Ken, next to a PlayStation, and she's never going to make it. If Barbie isn't better than Harry Potter, she's not going to get much attention, no matter how accessorized, scantily dressed, or anatomically adjusted she may be. The point is that it is much harder to be a well-made, educational toy and go to market based on that premise alone when you are competing for your customer's love and attention with offerings that are far closer to his or her values and the category Ideal.

Figure 2.5
Barbie's Dream Values

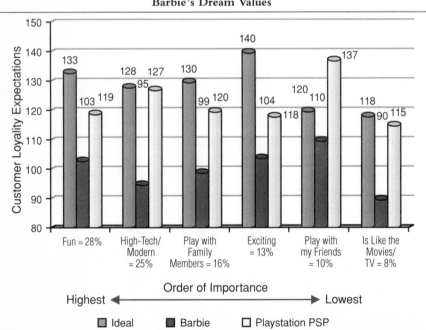

In the retail sector, the American Girl Store got the equation right: appeal to and encourage the collector. Allow extensive personalization or customization and emphasize the lifestyle—far more inclusively than any other retailer or any manufacturer could be.

At the American Girl Store, the doll becomes incidental, an ancillary to success, just one part of an event that is a masterpiece of integrated marketing, horizontal and vertical. Don't believe me? Just get within five blocks of one of their stores on a Saturday and count the American Girl Store shopping bags going by, or walk the aisles and watch parents shell out to have their daughters' hair styled in the fashion of the doll of the moment.

CHANGING EXPECTATIONS: GEN X VERSUS BABY BOOMERS

Advertisers and media planners who wish to provide more effective and profitable media plans have to forsake their historic reliance purely on demographics and add a new metric to their ad-planning tool boxes. Historically speaking, when customer expectations increase, it's a sign that customer needs are going unmet. When customer needs are unmet, customers defect to brands that talk to them in *believable ways* and fulfill their increased expectations. Rising expectations offer opportunities for brands, if they can just figure out how to capitalize on those trends. But how? Brands can identify and leverage opportunities by tracking the direction and velocity of changing customer values, so they can better communicate with their customers.

Decreasing expectation levels, however, are also a good index of consumer behavior, because they show that consumers are feeling disenfranchised and ignored by marketers, and are tending increasingly to think of products, services, and even brands as commodities.

As part of our *Customer Loyalty Index,* we examined consumer expectation levels among Baby Boomers and Generation Xers. The analysis revealed some surprising variations in expectation trends and some important implications that advertisers will need to take into account if they wish to have profitable, differentiated brands in the future.

For the past six years, Gen Xers' loyalty expectations (typically pretty flat) have been rising (see Table 2.4). The expectations of Baby Boomers (a group that historically logged the highest expectation levels of any segment examined), however, have been dropping. Expectation levels are indexed with 100 as the baseline.

These patterns reflect corollary trends in marketing, branding, and advertising initiatives. Industry observers have noted that until recently more

Table 2.4
Levels of Customer Expectations

Group	2001	2002	2003	2004	2005	2006
Generation X	106	108	108	116	116	117
Baby Boomers	128	125	120	118	117	117

time, attention, and marketing dollars have been spent against Gen Xers than Baby Boomers.

As we've noted, those recent attempts to emotionally engage the Baby Boomers have traditionally been anchored in stereotypes with references and symbols like peace signs and Woodstock images of rock and roll with positionings that imply (even take for granted) that Baby Boomers are self-centered. Brands that have based their development on targeting the youth dollar suddenly have to come to grips with a completely new market, consequently drifting away from the Baby Boomers. And Baby Boomers have been unable to escape the inevitable: time marches on, and it's someone else's turn to be the alpha consumer in certain marketer's eyes. But marketers have to realize this. They have to act accordingly and begin shuffling their ad targets, instead of just saying they realize it. Those who continue the old patterns will find that they are forcing a significant consumer group down a path where *only* a price will differentiate them from their competitors, moving away from brand status toward becoming a well-known Category Placeholder. To become such a Placeholder is risky at this time in marketing history.

AGE MATTERS: IN AND ACROSS CULTURES, AGE-BASED EXPECTATIONS MAY NOT BE WHAT YOU THINK, OR WOULD LIKE THEM TO BE

Age matters. The question is, for you and your brand, in what way does it matter? Marketers want to craft strategies that are able to meet or exceed age-based category expectations. So, why not just advertise product attributes and benefits and be done with it?

Because by more accurately identifying the real, age-driven expectations consumers hold for a category, marketers and strategic planners are able to *leverage* real brand values that result in more effective advertising.

Compared to 1998, we have found that *the order of importance* of the category drivers in the financial services category have remained relatively stable. This means the yardstick that consumers use to measure the category has not substantively changed in ways that would otherwise provide opportunities for brands to differentiate themselves. What's more, no differences reveal themselves when the driver's order of importance is examined by various age segments. Category expectations, however, have increased, and they vary, depending on the age segment being examined.

The variance in consumer expectations compared with the ability of brands to meet such expectations provides the foundation for the commoditization of financial services. It also provides an opportunity for brands that can accurately identify the changes in expectations, to leverage these insights to their advantage—to identify targets more effectively, to differentiate their brands, and to market more profitably.

Using this same approach, three age cohorts (18 to 29, 35 to 49, and 50 plus) for American Express (green) cardholders were examined in three countries (United States, Japan, and England).

Remember the five basic questions for which you should have answers:

1. What are the drivers for the category?
2. Which specific key attributes, benefits, and values form the components of each of the drivers?
3. What's the order of importance of the drivers?
4. What expectations do consumers hold for each of the drivers?
5. How does your brand stack up to a category Ideal?

After examining the cohorts, the four category drivers—in order of importance—were identified as:

1. *Usage and Payment Flexibility:* Includes values like "gives a reasonable time to make payments," "is widely accepted where you want to use it," and "is widely accepted abroad"
2. *Precision and Superior Support:* Includes values like "has accurate monthly statements" and "is provided by a company that has people to help you no matter where you are in the world"
3. *Company and User Imagery:* Includes items like "is provided by a prestigious company" and "is a technologically advanced company"
4. *Ease and Speed of Interaction:* Includes values like "posts payments to my account in a timely fashion" and "can get through to customer service quickly"

The order of importance of the drivers for the Ideal credit card was, as indicated in Figure 2.6, the *same* in the United States, Japan, and England. The order of importance of the drivers for the Ideal credit card was the *same* in the geographic regions for *each* of the three age cohorts by country as well. These findings meant that *how* consumers—of different ages and different countries—view the category are identical.

Although this is not an entirely surprising finding for a category that has virtually turned into a commodity, it also means that configuring effective, age-centric strategies based on what was important to the respondent becomes a nearly impossible marketing task.

Happily, the output of loyalty research *also identifies the levels of expectation* held by consumers for each for the category drivers (see Figure 2.6). And there *were* differences in the expectations held by certain age cohorts for one category driver over another.

Thus, age-based category insights founded on age-specific expectations could be leveraged to provide a more differentiated and effective marketing

Figure 2.6
Age-Based Expectations for Credit Cards

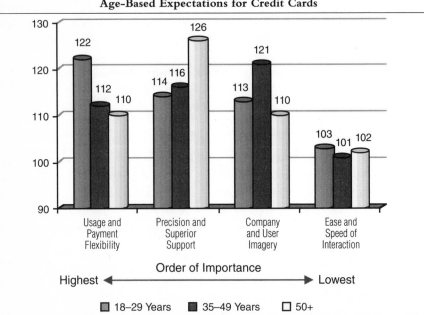

platforms for the brand, based on a new and more sophisticated way of interpreting how certain consumer segments are likely to behave in the marketplace.

Crafting strategies by age cohort has been proven to yield more effective positionings and, more important, more effective and engaging marketing programs.

Addressing loyalty expectations—or at the very least, making them part of the modern marketing toolbox—provides advertisers with more accurate targeting vis-à-vis brand momentum (i.e., what consumers are *willing to believe* about a brand) and a road map for designing, sequencing, and communicating such initiatives.

LOYALTY TALES FROM THE REAL WORLD

McDonald's and How New Employee Uniforms Affect the Brand

With wise consumers of the twenty-first century eating healthier at more and varied restaurants, traditional fast-food giants like McDonald's have been feeling the pinch. Fresh salads and premium coffee, after all, go only so far and remain fresh only so long. So, according to an article in *Advertising Age,* some fast-food companies have decided to migrate their image from *fat* to *phat* by commissioning the likes of Tommy Hilfiger and P. Diddy to turn their employees' uniforms into hip street wear. The thought is, presumably, to have uniforms so hip that they convert employees into walking billboards for the brand when they decide to wear them on the street. The logical reasoning behind this is that it has worked in Europe. Well, so did the metric system.

Let's take a quick side trip to Loyalty Land. First, values among American youth are different from those in Europe. Although American youth are more drawn to individuality, European youth seem to love uniforms. In most cases, uniforms are utilitarian, keep workers clean and safe, and make it easy to distinguish them from the customers. But the last thing an American teenager wants when he gets out of work is to go out with his friends in his polyester work clothes, no matter who designed them.

One managing director of Landor, a branding and corporate identity firm, supported McDonald's move, stating that how people feel about their company and brand contributes to their understanding of the "brand idea" and their ability to "live" the brand promise. According to this view, a new designer uniform presumably enriches the concept and experience of preparing fried food quickly and efficiently.

Second, one supposes that if McDonald's regards fashion as a useful mechanism to improve its human decor, and increase relevance and resonance with young adults, it presumably expects that, besides making employees more involved and invested in their jobs, it will get some ROI from the customers. Before we tell you what that contribution is, we'd like you to take this short test: Close your eyes. Think back to the last time you were in a fast-food restaurant. Keep your eyes closed and tell us what the employees were wearing. Okay, open your eyes.

If you weren't able to create a mental picture, don't feel bad. You're not alone. Uniforms (even haute couture uniforms) make a mere *0.5 percent* contribution to loyalty and profitability. "A Clean Uniform" makes a 1 percent contribution. On average, it typically costs $5,000 to outfit a fast-food restaurant with uniforms. You have to be confident that you will sell an awful lot of additional hamburgers to afford that kind of wardrobe outlay when you restyle an entire workforce across an entire franchise network.

Don't misunderstand us. It's nice to have employees look smart, clean, and hip. It's just that you'd like to be sure that you are going to get something more back for the investment than admiring glances from customers, positive reviews in the fashion pages, or even higher levels of employee morale. If boosted morale were your goal, a 75-cent-an-hour raise would go a lot further in that direction.

Loyalty assessments reveal the percent of contribution such efforts make to your bottom line. As it turns out, there are only three categories where the uniform makes a truly substantive contribution to positive customer perceptions, loyalty, and profitability. These are:

- Law enforcement (including the military)
- Pilots (but not flight attendants)
- Medical personnel (including doctors and nurses)

So, unless fast-food franchises plan to hire lots of moonlighting cops, commandos, aviators, and medical staff, their dollars would be better invested in other areas than spiffing up the behind-the-counter worker.

Talk all you want about the value of the brand experience, but the loyalty metrics *always* predict what return you'll get for your efforts. In the real world, you can't ask for more than that.

Q & A

Brands, Roots, and Loyalty

Lenore Skenazy, *New York Daily News:* *Can a brand get too far from its roots and start to dilute customer loyalty?*

Robert Passikoff: Yes. Some of these failures occur because consumers have become increasingly more knowledgeable and sophisticated about the plethora of choices; they know what they want and what something is worth to them. Other failures occur because what is coming out is "stuff" in which consumers have absolutely no interest. But here's the lesson: The biggest error leading to product failure is when a brand mistakes market opportunities for brand opportunities.

A recent survey revealed that 86 percent of all new product launches—including line extensions—fail. The real issue is whether companies can identify gaps in the market, but their actions are in response to the "can-we-put-it-out-there" question. Companies are expert at having the financial, production, and distribution wherewithal to get stuff out to consumers. New stuff rolls off the line all the time, but it misses far more often than it hits. The problem is that the failed brands could not actually sustain the opportunity—their equity was not strong enough among the target for customers to believe that the brands could deliver on their promises and meet real expectations and needs.

Brands often mistake image for equity. Image can be stretched quite a bit before the communications become dissonant. Real brand equity can rarely be extended that far. Even if sales and market share are strong for one quarter, or three, after a certain point, whatever does not align with the equity attributed to the brand will dilute it and the customer loyalty previously associated with it.

Lenore Skenazy: *Do older brands get perceived as trustworthy (as a brand to which we can remain loyal) or stale? Does a youth brand stay a youth brand or does it age along with its early users?*

Robert Passikoff: We have all lived through the brand version of a facelift, appearing as a new package, new or lower-in-something ingredients, a slightly more hip logo, or advertising in which today's music appears. In doing this cosmetic routine, older brands (especially those trying to appear young and hip) sometimes come across as being stale or forced. This is equally true for youth brands, whether they are trying to stay young or appear to be keeping up with their aging customers.

One of the shortcomings of research that measures how brands rate on image and personality items like trustworthy, stale, youthful, and so on is that marketers often treat these characteristics as being static. We should ask two questions when dealing with matters of brand perception: (1) Has the brand been able to track the direction and velocity of the values that customers are really using to define the category? (2) Is there evidence of what the brand can sustain in terms of customer beliefs about that brand?

Oreo Cookies has done a good job tracking the direction and velocity of multigenerational customer expectations and, as an older brand, has been able to avoid getting stale (no pun intended). AT&T is another story: They were so busy worrying about whether customers saw them as old and stodgy that they did not take the steps necessary to find out what they could change to better align with morphing expectations for the telecommunications category. The rest, as they say, is history.

"Then again, gentlemen, we're in complete agreement in the sense that nobody knows the answer to any of the questions that have been raised."

CHAPTER 3

How to Measure Customer Values, Expectations, and Loyalty

Things should be made as simple as possible but not any simpler.

—*Albert Einstein*

Good Research Means Asking the Right Questions

If the definition of insanity is doing the same things over and over with the expectation of getting different results, many marketers would have been institutionalized long ago. Business both big and small needs to awaken to *how,* not if, consumers are changing the way we should go to market, and, by definition, the way we should measure our efforts.

And, as usual, consumers are proving to be pretty robust at adapting and advancing knowledge, awareness, and understanding—and they are thriving.

Long no more for the sunny times just a decade ago, media and information channels were fewer, and life—even advertising—seemed simple, more easily packaged, very nearly Norman Rockwellian. Way back then it was much easier for the providers of products and services to manage and manipulate the information about their offerings, which consumers dutifully received and assimilated. The better the marketers managed and manipulated, the more they increased their chances of engaging the customer and developing a loyal customer base.

The times they keep a-changin'. With a mountain of offerings in every category, and information available 24/7 from a zillion sources, today's consumer is no longer at the mercy of the corporate party line. Some competing product, or a second opinion, is just a click or a conversation away. Forget multiplying; the information bandwidth increases exponentially every year—maybe every week. Whoever thought you'd be watching television shows—and commercials—on your cell phone or iPod? While the critical net result is that engagement loyalty is more difficult to create and maintain, what's interesting is the way in which many companies are trying to measure the consumer.

You can't greet consumers by asking them lowly, past-century questions as we try to cozy up to their agile, sophisticated sets of preferences: "Do you know about X?" "How likely are you to purchase Y in the next 30 days?" People can engage in much richer consumer conversations than that. Not only do they want to, these days people expect to.

As people get more complex and markets more crowded, the four P's (i.e., Product, Price, Place, and Promotion) become more similar and undifferentiated marketing activities. It's increasingly difficult to know who people are, what people value, and what they expect, whether you are using the traditional generational divides of Baby Boomers, Gen Xers, Gen XBoxers, or the burgeoning niche of groups based on ethnicity, gender, or sexual preference. If ever there was a call for a method to recategorize human groups and systematize the gathering of knowledge, it's now. Many people claim to do this, but interpretations are *not* leading indicators, no matter how much you wish them to be. They do not reliably predict purchase behavior and tie return on investment (ROI) correlation means trackable, quantifiable, "I-spent-and-did-this-and-got-this" kind of cause and effect.

A very real issue these days is that modern markets, and modern market makers, are fast moving. There are scads of consumer groups, and they're simultaneously less differentiated *and* more homogeneous in their preferences, profiles, values, and, more important, behaviors in the marketplace. Just when it seems you've got a bead on folks, there they go changing their direction again. There is more social and economic mobility in developed and developing nations than anytime before in human history. We as marketers stand at the edge of a precipice of real consumer profile change. We have no choice but to change how we examine consumers as well. For those with vision, will, guts, and curiosity, we have arrived at a new customer-marketing paradigm—and those who lack such vision will be condemned to putter along until the pain becomes intolerable.

We humans have tried to make sense of our selves, our values, and our world, and the underlying motivations for our behaviors—what makes us tick, why we do the things we do—for a great many years. Lately, modern marketing and commerce have certainly become very interested in answering these questions, just as anthropologists, theologians, and psychologists have been for a long time.

GOOD RESEARCH MEANS ASKING THE RIGHT QUESTION THE RIGHT WAY

"We knew what we needed to know, so we went out and asked what we needed to." Clients tell us that all the time. But usually, we're also having a conversation about how their information and insight needs weren't quite met by *asking what they needed to.*

The following dialogue best represents the pitfalls of relying on "ask-a-question-get-an-answer" traditional research. This conversation comes from the popular British TV show, *Yes, Prime Minister.* In this scene, the Prime Minister's secretary and Home Secretary (our version of the Secretary of State) discuss how to measure the merits of reinstituting Britain's version of the military draft:

Bernard Wolley (BW): He [the Prime Minister] thinks it [reintroducing National Service] is a vote winner.

Sir Humphrey Applegate (SHA): That's more serious. What makes him think that?

BW: They've had an opinion poll done showing that all the votes are in favor of bringing back National Service.

SHA: Well, have another opinion poll done showing that the voters are against bringing back National Service.

BW: Well, you can't be for it and against it.

SHA: Of course you can. Well, Bernard, you know what happens. A nice young lady comes up to you, obviously you want to create a good impression, you don't want to look a fool, so she starts asking you some questions. For example: Mr. Wolley, are you worried about the number of young without jobs?

BW: Yes.

SHA: Are you worried about the rise in crime amongst teenagers?

BW: Yes.

SHA: Do you think there is a lack of discipline in our comprehensive schools?

BW: Yes.

SHA: Do you think young people welcome some authority and leadership in their lives?

BW: Yes.

SHA: Do you think they respond to a challenge?

BW: Yes.

SHA: Would you be in favor of reintroducing National Service?

BW: Oh, well, I suppose I might . . .

SHA: Yes or no.

BW: Yes.

SHA: Of course you would Bernard, after all you've told them you can't say "no" to that. So, they don't mention the first five questions and publish the last one.

BW: Is that really what they do?

SHA: Well, not the reputable ones, no, but there aren't many of those. So alternatively, the young lady can get the opposite result.

BW: How?

SHA: Mr. Wolley, are you worried about the danger of war?

BW: Yes.

SHA: Are you worried about the growth of armaments?

BW: Yes.

SHA: Do you think there's a danger in giving young people guns and teaching them how to kill?

BW: Yes.

SHA: Do you think it's wrong to force people to take up arms against their will?

BW: Yes.

SHA: Would you oppose the reintroduction of National Service?

BW: Yes.

SHA: There you are, you see, Bernard, the perfect balanced sample. So, we just commission our own survey for the Ministry of Defense.

Reasonable questions, reasonably asked, yet there were two different results. This is not the kind of research conversation you want to hold. You need to ask—and answer—these questions:

- How do you know you are offering the right stuff, through the right channels, in the right way?
- Why does one brand lead over another?
- Why is one brand able to differentiate itself from the competition?

The answer is simple: Success comes to the brand that identifies consumer expectations and—via marketing and communication efforts—meets or exceeds these expectations by its position in a particular product or service category. The winning brand understands how high "up" really is for its category. The winning brand understands what consumers are willing to believe about it and how much people are willing to value it—after all, value is nothing more than a combination of belief, trust, desire, and, therefore, willingness to pay for something, anything really, from Calvin Klein's to Pirellis to iPods.

The reason for this is that a brand is an icon capable of securing an emotional bond with its user, and it should represent some guarantee of solidity in the relationship between customer and product. The common denominator of continued brand success—beyond price-of-entry issues like quality, availability, and even "value-for-dollar"—is the brand's continued ability to meet or exceed people's expectations about it.

Facts are facts: most customers leave a brand because another brand better meets or exceeds their expectations about specific attributes and benefits (although, as most marketers have discovered, exceeding even your competitors on an attribute or benefit basis has become nearly impossible in most categories) and values that they anticipate the product or service will deliver. Leave price out of it for the moment. For a brand (and the corporate balance sheet), that should be the option of last resort. Our bionic consumers, while informed, have morphed over the years into wise shoppers. Very few of them buy purely on price. The delivery of those attributes, from status to performance to beauty and quality, is what creates delight, builds or reinforces loyalty, and engages customers.

Just because some marketers have shed their ties and wear chinos doesn't eliminate the communication gap between companies and customers. No matter how in touch you may feel with your customer, if you are not anticipating shifts in values and expectations, you are just playing catch-up or, worse, follow the leader. To realize their full potential and life span, smart brands also know that the more their emotional identity is a reflection of their customers, the more they will be chosen. This is *loyalty* as defined by the people who put their money where their beliefs are. Companies that appreciate this dynamic understand and own modern brand equity.

Most companies (size doesn't matter, although it's likely that smaller companies have a better understanding of consumers than larger ones despite larger research budgets) are either not experienced at accurately measuring values, either what they're providing consumers or what customers really want. Cost accounting and standard financial analysis will not reveal the difference in expectations between new and mature customers.

Why established brands have collapsed in the face of aggressive competition should be old news. If you are surprised that General Motors (GM) reported a loss of $8.6 billion in January 2006, you shouldn't be. We can easily deduce its demise by tracing discrepancies between what a brand offers, what a brand *means,* and what the customer expects and is willing to believe about what is offered. In retrospect, it's a fairly easy and direct correlation to establish.

Ask yourself three questions about your brand, and three about the consumers to whom you're trying to sell. Be honest with these six questions:

1. What does your brand offer?
2. How is it substantively different than the competition?
3. What does it *mean*—what does the brand stand for?
4. What do consumers value and expect—what makes them feel valued and what do they really want?
5. How close does your offering come to that expectation?
6. What are consumers willing to believe about you?

Keep in mind that people tend to keep their jobs a little longer when they provide answers for what to do right when moving forward, not what they did wrong when they look back. The development of a modern brand vision must be inextricably linked to measures that continually and accurately *predict* what consumer values and expectations will be.

If you make that last statement to a marketing or brand team, the majority of the folks in the room will nod approvingly. But instead of acting on that idea, most of them nod off, adjust their rearview mirrors, or rely on the same old tricks. For many companies, most of the useful customer data that they do get isn't worth the trip to the photocopy machine. Because if those findings are not based on approaches that yield insightful, actionable, forward-facing, predictive results, the application of those findings—no matter how rigorously collected—can lead to brand strategies and marketing plans that are shaky at best. One of our pet mantras defines this condition as relying on *excellent answers to meaningless questions.*

Research approaches are usually based on points of view that are far too internally focused in the organization and as such, practitioners lack reliable methods to measure and capitalize on customer preferences and values. They do not go beyond direct-inquiry techniques like focus groups and standard polling and other dubious self-reporting. Here's another of our mantras: "You now know what they *said* they thought, not what they *really* thought."

It seems an obvious insight, but knowing what consumers really want and how they are really going to behave concerning your category or brand provides you with a substantial advantage.

LISTEN OR BE LEFT BEHIND

It's nice to see the resurgence of faith in the belief that corporations work best when people who are in them, from designers to managers to marketers, have the fullest understanding of everyday people—their customers. One neat, constant feature about human communication is that we do it through conversations: internal to our businesses, talking to ourselves, talking with each other, talking *to* others, and communicating to groups. And what we at Brand Keys have been suggesting for some time now is the adoption of sophisticated customer-listening devices to tap into both internal and external conversations.

Why the need for such a shift? Watch the market. Businesses are still mired in the tradition of *make it, move it, market it,* and *sell it at the right price* are having a hard time keeping up these days. If we can't agree that traditional advertising is dead, at least we can agree that it is on its knees, locked in a punishing customer chokehold. And the squeeze is on, whether customers are tuning in (TiVO) or tuning out (the Web).

Charles Darwin never goes out of fashion, if only by analogy, for brands and their survival in the economic jungle. In business, just as in biology, competition requires specialization, so when moving forward, survival of the fittest might easily be defined as those brands that evolve by identifying the values that will imbue them with enough meaning to engage the customers, and then meeting or exceeding customer expectations in their categories. But smart brands do more than survive. They grow through innovation, expansion, diversification, or specialization. This growth is rooted in an understanding of what drives loyalty: customer and category values, customer's expectations, and what customers are willing to believe the brand can actually deliver. Think of it as economic Darwinism.

Now is the time for businesses to re-create themselves through authentically and proactively meeting customer needs and values—by knowing how to listen. If you pay attention to successful businesses, you'll find that the truly wise companies are constantly moving further and further and deeper and deeper into a dialogue with the customer base, and using varying techniques to listen and learn.

You earn the respect of twenty-first-century customers by sincerely showing them you speak their language—not only their culture and vernacular but also their value language. Show them that you listen, that you understand, and that you offer them something they really want. Leading-indicator loyalty research methods let you make sure that you're getting the story straight, probing the core of their human values in this hypermodern life, category by category.

KNOWING WHAT TO MEASURE: COMMUNICATION, CAMPAIGN TESTING, AND TRACKING

The most aggressive minds in an organization rarely focus on measurement systems, or they haven't up until now. Most executives work with inherited measurement systems that distort their business strategies, anchoring their brands in the mid-twentieth century.

A number of approaches developed in the late-1950s and early-1960s laid the foundation for today's measurement and tracking systems. Three of the key, early models included the outdated AIDA (Attention, Interest, Desire, Action) model that assumed the message frequency or advertising tonnage (and associated awareness) would drive attitude change and, shortly thereafter, behavior. This has been shown to be a self-serving belief of most media-planning models. There's the obsolete Lavidge and Steiner's hierarchy-of-effects hypothesis but that was completely unable to link changes in consumer awareness to *any* changes in behavior in the marketplace. Then there's the questionable Colley DAGMAR (Defining Advertising Goals for Measured Advertising Results) approach that avoided issues related to sales and dealt only with communication effects. Makes you yearn for the days of long ago when you never heard or had to deal with "I-spent-and-did-this-and-got-what, doesn't it?"

You're welcome to look up the details of these approaches, but the basic assumption of these models was that the marketer was in control of most product or service information and persuasion that consumers received. Therefore, marketers should be able to manage and manipulate their own communication activities. Since, the theory went, marketers can influence consumer attitudes and ultimately consumer behavior, tracking of awareness and attitudinal change is a sufficient measure because the two ultimately result in future sales. That's why most people initially think, "they know my brand, so I have great brand equity." Generally, I ask people these two questions:

1. Have you heard of Tang?
2. Did you have it for breakfast?

Virtually 100 percent awareness of GM did nothing to thwart its recent losses.

A linear, one-way process *might have been possible* (and perhaps even practical) in the late-1950s and early-1960s. Today, it is highly improbable that advertising or brand communication works or can work in this marketer-controlled way.

The increasing number of competitive products and services available to the consumer, the diffused and cluttered media systems, the mediated effects of distribution channels, and the increasing amount of nonmarketer-originated information, assessments, and persuasion readily available to consumers at low or no cost challenge these assumptions. Just think about the effects of the simple blog.

Joe Plummer, Chief Research Officer of the Advertising Research Foundation (ARF), stated at the 2005 Advertising Effectiveness Council meeting that "the frequency and awareness-driven model has not been supported by robust research." He was being polite. More recently in a 2006 presentation regarding engagement, the ARF indicated, "the AIDA model of how advertising works will be put to bed."

The short of it is, advertising and brand measurement models based on an awareness-leads-to-behavior-change framework appear to successfully measure the *process*. They do not measure meaningful results or returns to the organization. And it is *results* that today's management is concerned with, not the process or procedure. They nailed that with satisfaction surveys, Total Quality management (TQM) initiatives, and process reengineering years ago.

Top management wants to know what return the organization got back from the resources invested and to relate today's spending to today's returns, or tomorrow's, or the next quarter's. So should you. The difficulty is that marketing and research managers and your local research consultants are still utilizing or recommending systems that measure results based on awareness and attitudinal change, not on likely behavioral changes that can predict *financial* returns to the organization as a result of planned spending.

So, the time has come to move to approaches that correlate with actual engagement, in-market sales, positive consumer behavior, and thus loyalty.

UNDERSTANDING THE NONTRANSACTION

While *measurement of actual transactions* is becoming increasingly common, it's not feasible for all product and service categories. There is a time lag or purchase-switching consideration period that makes the measurement of the direct effects of marketing and advertising and promotional activities difficult to correlate. You can't really be too disappointed if your automotive advertising "just" drives consumers into the showrooms, after all. On the other hand, you'd also like to be sure that the only reason that they've shown up *isn't* that you dropped your price (again), à la most American car companies. But while most car companies dropped their prices, Toyota didn't have to cut prices to sell cars. It expects to top $11 billion in profits in 2006. If you thought, "Well, sure, it's Toyota," you've proved my point.

However, *nontransactional behavior* (i.e., data that is not the final transaction but specifically relates to a purchase or predicts a reasonable level of a future purchase) *is* available. Loyalty-based engagement tools and measures can arm companies as they move forward and deal with the bionic consumers.

These realities have already sharply altered the ways in which some firms are regarding their businesses, *especially in environments where consumers have more options, and where information plays a greater role in driving consumer choice.* But as we've noted, this doesn't significantly shorten the list. If anything, it only lengthens it. It's more—rather than less—likely that your brand faces this same situation, whether you are Procter & Gamble or not.

How, do you measure such activities in light of the previously noted fact that not all the measures in use today are as dependable as needed? Remember the list of 13 questions we promised you that you would be able to answer? Here's where they come into play.

Even if you can't afford to conduct formal research, the questions give you a structure of how you have to *think* about your brand and the category in which you compete. You need to be honest in your assessment.

The answer is in possessing a set of basic, but statistically reliable and predictive, customer answers to seven of these questions. (You'll also possess answers to the remaining six questions, but even having just these seven will allow your brand to thrive.)

1. What are the *predictive drivers* of loyalty and profitability for your category?
2. What individual consumer and category attributes, benefits, and *values,* and communication elements (e.g., image, essence, assets, personality, and even DNA) make up the drivers?
3. What is the *order of importance* of the category drivers? How do consumers *view* your category? How do they *compare* brands? How, ultimately, do they *buy* (and remain loyal)?
4. What *expectations* do consumers hold for each of the drivers?
5. On which drivers is your brand strong and weak?
6. How does your brand compare to the competition?
7. In which driver(s) does your brand's equity reside? Does your brand *meet or exceed consumer expectations*?

This is not meant to suggest that we should ignore all traditional, reliable, and valid marketing and strategic efforts. Traditional brand measures just can't be configured to provide a corporation with *brand equity-based ROI because they don't correlate with behavior or profitability.* And that's where loyalty metrics can help.

If you measure your marketing efforts in terms of how those efforts affect, support, or alter brand equity, you *will* create a *predictive, leading-indicator measure of profitability.* Here's how.

Whether you are a Fortune 500 company or a one-person shop, your company's financial position is judged by its price/earnings (P/E) ratio, which links share capital with net profit. A high P/E ratio signals shareholder confidence and optimism in increased future benefits. Every business, big or small, knows that.

Although brand and corporation may be somewhat separate (although that separation grows smaller and smaller each year and is virtually indistinguishable in Europe), the same reasoning may still be applied by calculating a value called a *return on (brand) equity* (ROE).

$$\text{Corporation P/E} = \frac{\text{Market value per share}}{\text{Earnings per share}}$$

For those with a passion for diagnostics, the brand equity measures can be configured not only by category drivers but also by the individual components (expressed as the category attributes, benefits, and values) that make up those drivers. We'll show you how.

Evaluating the customer's nontransactional-but-highly-correlated-to-purchase reactions via loyalty metrics allows for a calculation of ROE and can also provide an ROE *based on your selected strategy.* This is a more precise and complex analysis that allows the marketer or planner to identify *precise* engagement effects of communications rather than just relying on reported message content playback (i.e., what did the commercial or print ad say, or *awareness*—did you remember that the brand advertised *something*?) Results can be *segmented* by various target audiences or evaluated based on current brand relationships. The trick is *not* to sacrifice exceptional, predictive customer intelligence on the altar of process by falling back on the "this-is-how-we-always-did-it" rationale.

The reason that the customer loyalty approach can be so broadly used is that it acknowledges that each category is unique. First and foremost, consumers view categories differently. They do not shop for colas in the same way that they buy hamburgers, no matter how much the two of them are gastronomically linked. No matter how interesting such research may seem, consumers do not decide to stay at a hotel in the same way that they decide to buy a computer.

The Brand Keys customer loyalty measurement approach can be adapted to fit *any* economic and communications system and it can be used in any format so that it provides apples-to-apples comparisons of results. That's why the ROE approach works so well in answering the question "What did I get?" From a top-management point of view, this has major advantages because comparisons can be made across initiatives and finite corporate and brand resources can be allocated in a more financially relevant manner and *without* trading away actual category specificity the way a number of brand assessment and valuation systems do. No matter how extensive the research, it doesn't help you to know that your airline falls into the same quadrant as a well-known mobile phone.

If the past decade's evolution of alternative customer information systems (Internet and interactive marketing) has taught us anything, it is that brand equity-based loyalty measurements (and attendant value metrics) will lead us more smoothly through the twenty-first-century marketplace. Beyond that, we can only speculate. What we do know is that it will continue to be based on the transfer of value and meaning between buyer and seller, and that the better you are able to measure those, the more profitable you will be.

Brand Keys Approach to Loyalty

We developed the Brand Keys loyalty system initially in response to the increasing difficulty clients had differentiating brands on a purely functional basis. The system is based on a combination of established psychological theory, factor and regression analyses, and causal-path modeling. Our basic tenet is that each customer or prospect has psychological tendencies and preferences that will determine his or her behavior in the marketplace.

Theoretical Framework or How to Think about It

During the development of this method, our research led us to thinkers who acknowledged the influence of both rational *and* emotional factors in interpersonal relationships. The theorist whose methods best served our purposes was Carl Jung, an early and highly influential disciple of Sigmund Freud. Jung's theory of interpersonal attachments was straightforward: The strongest relationships would be developed when powerful "locks" were established between individuals on both emotional and objective bases. The locks needed to be opened by the specific characteristics or traits of each person in the relationship—keys. These traits (keys) must mutually complement the other individual's needs.

Simply stated, we then extended Jung's personal attachments theory to the attachments that exist between consumers and brands whenever there is a high degree of brand loyalty. The details of Jung's theory led us to adopt a four-factor solution to brand loyalty—to identify the four most important drivers of brand loyalty in each of the categories that we study. We used the Category Ideal as the theoretical yardstick against which we'd measure brands or marketing initiatives or brands as they participate in marketing initiatives—you get the point.

We've been through the pitfalls of relying on direct Q&A. The challenges of differentiating a brand, having it meaningfully (and profitably) engage with consumers, and optimizing marketing and media opportunities are more complex and error prone than ever before. Accompanying a more complex marketplace is a far more sophisticated, hot-wired-into-the-Internet, cyberspace-traveling consumer, who has a far more multifaceted decision-making and engagement process in place.

Real engagement (marketing and brand activities that result in positive consumer behavior and brand profitability) is driven more and more by emotional values than rational ones. Recent Brand Keys assessments of 10 years of consumer value shifts indicate that today as much as 70 percent of the linked-to-sales, consumer-engagement process is emotional. We can argue that it's 65:35, or even 60:40, but it isn't a 50:50 proposition anymore.

Rational elements—even at a "table stakes" level—*do* factor into product and service usage, but to accurately *predict* consumer behavior in the marketplace, rational and emotional elements need to be fused together. You can't expect to ask a question, get an answer, and reveal an insight that will help to build a brand strategy that will engage consumers. You need to understand the emotional levers. But by utilizing a psychologically powered loyalty approach, companies can virtually guarantee that their brands will better engage consumers *and* predict returns on their marketing investments.

The methodological framework utilized is that of brand liking or brand bonding—a metric that reliably correlates to sales. Our approach permits marketers to fuse both emotional and rational elements in the consumers' category-specific, internal, decision-making process and accurately—predicatively—identify how the consumer will behave toward the brand.

The psychological questionnaire captures both the articulated and the unarticulated (perhaps even unarticulatable) elements that define a brand in the context of real marketplace behavior, but we also show you some ways of supercharging traditional research approaches to help you identify and leverage emotional customer loyalty and engagement values.

Twenty Questions

The development of our 20-item psychological assessment questionnaire was based on experience, testing, and knowledge in the field of cognitive psychology accumulated over decades. It has a test/retest reliability of .93 and has been used in 26 countries in virtually every B2B (Business-to-Business) and B2C (Business-to-Consumer) category you'd care to name. We constructed the questionnaire to tap into the most basic (therefore the most revealing) human personality dimensions or factors and category and consumer values. Examples of these variables include being impulsive versus reflective, active versus passive, rational versus emotional, and solitary versus social. All the things you need to know to engage customers. We acknowledge absolutely that the rational, functional aspects of your category are fundamental facts. You know them, and your competitors do, too.

Confirming the work we were already doing, the Copy Research Validity Project conducted by the Advertising Research Foundation determined that the best predictor of actual in-market consumer behavior across a wide number of product and service categories was achieved by a balanced model—a loyalty model that explicitly incorporates significant degrees of both rational and emotional components. It is just such a model that Brand Keys has now been using and improving for over 20 years.

And that's the theoretical foundation. Now, go and do the customer loyalty research. It's that easy.

Don't Panic

"Wait," you say, "how? How do I actually execute customer loyalty research?" Well, you could call Brand Keys or go to an extremely small list of alternative consultants who have developed rigorous and verified models that fuse the emotional and the rational and *are* able to provide loyalty and engagement metrics. You say:

> Well, that would be nice. You sound like a really smart person, but we're a very small company. We don't have the budgets that Toyota, Google, and the other big companies have. Isn't there something we can do on our own to develop real loyalty metrics?

And happily, the answer is, "Yes, there is."

BRAND KEYS METHODOLOGICAL FRAMEWORK: STEPS YOU CAN TAKE TO CREATE REAL CUSTOMER LOYALTY METRICS

We're going to take you through an overview of how to create loyalty metrics. We revert between a discussion of the Brand Keys methodology and the ways in which others—a small business doing this on a shoestring—can shape some traditional tools into a more emotionally centric, loyalty-based assessment.

Our psychological questionnaire does most of the heavy lifting, with the output being essential in providing predictive answers to the following questions:

- What are the predictive drivers of loyalty and profitability for your category?
- What is the order of importance of the category drivers? How do consumers view your category? How do they compare brands? How, ultimately, do they buy (and remain loyal)?
- What expectations do consumers hold for each of the drivers?

We get these answers by first identifying the category ideal.

Identify a Category Ideal

Remember from your school days how much fuss Plato made about a horse and how people conjured up the image of an ideal horse in their minds? With brands, it is no different. Creating an ideal is a natural, collective process based on experience and desire, knowledge and imagination—four very different realms that no one in my experience can fully describe in direct language.

We all do it, but we can't all talk about it very well. Let's step back from obsessing over the value of understanding what makes brands different in people's minds, why some people buy Adidas and others Puma, or why some prefer a PC and others a PowerBook. The most value for the research dollar, the first tier of critical information for market success, lies in identifying what people want *not in the market, but in their minds, their imaginations.*

With that Platonic ideal established, you have that reference, a yardstick if you will, as the basis of comparison for why your brand may be chosen over another—over and over again, if you've done it right. Ultimately, it all depends on how brands measure up to consumers' imaginations—their expectations. Luckily for us, imagination of an ideal still tends to run in large collective patterns in groups of people sharing the same values in a particular category, whether it be mutual funds, athletic shoes, sports teams, or pizza.

Wise brand management is the management of these differences. It is based not on quantitative shelf-research reports and computer-generated comparative spreadsheets or quadrant maps, but on a fluid, adaptable knowledge of brand ideals and value-based measures of realities as they exist in the minds and hearts and souls of customers describing today how they will behave in the marketplace tomorrow.

We don't want that ideal constrained by reality (importance ratings—stated or derived on their own—would give you that misleading data), so we use indirect inquiry (our psychological questionnaire) to get measures of unarticulated desires—a true picture of how high "up" really is.

Create Category and Customer Attributes, Benefits, and Values

When we create a component list of attributes, benefits, and values (ABVs), it comprises general product and category attributes, benefits, and values; customer service elements; specific product aspects or features; customer end benefits; corporate and brand imagery components; or any items thought to be useful to the customer- and brand-engagement process in the category in question.

Most large companies will have the majority of these ABVs readily available, extracting them from tracking studies, focus groups, and ancillary research. We generally urge clients to include what we've come to call *wish list* items—areas or questions that have been hanging around unanswered for a while or have been niggling at senior management.

Smaller companies may have to rely on old-fashioned, secondary research, sometimes called *desk research,* that is gathered through reviewing literature, publications, broadcast media, the Internet, and other nonhuman sources. Those companies who have small research budgets can avail themselves of a *focus group* as a way of capturing customer language and category values. Both secondary research and focus groups have their limitations, but we discuss how to optimize them later. With a little hard work, you can create a workable list for yourself and your brand.

In the Brand Keys approach, respondents then evaluate the ABV components for their importance with respect to brand delivery. These elements are then factor analyzed, and the identified factor groupings are regressed against the psychological factor scores. This provides a "best fit" or optimum relationship between the emotional and rational aspects of the category. An additional causal-path analysis locks items into appropriate drivers. Again, the two sets of items come from the psychological questionnaire (emotional) and the ABV ratings and attendant analyses (rational). Conducting the analysis in this way allows us to define the category loyalty drivers entirely from a customer perspective. The more you do that, the better you'll be able to measure engagement later.

Sole proprietors or small business owners can avail themselves of some traditional statistical analyses to identify category drivers. Two that can be helpful are *factor analysis* and *conjoint analysis*. They are readily and cost-effectively available, but they do have limitations of which you should be aware.

Factor analysis is a statistical technique used to reduce large data sets—in this case the ABV list—to the smallest number of factors required to explain the relationships in the data, in this case how the ABV components come together to form the category drivers of an ideal. Advocates of the analysis see it as providing neutral data analyses. Critics have sometimes called the techniques *the researcher's Rorschach* because it is something of an art form. Many decisions have to be made in interpreting the output. Some critics have suggested that corporate points of view have a way of coloring the data and that researchers can get out of it what is consonant with their current brand or category perspectives and that they are not necessarily psychologically meaningful. The Brand Keys approach obviates that approach, as the entire process is respondent driven and *not* open to interpretation. Still, factor analysis has it utility.

Conjoint analysis is a multivariate statistical technique that analyzes preferences for various combinations of attributes. Think of it as a trade-off analysis: "Would you rather have a cold can of cola, a glass of wine, or a cup of coffee?"

Conjoint analysis—derived from the phrase *considering jointly*—helps to separate, in this case, preferences for hot versus cold drinks, alcoholic versus nonalcoholic, color, and container. The objective of conjoint analysis is to determine what combination of a limited number of attributes is most preferred by respondents. For ABVs, conjoint analysis can be used to measure the perceived value of specific product features.

I intentionally use the phrase *product features* because the method is far more appropriate for circumstances where a strong case can be made that *rational* decision making will prevail. Conjoint analysis is a great example of the highest level of stated preference and is nearly 100 percent rationally driven. But as Brand Keys research has discovered, 70 percent of the decision process is emotionally based, and the need to take that into account when creating real loyalty measures cannot be overlooked.

Additionally, conjoint analysis works best when the ABVs are expressing bipolar characteristics like hot versus cold. These days, category ABVs are generally not that simple. To paraphrase architect Ludwig Mies van der Rohe, today "engagement and loyalty are in the details." The Brand Keys technique allows for the assessment of up to 80 ABVs, and the indirect, psychological techniques help to identify real, nuanced values that help to predict accurately customer loyalty and engagement. Even supporters of conjoint analysis acknowledge that respondents are sometimes provided with too much information to consider thoroughly. Again, used with due care, it can help to identify category loyalty drivers.

From the Brand Keys analysis or the output of the traditional statistical analyses, you can now name the drivers.

The Brand Keys psychological measures identify the importance of each driver. In the absence of those, you can rely on factor loadings that come out of the factor analysis and identify how well—or not well—defined the groups of ABVs are. There's some interpretation required here, too, but it's a lot better than relying on straight Q&A or basic importance ratings.

Of one thing, we are *absolutely* sure: All category ABV elements are important to today's bionic consumer—as well as being ubiquitous among brands in the category—and, therefore, relatively undifferentiating, which is why only 30 percent of the engagement and loyalty process rests on them.

Using the Brand Keys system, we conduct another statistical analysis involving the psychological weights and individual ABV importance ratings. That analysis provides a valuation of how much each component contributes to the engagement and loyalty process.

In the absence of those assessments, you can always use the factor weights and the conjoint analysis to estimate a contribution factor for each of your ABVs.

So, what metrics do we have right now? We have an identification of the category drivers that describe how the customer or prospect:

- Views the category according to his or her own definition of what is important
- Compares offering in the category
- Is best engaged (and the ABVs that contribute to that effort)
- Buys products in the category
- Remains loyal

For a complete understanding, you need three more items.

The first is an understanding of the expectations that consumers hold for each of the category drivers. This is a critical element since engagement and loyalty are measured by their abilities to meet or exceed customer *expectations*.

Another of the Brand Keys indirect, psychological measures is the expectation held by the consumer for each of the drivers in a particular category. Remember our definitions of brand equity and loyalty are expectation driven, so you'll have to provide some estimate of that as well. However, don't make it a rational decision process. People are far too constrained by reality. Let me give you an example. Suppose you were to ask a respondent, "How many miles per gallon (MPG) would your ideal car get?"

Here's the unarticulated thought process that would happen. It would only take a nanosecond inside her head, but it *would* happen this way:

> Okay, they want to know how many MPG my ideal car would get. I don't even know what I'm getting these days. I know I pay a fortune. They should do something about that! Well, I expect that I get 18 MPG and I know that there are cars that advertise that they get more. What? 35? 40?

Her answer: "45 MPG."

When it was added up and averaged, the report would come back and say that for an ideal car the ideal MPG number was 51.3.

But that's just math constrained by reality. What if we told the respondents that we had a car that got 150 MPG? We might have to prove it, but once we did, 150 MPG would be the new benchmark. So an ideal MPG isn't 51.3, it's nearly three times that. Maybe more, but you get the point.

So again, if you haven't employed Brand Keys-like metrics, you can always rely on a nonverbal, more-emotional-than-rational insight technique called a *photo sort*. It's a unique consumer-insight technique that provides consumers with a range of photos with the assessment task requiring that respondents indicate a high, medium, and low photo that represents expectations for each of the individual, previously identified drivers. An example of this might be photos of three automobiles (a Hyundai, a BMW, and a Ferrari) or three retailers (Kohl's, Macy's, and Bloomingdale's). Then you ask where your brand falls on that continuum.

The second missing element is an assessment of how your brand compares to an ideal? And the third is how your brand compares to the competition.

The Brand Keys approach allows the opportunity to measure all the relevant variables for the issue at hand: the brand, the competitive set, positioning statements, advertising executions, sponsorship opportunities, or virtually anything you can show to describe to the respondent. We then compare all of those results to a category ideal.

Once again, if you have followed our alternative recommendations for configuring customer loyalty and engagement metrics, you, too, will have a category-specific yardstick against which you can measure any of your marketing variables.

You can't just do this once. In repeat polling over the years, we have learned that changes in the configuration of Brand Keys data—the order of importance of the category drivers or the attendant levels of expectations about those drivers—indicate significant changes in the way customers are viewing the category. Companies ignore these changes at their peril.

We generally see these value shifts well before customers are able to articulate them—as much as 12 to 24 months before such changes show up on the radar screens of traditional research systems—especially focus groups. If you are ahead of these changes, it provides an extraordinary competitive edge in the area of brand management, customer engagement, loyalty, and profitability.

Follow our advice and you'll be able to track these shifts, too.

LOYALTY RESEARCH AND THE POLITICS OF BRAND EXPANSION

If you are asking yourself: Does a new product dilute what your brand stands for, either now or over time, you are asking the wrong person. You should ask the consumer, because adding brand extensions makes sense only when the marketplace demands it and consumers are willing to believe you can deliver what you promise.

Remember the Arch Deluxe? Only McDonald's had the budget to make such a golden mistake. Coca-Cola and AT&T made mistakes, too. But while all three were able to write off the expenditures, not all the accountants in the world could find a way to amortize the damage that resulted to the brands. Most other companies really cannot afford to get it that wrong, not even once.

Pressure from shareholders and the drive for short-term gain can be managed with less friction with predictive research into customer loyalty. This happens when the intelligent majority agrees that the brand direction should be founded on a customer-reality-based plan. Loyalty and values research as the basis for brand strategy is a very sharp tool to get teams to rally behind because it can help to align internal constituencies, not to mention keep detractors a bit more in their place. The proof will be in the numbers, correlating with where you choose to take your brand strategically based on leading-indicator insights and how much customers believed and bought. Then you should follow the process again, and again—the virtuous cycle of research-based brand-strategy development and execution that people like me dream of at night.

My colleague and positioning expert Jack Trout keeps it brief: "Differentiate or die." He's right. Companies that differentiate through knowledge gleaned from consumer expectations and values will unquestionably be those that run roughshod over the less-informed competition. But here's another quote: "Saying it don't make it so!"

So, the loyalty output answers two more of the questions we raised:

- What are consumers willing to believe about your brand?
- What market strategies and opportunities can the brand sustain?

The predictive nature of the loyalty metrics is such that the bars won't move if the customer doesn't believe what you are saying the brand has to offer. You can tell him anything, but if he is unwilling (or unable) to believe it about you, you'll know ahead of time. So, you won't fall prey to the "excellent-answers-to-meaningless-questions" trap like these:

Q: I see you are sitting here in McDonald's with your kids. They're eating [fill in the blank from the menu], but you are only drinking coffee. Why is that?
A: Because there's nothing on the menu for me.
Q: If we had something just for you, would you buy it?
A: Sure.

That kind of research (even conducted more elegantly) led McDonald's to mistake a market opportunity (increase consumption among an adult audience who wasn't eating much of anything) for a brand opportunity (offer a McDonald's adult hamburger).

But if consumers weren't willing to believe that they could do that, the market opportunity was just a "field of dreams." Figure 3.1 identifies loyalty metrics collected the day the Arch Deluxe was announced to the world.

That was then, but not many companies today can spend $100 million dollars on crash-and-burn marketing opportunities without being sure of their brand success. Loyalty metrics provide a picture of *what's going to happen* before you spend your money.

When Creativity and Research Make Beautiful Music

Design and advertising have a long history of putting down research because research is often hard to fit into the artistic process (or ego). It is often considered an intrusion on creative expression. If you are or know a copywriter or

Figure 3.1
Why the Arch Deluxe Failed

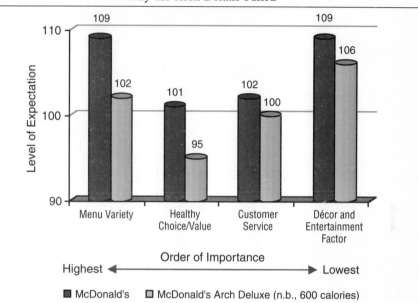

art director at any ad agency on the planet, you have most likely heard the ral-
lying cry, "To the barricades! The researchers are coming!" I doubt that there
are many creative folks drawing breath who do not believe that research
squashes their great work, short-circuits the emotional punch of a great ad,
and reduces the brand message to a series of sterile Morse-code-like sound
bites approved by focus groups. Forward-looking, predictive research that
probes consumers' emotions can be far more revealing and helpful.

Creative professionals know that striking an emotional chord with people is
the most effective (and enduring) way to involve them with a brand (or in
Madison Avenue argot, "telling isn't selling"). Predictive loyalty research is
designed to deliver the insights the ad department needs to yank the emotional
levers of its target audience. Creativity is always better served when it is
guided by consumer expectations and preferences. Those are the very elements
that make up what we call consumer emotion. The magic and finesse of creativity can now be reinforced by science in a way that complements the rational, logical, and attribute-focused side of brand communication.

Creativity open to this new form of customer guidance will ultimately be
the most successful. Creativity was formerly subjective. That is until it hit the
world outside the ad agency's carpeted hallways, where customers' expectations

and ideals are often quite different from those of copywriters and art directors. That is where the discrepancies really show up in the marketplace—in unsold goods and services. With today's customer loyalty measures, creativity can be fed and informed by research throughout the whole life cycle of a brand, resulting in more effective executions.

RESEARCHING YOUR WAY TO A RELIABLE BRAND MODEL

Like leaves, snowflakes, and children, no two branding efforts are completely alike. Yet, they can succeed or fail for surprisingly similar reasons. Most succeed by either chasing or anticipating the values and preferences of the customer. In this customer-centric branding network, the epicenter is the customer as much—or more so—than it is the company.

The research that gives you the insight into what drives one (the customer) by definition instructs how to drive the other (the company). That research, be it provided internally or by a hired gun, should provide predictive road maps about customer values and expectations.

Product innovation makes sense *only* when it meets or exceeds expectations that other similar offerings do not meet or exceed. It can get a foothold in the marketplace only when it positions and delivers in ways that accurately reflect how consumers view and compare offerings, and what they really expect.

In this light, examine the efficacy of your ideas. Innovation will always be part daring, part imagination, part will, and all gumption. But every innovation also needs solid consumer research supporting the conception, confirming that folks are ready, willing, and able to accept it. Research applies to each portal that brands go through to get to the customer:

- Product design
- Advertising
- Direct response
- Promotions
- Point-of-Purchase (POP) displays
- Public relations
- Identity
- Events
- Naming
- Web design
- Packaging
- Sponsorships

- Licensing
- Media planning
- Product placement
- Brand extensions
- New products

No, people are not entirely predictive any more than they are behavioral automatons, and what shapes and governs our free will is not our concern as businesspeople. However, *how* free will expresses itself in the marketplace is. No matter how we dissect language, craft questions, or wire feedback to our foreheads, fingertips, eyeballs, not everything about us is knowable, or even needs to be. Just ask any philosopher or social scientist.

But methods of identifying ideals and expectation *are* knowable. There's ample reason to trust enlightened loyalty research because of its predictive accuracy, the best litmus test of all. Behavioral trends can be spun out of emotional yarn. But the weaving process involves new ways to process information, looming raw data into patterns that we can recognize and act on more quickly. And moving more quickly than the competition is an enormous advantage these days. We do it every day, getting more nimble as we go. Make the magic by deliberate design, by informed intention, via systematic methods—not by luck, gut feel, trial and error, casting bones in the sand, or hovering over a Ouija board.

I entice my colleagues and clients with a chillingly basic proposition: *Would you like to be able to know the customers' preferences in your category six months to a year before anyone else?* It's a loaded question—a pay-loaded question. If you can regularly deliver the payload, the relationship between research and brand strategy (and even creative development) will change in one generation.

If you have any doubts about the wisdom of this, consider the great contributions an aversion to, or misunderstanding of, research has given us:

- The Edsel
- The Yugo
- New Coke
- Pets.com
- The Arch Deluxe
- Atkins-based food products
- Lifesavers soda
- Frito-Lay lemonade
- Virgin Cola
- Earring Magic Ken doll

- RJ Reynolds smokeless cigarettes
- Pepsi AM
- Thirsty Cat

Confirm market hunches via your consumers before you act on them, because gone are the days of dreamy fields and creative sessions when a company could build it and see if folks would buy it. Today, those are the fields in which we see many well-fed daisies growing among the tombstones of yesterday's brands that failed to:

- Listen to the customer.
- Validate that what is being offered is in line with what the customer wants.
- Cultivate a customer dialogue (a values-based feedback loop that projects engagement and future behavior).
- Innovate in those aspects of the brand that will meet or exceed customer expectations.
- Differentiate through knowing the hearts and minds, values, and expectations of customers.
- Collaborate internally to leverage knowledge gained through predictive research.

LOYALTY TALES FROM THE REAL WORLD

9/11 and Fahrenheit 9/11

The fear and uncertainty spawned by the September 11 attacks, and the bombings in Madrid and London, are still very much with us. We all wish it were different, but one unexpected *positive* result seems to be the acceleration of certain customer loyalty trends, trends that were already making business-as-usual marketing less and less effective.

At first glance, this idea might surprise you. Take a closer look. Historically, great, unforeseen national shocks (e.g., wars, market crashes, plagues, and amazing scientific or technological breakthroughs) had the effect of sudden adrenaline infusions pumping through the socioeconomic system.

Bolstering customer loyalty (which fewer and fewer companies were successfully executing before 9/11) has *always* required a clear understanding of customer values. On the surface, the 9/11 catastrophe would seem to have made it even more difficult to do so successfully since customer values, and loyalty, radically shifted in minutes.

Once again, let's look closer. Customers are people. At the time of the attacks, they were people in a state of shock that led us all to take stock, to reexamine the values we hold dear.

These rediscovered—and probably heightened—values will now include freedom, personal safety, and love of country, authenticity, and family. American traditions are expressing themselves strongly, like a desire to return to simpler times, basics, a balance between career, family, and community. In London, the British values of the stiff upper lip and "carrying on" rose to the surface. But to be meaningful and lasting, the values have to take the form of something more substantial than a flag-waving, chest-pounding, return-to-basics brand position. This means that researchers have to dig deeper than simplistic patriotism for their answers.

In this context, marketers kept scrambling to measure postattack customer values in terms of the challenge of real-world marketing profitability. We did this successfully, and a trend of major moral and economic value emerged to help us recover from such devastation. Directly after 9/11, effective marketing and advertising had to reflect a return to a *new* normalcy. To do that we had to base our marketing on what our customers really thought, not just what they said or what we would have liked them to think, about an event as awful as 9/11 or the bombings in Europe.

Fahrenheit Market Research: The Temperature at Which Your Findings Go Up in Smoke

Let me ask you a question you were probably asked more than once back before the past presidential election: "Have you seen *Fahrenheit 9/11?*"

Wait a minute. On second thought, don't answer that.

Why? Because the way you answer could reveal more than simply your intention to have seen a film. It could reveal your deepest political leanings, or at least, be interpreted that way. The key here, as with all research that accurately predicts future human behavior, is in how we ask the questions *and* interpret the answers. The emotions behind our politics, and our answers, are hard to hide. If you answered "yes," to the above question, you risked being branded a liberal by some, maybe even a national traitor. If you said "no," then you're maybe just a step away form being one of the quasi-informed, insensitive neoconservatives on the far Right. Now, for a reality check: If you answered "yes," it could just mean you're open-minded, curious, wanting to keep up with all sides of the argument. Similarly, "no" might mean you are dying to go, but promised the kids you'd take them to see *Shrek 4.*

Do you see the problem? Traditional, off-the-rack polling techniques have no way of drilling down deep enough to reveal those nuanced truths, the emotional places inside each of us where our deeper realities—true feelings and motivations—lie and where they shift and evolve.

The movie industry knows the results it wants. It sends its legions of polling minions to find folks who say they're likely to go to the movies in the upcoming weekend—people who are already familiar with the movie titles. Then they pop the question: "Are you planning to see?" From these answers, they project which blockbuster will come in first, second, third, and so on at the box office. Many decisions are made, and screens allocated, based on these findings. Much media money is also spent.

More than every so often, a glitch shows up in predictive paradise. In this historic case (by no means unique), reality did not jibe with what Hollywood, or Karl Rove, predicted. This was a mistake with rather serious implications for planning and the bottom line. Traditional market research projected that Michael Moore's documentary *Fahrenheit 9/11* would come in third for that particular period in time, behind two mainstream summer comedies.

Only that didn't happen.

The film that mocked President Bush, criticizing his decision to invade Iraq, became the highest grossing documentary of all time, coming in first at box offices nationwide. It beat out films that were playing on almost triple the number of screens, grossing $21.8 million. That's $2.2 million more than the predicted screen hit at the time, *White Chicks,* and $3.3 million more than *Dodgeball,* which came in third.

In the research world, that's a pretty big margin of error. And it didn't just happen in the liberal precincts of New York City. The film sold out in military-base towns and in the reddest of Republican strongholds. Why? We can't answer that (yet).

What went wrong?

We *can* answer that one. We see it all the time. The movie industry measured what we call a *moderated response*—what people wanted the interviewer to think about them and their politics, as well as the politics of movie going at that particular place and time, and not how they were actually going to behave when it came to choosing which movie to see. It's unfortunate, sometimes even tragic, that this outmoded research continues to be the foundation on which many companies base their planning processes. Worse still, as with *Fahrenheit 9/11,* it's the only way movie distributors attempt to translate consumer likelihoods into actionable insights that yield greater profits. With box office numbers as big as these, a little more accuracy in the research means a lot more money in the till. This is the ideal state of market research: *highly reliable findings that correlate to your bottom line.*

Those weeks were a great success for Michael Moore. From a research point of view, it was a disaster. Shortly after the opening of the film, Moore was quoted as saying, "Clearly something happened here that no one expected." More correctly, what happened was something that *no one properly measured*. And researchers could have done that, for about the same cost they spent asking loads of people the meaningless "did-you-see-it, are-you-going-to" questions.

There's a lesson here for more than just the Hollywood moguls: Unless we use the appropriate method of projecting consumer behavior, many companies out there stand a good chance of getting burned when the reliability of their market research, and potential profits, go up in smoke.

Q & A
Loyalty's Evolution

Becky Ebenkamp, *Brandweek* magazine: *What does the term* loyalty *actually mean these days? What does loyalty entail and how do you measure it in the current marketplace?*

Robert Passikoff: *Loyalty* means just what it has always meant. Behaviorally, it means that your customers are going to stay with you (read, make future purchases), even in the face of lower prices or newly upgraded products and services offered by your competitors. Attitudinally, it means that there's an emotional bond between your brand and the consumer, the strength of which is based on the ability of the brand's ABVs to meet or exceed customers' expectations and real desires as they pertain to the category.

Most planners acknowledge that brand values and customer expectations play an essential part in understanding the loyalty process. In our experience, however, few firms can clearly define where their brand equity lies. Most firms tend to define the brand essence, personality, or culture in terms of imagery. You need imagery, but it fits better in the context of communication models. You should view brand equity as the strengths (and weaknesses) vis-à-vis the real values and measures that consumers rely on to make loyalty decisions between you and your competitors. At the very least, you need both competitive context and expectations to measure loyalty in the current marketplace.

Becky Ebenkamp: *How, then, does brand image relate to measuring and building brand equity and loyalty?*

Robert Passikoff: If we examine the ways many companies identify brand equity, most of the definitions would refer to image and positioning. Here's where many people get confused. Image and positioning are the advertising agencies' and design firms' best attempts at creating manifestations of a brand's equity. These are creative expressions—but as entertaining, eye-catching, funny, moving, and visually differentiated as they may be, they are still completely underpowered to move a brand closer to its strategic loyalty goals.

We provide a solution: A definition for brand equity that is established in the context of the category, captures the direction and velocity of customer values and expectations, and correlates with market activities and loyalties.

There is yet to be an image assessment that can deliver those insights.

That is why core brand equity exists only at those points where the brand exceeds customer value expectations. Correctly measured, those expectations identify how the customer and category values merge to form the dimensions of purchase and loyalty, and precisely how high a hurdle the brand and marketer face. The results are statistically reliable assessments of potential behavior, not just imagery items ranked for importance or compared to the competition.

Effects of Consumer Ratings on Loyalty

Roxanne Roberts, *Washington Post*: *To what degree do independent consumer ratings like those on Amazon.com affect consumer loyalty to brands?*

Robert Passikoff: Independent consumer ratings have taken the high ground from advertiser-controlled information and persuasion. Consumer evaluations and comments are usually a better synthesis of customer values, so the posted comments are better noticed than paid advertising, and the fundamental nature of the insights resonates better as well.

And that's the secret of loyalty. If you successfully address the values, you'll have loyal customers. But as we've pointed out, capturing values is a tricky exercise. Having customer loyalty metrics allows you to possess these insights ahead of the competition and in time to insert them into your strategic and communication planning processes.

"A final question. Would you put your money where your mouth is?"

CHAPTER 4

LOYALTY IS 70 PERCENT EMOTIONAL: AN EMOTIONAL BOND ENGAGES CUSTOMERS AND MAKES MONEY

At the heart of an effective creative philosophy is the belief that nothing is so powerful as an insight into human nature, what compulsions drive man, what instincts dominate his action even though his language so often camouflages what really motivates him.

—*Bill Bernbach*

By now it should be clear that a loyalty approach leads to continual movement for your brand: With each visit to consumers in a category, the danger of drifting from an exceptional brand to a commodity is systematically avoided.

The Holy Grail for marketing research has at its core a continual early warning system that yields a competitive advantage. At Brand Keys, the system entails the measurement of customer expectations, which includes understanding the emotional bond that can be created between a brand and a customer, the identification of values that customers appreciate (and that makes them feel valued), and whether a customer is willing to believe what you're telling him.

A BRAND'S DNA DOES NOT ORIGINATE IN THE BRAND

It has become cool, trendy, and sometimes even useful to use the language and metaphor of evolution and genetics in brand speak. If Darwin imbued us with the metaphor of specialization and brand survival, Craig Vetner is the genetic pioneer responsible for marketing the metaphor of brand DNA.

Building brand DNA is indeed about creating a sequence. But, as *build* implies, it involves construction, not deconstruction. Building good brand DNA means designing or producing *according to a set of values that are fundamentally external to the brand*—customer values and expectations.

We have entered the age where the customer's values are the brand's values. Or they should be. Brand characteristics, from design to slogans and catchy copy, are antecedent to the customer's values and expectations—they are what you do *after* you understand your target's expectations and how to satisfy them.

So, if you isolate the strands that reveal how customers see your brand and the category, you can gauge how well your brand jives with their needs, desires, and emotions. Modern brand strategy should be based on the untangled DNA of customer expectations and its representation of category ideals—the ultimate brand that may, or may not, be possible to deliver. The task is to measure, design, and build the brand to match an ideal as closely as possible. Then do it again and again, generating the fit between brand and customer in a way that is completely believable.

Think of it this way; suppose someone was talking to you about a luxury car. One with a powerful engine and great aerodynamic lines. Plush leather and wood interior. All the amenities you'd want. Good gas mileage and front and side airbags. The whole, as we say in New York, schmear! Have you got all those values fixed in your mind?

Now, I'm going to tell you that the brand is a Kia—yes, the car company in Seoul, Korea. If you had a nanosecond of "wait a minute that's not the car you were describing" rushing through your head, you're not alone. Kia may be many things, but it's not the car being described in the previous paragraph. The DNA just isn't there. People are just not willing to believe that description fits a Kia.

Contrary to many well-respected and well-intentioned business gurus, customers *do* know what they like, want, value, and therefore what they will buy. Contrary to many others who understand this truth but lack reliable methods for accessing this information, it's not about holding focus groups to reach conclusions that tie to sales and return on investment (ROI).

Have we taken the fun out of branding with this dissection and measurement of consumers, how they really feel and behave? Absolutely not. By gaining a firmer grasp on our target and the future that consumers prescribe for our business, we are adding fun by reshaping how the branding process unfolds. We look at the fundamental drivers of change and innovation as being pulled along by the customer. Developments in technology—new foods, fabrics, electronics, whatever—are the nouns and customers are the verbs. People's belief-based behaviors, value perceptions, and emotions pull the buying process, so that brands more often serve markets (people) rather than create them. Categories emerge and evolve to meet consumer needs, and those that succeed do so for one primary reason: The brands in the categories have figured out and stayed on top of their customers' values.

Postmodern branding (anything after 1985) is more about anticipating customer thinking and values than it is about influencing it. This should be inspiring news for marketers and their agencies alike. Once you know the difference between a brand-driven marketing opportunity and a consumer-led brand opportunity, deciding what to bring to market and how to advertise it becomes infinitely clearer and more creative for all parties. Conventional business speak advises us to think category first, and brand second. At Brand Keys, we define brands in terms of *customer values first*. And as we've said (most of the time), the really meaningful values are emotionally based.

EMOTIONAL BRANDING

It may surprise you that in this information-filled world where endless data are at our fingertips, the consumer economy is more emotionally based than ever before. Brand design, from store to product to customer service, has to answer expectations and preferences as the customer defines them. Demand is increasingly consumer pulled rather than brand pushed.

Remember when television commercials often ended with, "Ask at your favorite store—if they don't have Quickie Cooking Lard, they'll get it for you"? Not today, they won't. If consumers aren't buying a brand, and buying it frequently, retailers aren't stocking it—no matter how hard marketers push or how much they pay. And what drives consumers to create that pull? Their emotions and expectations based on a staggering amount of information. So, rather than try to control the information through conventional communication channels, why not put the emphasis more on tailoring the information to give it greater emotional appeal? Expectations and desire are often synonymous. All it takes for a company to speed by the competition and into the lives of consumers is identifying how to fill the gap between what is and what is wanted.

Knowing preferences serves as a solid foundation for creating an emotional association. The more we systematically anticipate what will engage consumers on functional, sensory, and emotional levels, the less we leave the success of our creations to chance. We know that people will pay a premium when their expectations of value or service are met or exceeded. Diesel jeans are just not *that* different from Levi's. But what people want and expect from a $400 pair of jeans and what Diesel delivers compared to Levi's is a totally different set of values and an ability to meet or exceed expectations. There is a willingness on the part of the customer to *believe* that there is a difference worth paying for.

The call from Marc Gobé is spot-on concise:

> Understanding people's emotional needs and desires is really, now more than ever, the key to success. Corporations must take definite steps toward building stronger connections and relationships that recognize their consumers as partners. Industry today needs to bring people the products they desire, exactly when they want them, through venues that are both inspiring and intimately responsive to their needs.

PREDICTING LOYALTY, BEHAVIOR, AND PROFITS

If the shift in power favors the customer, a corresponding shift to informed customer insight is critical to striking the emotional nerve that will keep a brand popular and competitive. Emotional branding is based on engaging consumers to create an emotional bond, which itself is at the heart of the Brand Keys approach to predicting customer loyalty. Until recently, the systematized study of emotion really has been largely uncharted terrain. However, emotional intelligence, though a little more difficult to access and quantify than intellectual intelligence, can be recorded in the form of reliable associations and preferences.

We adopt the same methods of inquiry used in modern psychology and apply them to increase our understanding of the ubiquitous relationships between people and brands, because, as Mr. Bernbach so eloquently pointed out in our opening quotation, "language so often camouflages what really motivates" the consumer.

Loyalty approaches can tap into and measure the drivers that underlie human motivation and identify the characteristics of things that inspire people to choose them as part of their lifestyle. Marketing success is as much about measuring the role of our gut-raw emotions as it is about interpreting the conscious feelings that contribute to choice. If people are at the heart of everything we bring to market, our efforts should be a collaboration based on identifying the attributes that make possible strong emotional bonds between people and brands—the values that lie in the deepest recesses of the heart.

This is creativity at its best: making the magic of human emotion the foundation of brand marketing and all that goes into it. Follow this process and you will find yourself viewing loyalty as an emotions-based customer hologram, a virtual tap into the future behavior of your target audiences based on specific measures such as:

- Material satisfaction and product utility
- Emotional fulfillment
- Aspirational drives
- Feelings about the category or brand
- Feelings about the company
- Feelings about themselves

Brand vision is customer vision. Or should be. Legally speaking, corporations do *own* brands. But in the age of choice and information, brands should be forged very specifically for certain people with certain values. In a sense, brands do indeed *belong* to us—the people that use them and are willing to believe in them.

BRANDING FOR LIFE—A STRATEGY FOR OPTIMUM POSITIONING AND DIFFERENTIATION

Predictive research pulls information on consumer emotions and can bring magic and creativity to all aspects of the branding process. After all, what's more magical for a brand than weaving a bond with people that touches their needs and desires—their hearts—to the point where it is impervious to baser elements such as competitive price and product features?

The age-old tendency to assume that customers captured early in their lives would remain loyal is playing out differently these days. Attention spans are short. There is a sense that we ought always to be excited, fulfilled, satisfied, and even rewarded or loved a little. Expectations and relevance, regardless of age, shift very quickly depending on the category or product.

So, the new branding is a lifelong affair. It is somewhat like getting a physical. If you haven't had one in a while, a physical reveals short-term tweaks that may correct immediate problems—like market share loss, if you were a brand. You can then increase the frequency of your physical, making it an annual event, because your body (like your customers' values) changes over time and you get a longer view every time you do it—identifying what to track or alter so that your longevity increases.

What happens to those who do not take this dictum seriously? Case in point: Life cereal. Rather than take an anticipatory stance toward the generation it originally attracted and wanted to keep loyal, Life stayed where it was, changing little more than its box design. Life's consumers' needs and desires changed, a whole industry of enhanced foods and nutri-ceuticals sprouted to meet those needs—and Life's reaction to falling sales and share was to relaunch the "Mikey" TV campaign in an attempt to shore up the brand through a misplaced bet on *which* emotional platform? Nostalgia. Too late—the brand was no longer differentiated from its competitors or relevant to its target based on that emotion.

Here are some other areas where you need to maintain a better emotional balance if you want to ensure loyalty.

Hispanic Marketing

Latinos demand more than just Spanish language from their brands. They want Spanish (Latin) values. Marketers seeking to capitalize on the flourishing Hispanic market ought be more concerned with Hispanic values, and less with Latinized venues.

According to the findings of the Brand Keys *Customer Loyalty Index,* Hispanics are more likely to purchase brands that make them feel valued as customers. Brands that better understand them, and use emotion-based vehicles to reach them, benefit from the endeavor. You need to be able to reach them just as you would any other consumer segment, but that means going beyond Hispanic television and magazines to seek out vehicles to help reinforce the values that make the difference between buying your brand or a competitor's.

There are key emotional values that need to be factored into any strategic decision-making process. Loyalty-based values help to craft truly resonating differentiation. Here's some of the interesting value statistics for Hispanics relative to the general market (see Figure 4.1):

- Hispanics are 21 percent more loyal to brands that were seen to be relevant to them, especially those that had a real sense of family about them.
- While 2 percent less likely to actually be *brand loyal,* Hispanics were, in fact, 7 percent more *brand conscious* than non-Hispanics.
- Hispanics were 9 percent more likely to regard shopping as a *social experience,* one in which the entire family may be involved, because shopping was a more emotionally based activity for them.

Figure 4.1
Hispanic Values

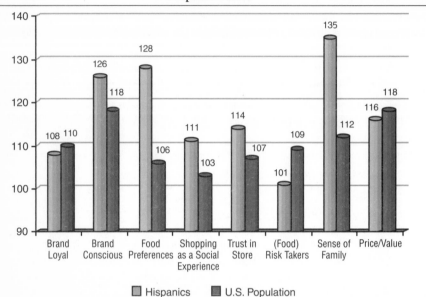

Depending on the marketing vehicle selected, the choice of communication vehicle itself could contribute as much as 10 percent more toward creating the loyalty bond between Hispanic consumers and the brand, and could provide negative effects that degrade the brand-to-consumer bond by as much as −18 percent.

Just being available and in Spanish clearly doesn't cut it and establish a firm basis for being believed. The reality is Hispanics don't just see it, like it, and buy it. They don't just want to be reached, they want to be *touched*.

To do that, marketers need to understand the emotional values first, and the category attributes afterward.

The Importance of Being (and Staying) Relevant

Customer relevance follows in a similar vein. Being different only works as a brand strategy if that (i.e., how and when you are different) is relevant to the customer base. And you have to know it in ways that consumers usually can't even consciously express.

But that isn't the whole customer picture. You also have to know *what people are willing to believe about your category and brand*. Why? Because how loyal they are rests on how much they trust you to deliver a new offering, or how willing they are to suspend disbelief if trying something new from you was not already on their expectations radar.

Clearly, the limits to brand positioning, innovation, communication, and so on are defined in terms of what the customer wants, not what R&D, bleeding-edge technology or imagination says is feasible or appealing.

Consider the success of:

- Ten-bladed razors
- Apple's cube
- Half-carb sodas
- Wristwatch TVs
- Apple's Newton

But perhaps customer and their expectations are willing to meet you halfway. In 2006, Gillette escalated the razor wars, unveiling a razor, the Fusion, with five blades and a lubricating strip on both the front and back. This was in reaction to Schick's 2005 launch of a four-blade razor, the Quattro. This year, Schick is introducing a battery-powered version to its lineup. The Fusion will be available in a power version and will feature a microchip that regulates the voltage and blade action with a low battery indicator light and a safety switch that shuts the razor down after eight minutes of continuous operation. The reality—and the test—is whether this is all relevant or meaningful to the customer.

Relevance is a manifestation of emotional values. Human emotions come first, then economics. But it's a moving relevance. How fast or slow the values that define relevance shift is a function of the category and customer's expectations for it. The rate of change is different for each category. Which is why if you are in the hotel business, it doesn't do you a whole lot of good to compare your brand to a hamburger chain, magazine, or cell phone.

Differentiation and relevance go hand in hand. Both are critical to brand loyalty. If a brand has no meaningful difference from its competition and consequently offers no incremental benefit, or if it proffers a difference that is irrelevant to the target and its expectations for what the brand should be, there's no reason for customers to be loyal. Fortunately, the magic of the new branding process is that the emotional values that determine loyalty in every category, in any market, anywhere in the world where people buy stuff can now be tracked and, without exception, anticipated.

TRACK VALUES AND EXPECTATIONS, NOT FADS

Hardly a week goes by without a business journal or popular consumer magazine missing the opportunity to trumpet the latest trend in fashion, music, food, diet, or exercise. We as a people are fad obsessed. If there is a mere glimmer of a new trend on the horizon, we jump on it. If there's not, we make one up. Where did this low-carb madness come from, anyway? It seems as though we went from anti-fat to anti-carb in about one month's time—just long enough for food manufacturers to change their packaging.

While the fad/trend thing may be mildly entertaining, it is not a firm foundation on which to build a brand strategy. Fads are only fads. And if a brand gets caught up in the frenzy, it may not be around when the fad runs out of hot air. Better to look at values and expectations as the strategic underpinnings that may shift, yes, but that will support the brand as trends come and go because they are consumer centric.

In doing this, it is important to distinguish between a value, expectation, trend, and fad. For example, people talk about convenience and customization as trends. Trends they are not. They're expectations that have been increasing over time as consumers have become more empowered. These expectations are so pervasive that they are almost category agnostic. They exist at so many levels that they will *never* go out of style the way a fad or trend will. Let's take a look at our findings in this area.

Low-Carbohydrate Craze or Research Lite?

The food and beverage industries had to scramble to get on the low-carb train before it left the station—I just hope they had return tickets. After only 9 months of frenzy, companies like PepsiCo, Unilever, and Kraft were retreating from the shrinking category. They all cited dismal sales and the low-carbohydrate food market that was once predicted to hit sales as high as $15 billion, topped out at just under $1 billion, with products being pulled off store shelves.

On August 1, 2005, Atkins Nutritionals, Inc., filed for bankruptcy, citing "waning interest" in the once-popular diet. "The low-carb fad has gone," said

Michael Steib, a consumer food analyst for Morgan Stanley. "Dieting habits are very short-lived." But if that's the case (and we agree; dieting is a trend, and the diet of the moment is a fad) how did these companies get caught short?

If they had done some predictive, values-based loyalty research they'd have been able to see what was coming as consumer expectations change, rather than ask the comic question "Is that daylight at the end of the tunnel or an on-coming train?"

People make a lot of excuses for not dieting. That's not news. What is unique was that suddenly dieting in the Age of the Low-Carb Craze was being used to excuse—or at least to explain—the slimming of corporate prof-its for carb-heavy brands.

The low-carbohydrate craze *was* a fad. And fads are unpredictable. Fads are leanings, human propensities over time, not absolutes. They are temporary. They are also hugely profitable. If, like waves, you see them coming, catch them, and ride them until you see the rocks or the beach. The crucial un-knowns are constant: just how temporary is the fad? What accounts for it? Where and when will the trend peak, and, most important, what are the im-plications for the brand involved?

Companies *could* anticipate the degree to which fads and trends are going to impact their businesses. But this will never happen by asking consumers "Is it important for you to lose some weight?" or, worse, "If we had a tasty, low-carbohydrate, sugar-free doughnut, would you eat it?"

What companies really needed to know was exactly how important the fad (in this case, the low-carb mania) was going to be to their category. They needed to know how consumers viewed the category—for example, how they ate, did not eat, or found a suitable substitute for doughnuts. That is what we want: the percent of contribution the fad makes to behavior. Knowing pre-cisely how large a contribution the percentage of this particular attribute in the category makes to your business reveals a very clear brand and product de-velopment road map: What you should and should not be doing to your doughnuts—or sneakers, colas, or cars.

Table 4.1 shows percentages of contribution that carbohydrate awareness makes to selected food categories, and you see that the output of customer loy-alty metrics provides these insights. Here's where I put the Boston Creme where my mouth is. We predict and track just such fads, including the low-carbohydrate dimension, as they apply to appropriate categories in our *Cus-tomer Loyalty Index.*

Found what's surprising? Even taking low-carb hysteria into account, doughnuts didn't fare all that badly. Not when you figure that there are other

Table 4.1
Carbohydrate Percent Contribution
to Selected Food Categories

Food	Percentage
Apples	5
Bagels	11
Beer	4
Bottled water	1
Chicken	6
Doughnuts	5
Hamburgers	12
Light beer	2
Milk	4
Pizza	10
Soft drinks	2
Soft drinks (diet)	1
Sub/Hero sandwiches	7
Tacos	12

categories (e.g., pizza, hamburgers) where high carbohydrates (or, more appropriately, *the appearance of being high in carbohydrates*) make a much bigger impact on the business.

So, it turns out that even in food, nutrition, and diet-related categories, there may be ways for brands that do the right type of predictive research to have their doughnuts and eat them, too.

CONVENIENCE AND DIFFERENTIATION: THE ROAD MOST TAKEN IS NOW FIVE TIMES AS IMPORTANT

To paraphrase Robert Frost, "Two consumer trends converged in the forest of retail and service, and I took the one most convenient."

While not as polished as Frost's verse, the sentiment captures what we are all currently witnessing: consumers' heightened feelings of time stress, resulting in their need for all things in a hurry. This has naturally resulted in an increased desire for more convenient products and services. The percentage of contribution that convenience makes to product and service consideration, adoption, and loyalty—and therefore profitability—is currently 19 percent (see Figure 4.2). This is a nearly fivefold increase since the value was first measured in 1997, when it made only a 4 percent contribution.

Figure 4.2
How Convenience Contributes to Loyalty

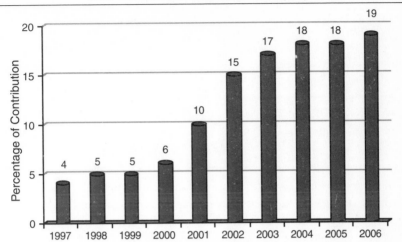

It's not that "convenience" has always been part of most of today's product and service offerings. It's just that, that particular item on the list of attributes, benefits, and values has become more important to consumers as one that will actually differentiate category and brand offerings. There was a time when some of the more basic category attributes—like availability, variety, online access, or even taste—made a larger contribution to consideration, purchase, and loyalty.

Not any more. Because nature abhors a vacuum, and because the consumer world has dramatically changed, other values have become more important to customers. In this case, convenience has become king. The form that convenience takes depends on the category and brand. For each of the following categories, convenience could be defined as:

- *Online:* "instant account access"
- *Airlines:* "selecting your own seat whenever you want"
- *Restaurants:* "delivery in under 20 minutes"
- *Food Shopping:* "24-hour online ordering and delivery"
- *Hotels:* "automatic check-out"; "room service 24/7"
- *Retail:* "convenient/close parking"

Of the 35 categories that currently make up the Brand Keys *Customer Loyalty Index,* the top 10 categories where convenience has become one of the largest brand differentiators are:

1. Car Rental Companies
2. Hotels
3. Online Retailers
4. Online Travel Sites
5. Banks
6. Clothing Catalogs
7. Wireless Service Providers
8. Quick-Serve Restaurants
9. Parcel Delivery
10. Coffee and Doughnut Stores

Because convenience is so very important to the car rental industry, a growing number of companies are creating partnerships with retailers to provide new, more convenient locations that rent cars. Budget and Enterprise are partnering with Wal-Mart, and Sears with Avis. Avis, a company that has excelled at building customer loyalty, planned to have 986 additional locations by the end of 2005.

What marketers need to do is actually understand how the characteristics of their category are *translated* into convenience assets. If marketers identify the characteristics correctly, they can effectively communicate value. They will then be able to better engage consumers and convey brand differences that get people to buy.

It sounds simple enough. But the process is a bit more complex. Marketers are much more nimble today than a decade ago. What used to be a real, six-month market advantage has dwindled to less than a week. In this time, a competitor could be offering similar conveniences.

Convenience is the newest of brand differentiators. Make good on your convenience promise and consumers will beat a path to your proverbial door, wherever it may be. If not, they'll beat a path to whichever other door they perceive as most yawningly open and inviting. And when it comes to loyalty, to quote Mr. Frost, "that can make all the difference."

All Differentiation (Emotional or Not) Is Not Created Equal

Remember Trout's law: Differentiate or die. However, *how* to make differentiation a more robust, accurate, and believable customer-driven process is rarely addressed. If you as a brand are all about a lot of message and not much product, pretty soon no amount of marketing—whether through traditional media, product placement, or sponsorship—will keep a productive and profitable brand-customer conversation alive. Messaging is important only if you are doing it in a way that resonates with the majority of customers, hitting on what they *like,* the street term for what resonates with their values and expectations. Nothing is as effective a loyalty and sales builder as the ability to stand apart from the crowd by saying who and what you are when both of those qualities are what people expect and truly want.

If you're following this leading-indicator argument, you can probably anticipate the answer to how differentiation is identified.

Being different from the competition means nothing to the consumer unless being different becomes synonymous with being able to produce, and deliver on, what he or she values *better or before anyone else does.*

Let's state it as law:

Being different, or new, is no guarantee of competitive advantage or success. Brands are competing to meet or exceed customer values and expectations first, and against each other second.

Plenty of companies use important-sounding but resonance-free offerings as a basis for brand success in their category, from discount coupons to free home delivery. The best quality products, the best possible manufacturing processes, even the highest quality ingredients are not the answers to deliver to a questioning market if those were not the customers' questions in the first place.

To differentiate properly, you need to identify and capitalize on customer values *before* they become entrenched, obvious, and therefore available to everyone and every brand. You have to select the ones that not only *sound* good, but are going to be believable to your customers and prospects. Research must ask if these qualities are what people are expressing as preferences for a brand, measured as unfulfilled expectations. How much you need to address a particular value depends on the percentage of contribution it makes to brand loyalty.

For a sense of general patterns of values and expectations, track all the hot spots by asking if there is a measured preference that is currently going unfulfilled in areas like:

- Hip/cool
- Original
- Flashy
- News
- Creative
- My community

- Me
- Sexy
- Honest
- Fun
- Interactive
- Cynical
- Stylish
- Humorous
- Real

There is no free ride. Even when brands compete on the level of generics or as price-differentiated commodities, unless the price or features of the offering match or exceed customer's perceptions and expectations for value, they simply will not significantly move the sales needle.

LOYALTY TALES FROM THE REAL WORLD

The Magic of the Harry Potter Brand

On Saturday, 12:01 A.M., July 16, 2005, the sixth volume of the *Harry Potter* series was released to even more fanfare than the fifth volume. It had an initial print run of 10.8 million books, and sold 6.8 million copies in the first 24 hours. Try to imagine old Mr. Gutenberg's jaw dropping.

So we were amazed when an independent global branding consultant proclaimed "*Harry Potter* is headline news today because of the media blitz surrounding the new book. Six weeks later, you won't hear anything."

The consultant based his insights on the results of a 2003/2004 18-country survey of 20,000 kids between the ages of 7 and 12 that he conducted along with U.K.-based market research firm Millward Brown.

Apparently, they asked kids whether they thought *Harry Potter* was "a fading phenomenon." And 69 percent said they did. In July 2005, the consultant felt that the percentage "today was probably closer to 80 percent." The statements raised a number of loyalty and research issues and questions:

- Did 7-year-olds even know what a "phenomenon" was?
- Before asking the question, did they consider the category drivers and the rhythms involved in the category? Books, toys, and all the stuff related to books and movies have real half-lives. People rarely think about the category or a brand until the time is right—when a new book is being published or a

new movie being released. This is particularly true of children, who are more in the moment than most consumers. Attitudes are fine, but behavior is magic.

• Did the researchers suggest that the consultant consider including a *behavioral* question? They didn't even have to report the findings if they didn't like what they learned, but they should at least have considered it. Having been children, and having children of our own now, we are well acquainted with the notorious fickleness of children's attitudes. They should have asked something that followed the "fading phenomenon" question with a question like: "Even though you think that *Harry Potter* is a fading phenomenon, will you buy the next *Harry Potter* book (or go to the next *Harry Potter* movie)?"

• History is wonderful because it allows you to recognize a mistake when you make it again. That's why loyalty metrics are so useful—they predict what's going to happen. Although you didn't have to be the prophet of Delphi to have guessed that—as the number of copies increased with each volume of the *Potter* series—it was extraordinarily likely that the sixth volume was going to be a hit, too.

• As to the statement that "six weeks later you won't hear anything," this was likely true only to the extent that everyone was going to be thoroughly engrossed reading the book. The consultant also said that kids today are not as enamored by the magic of *Harry Potter* as they were when the author first introduced the boy wizard almost seven years ago—what a muggle. Values define the degree to which customers are loyal to brands, and *Harry Potter* is imbued so richly with values that it has become an instant classic, like *Winnie the Pooh* and *Mary Poppins*.

It's true that for many consumers some categories and brands are, indeed, not held in the top of mind, and we suppose that we could take the jaundiced view that as such, these categories are fading phenomena. But the phenomenon fades only until a friend or colleague is due to have a baby. Then our thoughts turn to *Goodnight, Moon,* and *Pat the Bunny,* and virtually anything by Dr. Seuss. We remain loyal to the end to books we bought for our own little ones.

Starbucks and Dunkin' Donuts: How Far Would You Drive for a Latte?

Chatting recently over coffee with a senior member of the Advertising Research Foundation, we commented that values that account for loyalty in the "Coffee and Doughnuts" category (among others) were shifting in interesting ways.

"What values?" he declared. "I come to work and buy coffee at the place that's most convenient." And that may have well have been the case. But as researchers, we are (or should be) wary of generalizing from single-person samples.

Looking at the most recent loyalty drivers for the category, we noted that "Location" had become the first most important driver for the category, and the driver where customers held the highest levels of expectation.

This was followed by "Quality and Taste" (suggesting that the coffee and preparation in a coffee shop is superior to that of home-brewed coffee), "Service" (it's easier to have someone wait on you than to do it yourself), and "Variety" (as in small, medium, and grande, with and without foam, in one of 10 types not available at home—you get the point; see Figure 4.3).

The availability of better or more preferred coffee from coffee shops and specialty stores has largely replaced the in-home activity of brewing your own cup. And in many, many cases, the home brew preparation has been replaced with a walk, or even a car trip, to a favorite purveyor. Indeed, today cities and suburbs are thronged with white- and blue-collar men and women toting cardboard containers of coffee into their shops, offices, and trucks.

This has compelled us to consider adding the following to our list of loyalty mantras: "Loyalty in the 'Coffee and Doughnuts' category can result in gridlock."

Figure 4.3
The Coffee and Doughnuts Category

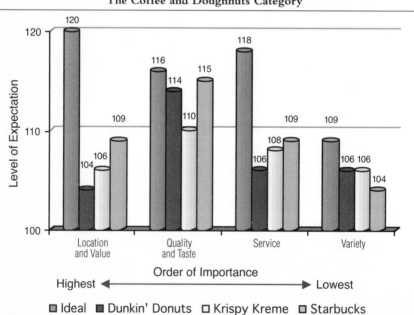

If behavior in the marketplace is everything, here's the proof: the U.S. Department of Transportation (DOT) has noted that Americans have tacked personal errands onto their commutes. In drilling-down into the data, it turns out that more and more consumers, especially men, are devoting many of their morning trips to coffee and portable breakfasts like doughnuts and bagels. Instead of their usual beeline to the workplace, they have begun making more side trips to their favorite quick java-and-carb purveyors.

This increase in customers side tripping for coffee and doughnuts has increasingly thwarted attempts to forecast travel patterns that have traditionally been based on computer models that rely primarily on the predictability of the morning commute.

A growing percentage of commuters, driven by their lust for caffeine and carbohydrates, seem willing to go out of their way, and add time to their morning commute, to satisfy that lust.

The DOT would much prefer that all commuters were like my colleague at the Advertising Research Foundation: take the shortest, fastest, most convenient route to work, and not deviate in unexpected directions dictated more by coffee-shop loyalty than by time or motion considerations.

Restaurant industry analysts reveal that it's no accident that commuters rarely have to make a left turn to get coffee. Coffee shops try to make sure that they are on the right side of the street for the morning commute, boosting their chances for a pit stop.

So now you know why Starbucks will have two locations across the street from one another. It accommodates traffic patterns in both directions, reinforces loyalty, and capitalizes on another important twenty-first-century value—convenience.

And as shown in Figure 4.3, Dunkin' Donuts is capitalizing on its strength in "Quality and Taste." Its new campaign is based on real-life stories about consumers who'd walk a mile (or make an unscheduled stop in a locomotive) for that great-tasting Dunkin' Donuts coffee.

Q & A

Customer Experience + Brand Loyalty = ??

John Gaffney, *1to1* magazine: *How does customer experience relate to brand loyalty?*

Robert Passikoff: Customer experience, now huddled under the umbrella of experiential marketing, is an approach that permits marketers more leeway for increasing the emotional bond between consumers and their brands. The trick is to know which experiences your customers want (or expect you to create) and that will contribute most to loyalty and sales.

Traditional product-centric marketing represents a left-brain approach to the consumer. It generally seeks to persuade consumers by invoking rational factors that position the advertised brand as better than competing brands. This rational approach is not entirely unimportant. But it has become increasingly difficult for brands to find rational product and service attributes that are different/better/more compelling than those of the competition.

It's all part of the ongoing commoditization epidemic.

On the other hand, the idea of experiential marketing reflects a right-brain bias because it is about fulfilling consumers' aspirations. We often shorthand these aspirations by asking whether the activity will make the customer feel valued. As customer decisions are much more influenced by emotionally generated feelings than by rationally derived thoughts (see our 70:30 rule), experience plays a big part in producing better loyalty bonds between customers and brands.

Social Responsibility and Customer Loyalty

Garrett Glaser, NBC News: *To what extent does awareness of a company's record on social responsibility impact customer engagement and loyalty to that company's brands?*

Robert Passikoff: It depends. Corporate social responsibility (Cause-Related Marketing) is something that most companies participate in to one degree or another. Problem is it isn't all that easy to identify a cause with a credo that realistically enhances the bond between brand and consumer. From a brand loyalty perspective, social responsibility is a tactic companies have used to link brands to charities and causes that they feel enhance and differentiate corporate reputation.

In the current environment, where real and even perceived differentiation is more difficult to attain, many companies have felt that such acts of social responsibility move their brand beyond the rational arena of product attributes and benefits into the sphere of creating actual belief systems that will more emotionally bond consumers to brands.

It's a relatively new marketing typology, and why not give back to the community that includes your customers? And if, at the same time, you add a little to the bottom line, who would say no to that? So, if it's such a good idea, why was my answer: "it depends"?

Because there just isn't enough money to support all the worthy causes out there. Corporations don't have unlimited coffers. Issues of accountability are being discussed more heatedly, and it isn't all that easy to decide on a cause valuable enough to guarantee bolstering the brand-consumer bond. Today's consumers expect this sort of activity as a corporate behavioral benchmark, like not testing on animals or recycling. So, you can be dedicated, you can be sincere, you can market the heck out of your kindhearted activities, and you may get a hearty "thank you" from the organization you've sponsored—but zip from the market.

There is nothing wrong with "doing well by doing good." Still, the question remains: How can you ensure that your efforts pay off in a way that you like?

In just the same way that we can identify the components that best reinforce the brand's equity, we can identify the causes that make the largest percent of contribution to brand equity and customer loyalty.

One of our surveys showed that, for a particular brand, sponsoring a literacy program would result in a 2 percent increase in brand loyalty. The same survey showed that sponsoring a local baseball team would yield a 10 percent increase in brand loyalty. Given that both organizations were actively looking for sponsors, would you rather a 2 percent or a 10 percent ROI?

That's why it depends.

Q & A
Groups and Brands

Amy Chozick, *Wall Street Journal*: *What makes one ethnic group respond to a brand differently than another?*

Robert Passikoff: There is a finite collection of values that defines the loyalty parameters of a category (although some categories have more comprehensive lists than others). Even more interesting is that the composition of these lists doesn't really change from one ethnic group to another: the collection of category and consumer attributes, benefits, and image items that form the yardstick consumers use to measure and buy brands stays relatively the same.

What does change from ethnic group to ethnic group are three things:

1. The order of importance of the category drivers
2. The percent of contribution that the individual value components comprising the category drivers make to loyalty for one group versus another
3. The level of expectations that one group holds for a particular driver compared to those held by another group.

These differences *do* create different category yardsticks. Their configuration causes one group, drawn along ethnic lines or otherwise, to behave (read: identify and buy) differently from another. Because of the predictive nature of values-based metrics, good measurements also define how value-defined groups, ethic or otherwise, will respond in the future.

Take frozen foods. Hispanics are just as brand loyal in this category as other consumer groups. However, "Trust in the Store" is the most important driver for Hispanics compared to third most important for Caucasians—and that trumps brand loyalty. Hispanics also have much higher expectations for a brand's ability to provide a range of products than Caucasians, nearly 21 percent higher, and the value "enjoy the shopping experience" makes an 11 percent contribution to Hispanic loyalty, compared to only 3 percent for Caucasians.

Brand versus Store Loyalty

Jim Ostroff, *Kiplinger Letter*: *Why is it that consumers are more loyal to a particular brand than to a particular department store?*

Robert Passikoff: Jack Trout pointed out that today differentiation is the one aspect of a brand that helps fuel loyalty. Brands have spent a lot of time and money trying to do just that. And even though they are having a rough go of it, they have done it better than most retail outlets, including department stores.

Retailers have relied on brand awareness and store location as the items that they feel will engender loyalty, but given the sameness of the inventory and the shopping experience and generally ubiquitous distribution, it's no surprise that department stores don't really do a good job differentiating themselves from their competition—let alone e-tailers. These days it is more likely that a consumer wants a particular brand and does not care where he or she buys it (this does not hold true for some Hispanic consumers, as noted previously).

Jim Ostroff: *Are there specific things a retailer can do to build (or rebuild) loyalty?*

Robert Passikoff: Here are the Top 10 Rules for Retailers:

1. Know and respect thy consumer.
2. Understand them *way* beyond just demographics and the holidays they celebrate.
3. Know what consumers really expect, thereby keeping ahead of the competition.
4. Know how to manage your operation to meet or exceed customer expectations.
5. Know what consumers are willing to believe about you.
6. Recognize that a marketing strategy is not necessarily a brand strategy.
7. Pricing, distribution, and quality constitute the twenty-first-century price of entry.
8. Capitalize on any opportunity that presents itself. Can you spell convenience?
9. Inventory has to be in stock.
10. Location does matter—only with the Internet, not as much as it did.

"Confound it, men! If they don't respond to hard sell and they don't respond to soft sell, what the hell sell <u>do</u> they respond to?"

CHAPTER 5

EASY-TO-IMPLEMENT CUSTOMER LOYALTY METRICS: HOW TO SUPERCHARGE TRADITIONAL RESEARCH AND MARKETING

Even if you are on the right track, you'll get run over if you just sit there.

—*Will Rogers*

What do we know about what we *know*?

Thirty percent of what we know comes from using direct, traditional questions and answers or some other traditional methodology or medium. Seventy percent comes from a subtle, nuanced, and indirect approach. Be aware that even in the face of difficult-to-attain profitability and nearly impossible-to-attain brand differentiation, not many marketers are brave enough to jettison their roster of traditional research approaches. Whether it's at the 30 percent level in your business or not, there is ubiquitous agreement that traditional research approaches can, by their very design, provide only a portion (ever diminishing though it may be) of the insights modern marketers require to be competitive and successful.

We find three main elements underlying most marketers' hesitation to use twenty-first-century tools to deal with more-difficult-to-read, twenty-first-century consumers:

1. A lack or conviction regarding the efficacy of the new approaches
2. A comfort level with older approaches despite their limitations
3. A lack of urgency, and corporate inertia

Although given the state of many brands, we recommend adopting loyalty metrics. They work, are leading indicators, and correlate with consumer engagement levels that, in turn, connect with profits. Those issues aside, there are ways in which some very basic predictive loyalty metrics can help to optimize or supercharge your traditional research tools.

OVERLAY LOYALTY RESEARCH ON OTHER MEASURES TO TIGHTEN UP THE CUSTOMER FOCUS

Next I share some recommendations regarding some of the basic traditional research tools. If the recommendations sound a little self-evident, keep in mind that we're optimizing these techniques based on *totally consumer-driven, predictive, linked-to-profitability loyalty and engagement metrics*. You can't just say, "Okay, we'll make these changes using different traditional methods and get on with it." If you do that, you'll end up spinning your wheels.

That last point is important. Try to imagine what would happen if you tried to institute the recommended, optimized changes based on internal decision making alone. It's difficult to attain strategic alignment at the best of times, no matter how well-meaning your colleagues. Ask "what drives a category?" and you're likely to get as many answers as there are committee members. "Which items do we think are important to the consumer?" will result in an endless discussion of why the issue regarding the color of your packaging absolutely needs to be asked, while someone else will want to know if the consumer can accurately report what your brand name used to be before you changed it eight years ago. These are not exaggerations but actual questions that have appeared on actual questionnaires. You've all sat in meetings where issues like these have been discussed ad infinitum.

So, our recommended optimization approaches are practical and allow you to recalibrate your traditional research to customer loyalty standards that allow you to predict brand success.

THE BASICS OF LOYALTY MEASUREMENT

When discussing how to optimize your traditional measures with customer loyalty metrics, I refer to the following customer loyalty outputs, all of which can be derived from the most basic customer loyalty survey:

- The drivers for the Category Ideal—how consumers view the category, compare offerings, and, ultimately, buy.
- The order of importance of category drivers.
- The category and customer attributes, benefits, and value components of each driver.
- The percentage of contribution each driver—and its components—makes to consideration and purchase.
- The levels of expectation consumers hold for each of the category drivers. (Remember, a consumer can hold higher expectations for a less important driver, so the difference is critical to include in your research and planning approaches.)
- Overall brand assessments that are predictive of positive consumer behavior in the marketplace—that positively correlate values to the purchase of goods and services embodying those values.

More information can be derived from a more sophisticated loyalty survey design, but for the moment let's rely on the basic outputs to help optimize some of the most popular traditional approaches. In all cases, I assumed that we would avoid making the kind of design and semantic mistakes mentioned previously, and that—in all but one case—you actually *know* whom you want to interview.

POLLING AND OVERALL QUESTIONNAIRE DESIGN

I have had a framed cartoon hanging over my desk for over 20 years. It's a picture of what I have always judged as a central location interception: A woman with a clipboard approaches a man with a shopping bag. The caption reads, "Excuse me Sir, do you have a quarter of an hour to waste on some fatuous questions?" It has acted as a reminder to me that in today's 24/7 media and technology-driven world, getting *through to* consumers is already tough enough, without actually wasting their time answering questions for you.

We've noted that consumers are smarter than they used to be about marketing. Advertisers, marketers, research houses, and the Internet are to blame. We educated the heck out of consumers and they are *on* to all the old methodologies that used to work so well. We get at least five calls or e-mails a week asking to be listed for participation in focus groups. So, this new consumer—intelligent as the average researcher—isn't going to put up with wasting time or fatuous questions.

Brand Keys is also at the point where we augment *every* study we conduct—telephone, mail, online, central location tests (CLT)—with central location intercepts of "cell-phone users only" (i.e., no land line), so that we do not miss a portion of what's turned into an ever-growing segment of the population. You didn't have to worry about that even two years ago. Many people now have cell phones but no land line—an issue that more people shopping for research firms need to know. It's a statement about the markets today, yet we're willing to bet that most of your research suppliers haven't incorporated that fact into their standard polling approach.

Before beginning with some of the customer loyalty basics—like optimizing your overall questionnaire design and the time spent with your respondents—I want to address my personal bête noire and an issue that modern-day researchers must address. Questionnaire design comes down to a question of *what* you ask, *how* you ask it, and asking what's important to *know*—what will best benefit the brand and the marketing strategy. Let's discuss some examples of how questionnaire design determines the marketing strategy.

How about Them Yankees?

Suppose a client bought significant signage in Yankee Stadium. Contracts are generally multiyear. In your regular local tracking survey, you might wish to determine who had seen and remembered the sign. It probably makes sense to drop the question during your winter wave because nobody's at the stadium in January. If you are really, really compulsive about your chart continuity, you might keep the question for respondents who live in the Bronx, but you wouldn't want to compound the issue and weaken the results by asking the question of respondents in Queens, where it's dramatically unlikely that Mets fans were sneaking into Yankee Stadium in the dead of winter.

Significant signage is an expensive, long-term commitment. It makes sense to ascertain a benchmark measure of awareness and take another measure, say, six months *before* contract renewal discussions begin rather than asking the same awareness question whenever you field your tracking study. If your initial awareness was 1 percent and five years later, it's only 3 percent, you may want to reallocate those marketing dollars where they will do more good, or you may now have a good negotiation point with the Yankees.

Lesson: Don't make the interview long (and more expensive) by asking questions, wave after wave, that you can't do anything about or when there is nothing to learn from reams of interim data. You're just asking fatuous questions, and wasting, or paying for, the respondents' time.

Why bother your respondents with that? If the objective of the signage exercise is just being a good corporate citizen, the awareness effects shouldn't factor into the decision to make the investment in the first place.

If you add a few more questions like that to your tracking questionnaire, you add five, maybe more, minutes to the length of the study. You do the math. Longer questionnaires, wave after wave, cost more, but more important, you begin to "piss off" (that's the research insider's technical term) your respondents, and then it gets harder and harder to involve them the next time you want to talk to them.

Amex and the Magic 77

American Express had a questionnaire that—once you got past the screener—was made up of 77 individual metric points—questions that it had forever measured in its tracking.

It's a worldwide company that tracks in many places among many cardholder segments. It gets expensive after a while. This would perhaps be even truer if you're a small company. If you are not willing to give up the number of areas in which you track or cut down the number of segments you interview, the only way to make the survey more cost-effective is to either decrease the number of annual waves or decrease the number of questions you ask. You can argue about the merits of how many multiple waves, but if you reduce your time in field, cost of tabulation, time required to report, and so on you can actually see some real savings.

The company chose to look at the latter option.

By putting the 77 question areas under a customer loyalty microscope—identifying the percentage of contribution each individual area of inquiry made to loyalty—we discovered that (depending on the particular cardholder segment) only 22 to 28 questions accounted for over 85 percent of the variance. That meant that even with some of the legacy questions *forced* into the design, it was likely that you could literally cut the survey length in half and still capture the aspects that most highly correlated to loyalty to the brand.

Asking Questions: How Confused Were You?

Now, *how* you ask the questions is about getting behind their defenses, dropping below their radar; it isn't just an issue of being elegant or clever when interviewing consumers. It's sometimes just merely a question of being clear and polite.

The following questions were crafted and fielded by a large and well-known market research firm for a division of a well-known company that would normally service—for the purpose of this story—your cable TV box.

The name of the client and the research firm will remain anonymous. The quality of mercy is not strained even in the market research industry, but the questions were actually asked in this manner:

> First, I have some questions about the Sowanso Corporation name.
>
> Before the Sowanso Corporation came out to do the service work it has recently completed, would you say you were very confused, somewhat confused, or not confused about what the name of the company actually was?
>
> Now that they have been out, how confused are you about what their name actually is? Would you say very confused, somewhat confused, or not confused?

They must have thought, "We've done some rebranding, so there might be confusion about our name and our brand, let's find out." It was a reasonable enough question, so they just asked—precisely as indicated.

It never occurred to the Sowanso Research Director that consumers might be just the tiniest bit hesitant to admit to a stranger on the telephone that they had been confused about the company they called for a service appointment and whom they actually admitted into their homes. The interviewers also cued the respondents in the introduction by telling them about whom they were going to ask some questions. Perhaps, the Research Director knew that and figured that he'd be able to go back to his management and say, "See how low the confusion numbers are. Aren't we doing a great job?" That, of course, raises ethical issues beyond the scope of this book.

As the client company *knew* whom they had actually serviced—these weren't, after all, random visits by their technicians—all they had to do was call up and ask: "You recently had your cable box serviced. What was the name of the company that came to your home?"

That's it—no cues and no suggestions of confusion. The respondent would have (1) either known the name right away, (2) had to think about it a while, or (3) not known the name. But the tallying of just those responses in that way would have been enough to tell the client whether there was any degree of confusion about the brand name. It also would have had the added advantage of *not* making the respondent feel stupid. This is an added bonus when most businesses these days spend a great deal of money on programs that try to help them keep all the customers they can.

SPECIFIC QUESTIONNAIRE DESIGN (TRACKING OR OTHERWISE)

The issue is *what* you should ask about and in *which* order you should ask your questions. Everyone always wants to ask about everything. Many of the issues that are looked at tend to be legacy measures (i.e., they were asked about in the past, so why not just continue to ask about them?). Sometimes legacy measures are germane to the brand problem at hand, but mostly they are asked because of tradition and habit. This creates great historical tracking charts in the report to management, but it is of no use to the brand in any predictive or monetary way.

Category and consumer values continue to shift and morph faster and faster. Both change regularly. You want to make sure that your questionnaire considers those shifts. Asking about trends from two years ago wouldn't help you today or tomorrow.

Knowing the precise percentage of contribution each of the category components—the attributes, benefits, and values—make to consideration, engagement, purchase, and loyalty allows you to measure what *is* important to the category and the consumer. It makes for a shorter, more useful questionnaire and results in a more time- and cost-effective effort.

ORDER MATTERS

So, we use customer loyalty measures to identify *what* to ask—now let's turn to *how* to ask those questions. We don't specify which language to use—that we leave to you (although we *do* advise not insulting your respondents, intentionally or otherwise)—but loyalty metrics can help with the order in which to actually ask the questions.

Remember, the loyalty measures show you the components that make up the drivers themselves. All we need to do now is set the order of the questions asked, or the attributes and benefits measured, according to how the consumer truly views the category.

"Why do that?" and "If I already know *what* to ask, why should I concern myself with the order in which I ask the questions?" are both good questions we hear often. Issues of continuity and comprehension are often overlooked in research design. Researchers are trying to communicate as cogently (and engagingly) as possible with the respondents. Customer loyalty studies worldwide reveal that *consumers process information better if the questions are asked in a sequence that most reflects the order of the category drivers as perceived by the customer,* not the client, marketer, or the researcher team.

Communication theory suggests that the more consonant any communications are—be it Q&A, conversations, or online chat—the more the communication flow is enabled. That's a fancy way of saying that if there's more flow, the conversation is smoother. If you are disjointed or dissonant in terms of how people look at a category (even if that view is taking place in their minds), the results tend to be equally unbalanced. If you're consonant with the way people think about the category, you get answers that reflect what they really think. There's less of a stretch, mentally speaking, about answering the questions.

If you order your questions in this manner, you get more truthful, more accurate answers more quickly, and you *reduce the length of an interview by 18 percent to 25 percent on average,* depending on the complexity of the category and how neurotic your marketing team is. There's also a big difference in cost between a 10-question and a 20-question survey.

SATISFACTION SURVEYS

Satisfaction surveys have become very popular in the past few years. They were useful back in the 1980s when companies *needed* to fix products, services, and processes. However, most companies that managed to make it to the twenty-first century are already doing it right, so, in reality, satisfaction measures remain mostly another legacy metric.

But more than just being a legacy, they are also lagging indicators. You may have satisfied a customer yesterday, but values shift quickly and now they're not so satisfied and they've moved on to your competitor.

Doubt me? Hop into the "Way-Back Machine" with me and let's return to the glory days of 1997 for a history lesson. True, it was only a few years ago, but in customer loyalty terms it is like going back to the time of the dinosaurs.

Let's look at IBM: Of the customers who had been interviewed for a satisfaction survey. A really impressive majority said that they were "deeply satisfied with current (1997) IBM products." Shortly thereafter, when these same customers replaced their equipment, an equally impressive majority turned to other suppliers. It cost IBM nearly $7 billion. This was a shock to Big Blue.

What do we learn from this history lesson, besides the fact that $7 billion is painful to lose, no matter how big or how rich you might be? As astute observers might have suspected, customer satisfaction, though important, *doesn't necessarily translate into repeat sales and bottom-line profits.*

In the IBM case just cited, traditional measures didn't alert IBM to the fact that customers no longer valued the satisfactory products they were providing. It turns out that customers valued personal computers, PCs—a new value. Since IBM didn't have a clue about that particular value, it hadn't any PCs to sell. *So, millions of those entirely satisfied customers went elsewhere.*

IBM made a mistake, but in the interest of historical fairness, IBM *did* include the traditional questions that are *supposed* to capture customer loyalty information as part of its satisfaction survey. It did ask, "Do you plan to buy from us again?" "Would you recommend this product to a colleague?" A "yes" to each question still would not have prepared it for the right course of action, because it was smiley-face, honest and excellently tabulated answers to irrelevant questions. I start to lose sleep when I consider how many other large companies still ask those same questions and mistake positive indications for leading indicators.

IBM is not alone in its research-induced malaise; there are many other firms (most without the financial armor of IBM to deflect the disloyalty arrow) in many industries that risk failure on one or more fronts because they are not using values-based research and rely primarily on satisfaction surveys.

Largely due to the excellent marketing prowess of J.D. Power and Associates, satisfaction has become more of an advertising differentiator than a measure that allows companies to manage their brands strategically.

Consumers deserve—and companies should be proud of—exemplary levels of satisfaction. But you want to be careful of falling into the we-are-a-differentiated-brand-because-we-won-an-award trap. I quote from an old Enron press release:

> Enron Corporation was named today the "most innovative Company in America" for the sixth consecutive year by *Fortune* magazine. Said Kenneth L. Lay, Enron chairman and CEO, "we are proud to receive this accolade for the sixth year. It reflects our corporate culture which is driven by smart employees who continually come up with new ways to grow our business."

But there it is. Many companies are still intent on determining how satisfied their customers are and using it to differentiate themselves from their competition (who have *different* satisfaction awards of their own). If you, too, are intent on keeping the measure in place, we believe that the most useful customer satisfaction model is one that examines traditional measures from the point of view of how they affect customer values, contribute to loyalty, and affect company profitability. Over the past decade, your company has likely developed finely tuned satisfaction measures that move in this direction. Your competitors have done the same:

- We've found that twenty-first-century customer expectations are such that all items being measured can be deemed to be important to the process of both satisfaction *and* loyalty.
- Most of these items are viewed as the price of entry to the category by the majority of customers and prospects. It's probably fair to say that satisfaction is table stakes. Either you have a stake or you don't, and if you don't, you don't get to play.

The facts of modern markets are simple. To gain a competitive edge, therefore, it is necessary to move beyond standard statistical analyses—splitting hairs to identify significant differences between 5.8 and 6.1 ratings (most sample segments aren't big enough to do that anyway and if they are, and there are no differences, you are just burning your marketing budget)—and the rank-ordering of the price-of-entry satisfaction items on the basis of claimed or derived importance.

Some clients have tried to expand the bandwidth of their satisfaction ratings to identify greater degrees of differentiation. Often the rating scale ends up looking something like this:

- Very excellent
- Excellent
- Very good
- Good
- Well above average
- Neither good nor bad
- Poor
- Very poor
- Really extraordinarily poor

Okay, I exaggerate, but not by very much. Expand the scale all you want, even the most sophisticated customer satisfaction measures *cannot* predict future behavior, and in fairness, don't purport to. By definition, satisfaction measures are at best a look at the past—at how customers feel about the transactions that they've already made. You discover very little, statistically speaking, about whether your current customers will be repeat customers. At the risk of sounding repetitious, a current satisfied customer is not necessarily a loyal future customer.

How do you rank the importance of the drivers and the characteristics in such a way that you know exactly what your next steps should be? How do you create a model that provides leading-indicator data that correlate to market behavior that drives sales? You know the answer because you're reading this book: customer loyalty metrics.

Most, if not all, of the satisfaction items you want to know for whatever reason can by found in one or another of the category drivers. Examining these drivers, and their percentage of contribution to loyalty, allows you to configure a true value equation with which to measure what is going to make a real difference in how people become engaged with and purchase the brand.

It allows you to more predictively sequence your initiatives and do so in a more time- and cost-efficient manner. If there are 30 attributes, benefits, and values in your study, customer loyalty metrics allow you to focus marketing on just the most valuable.

Additionally, the metrics allow you to make your process and marketing investments based on what will (or will not) contribute to loyalty, positive behavior, and therefore profitability, without falling into the trap of "We're in trouble because the satisfaction numbers aren't so high. Let's do something immediately to remediate the situation before someone in management finds out."

FOCUS GROUPS

One of the most popular research techniques today is undoubtedly the focus group. The technique grew out of the psychiatric group therapy interviews of the early-1960s. It was based on the theory that individuals who shared values would be more willing to talk about issues related to those values in a group setting. It was designed to provide insights into the behaviors and attitudes of a particular segment of the population in which the researchers were interested. That was then. This is now, and the game has changed.

Do not confuse focus groups with predictive methodologies. Focus groups were *never* supposed to be the only element research on which marketers depended. They are one tool among many, and more often than not, by virtue of their structure they obscure clarity rather than lead to insights and innovation.

The problem is, focus groups are the most accessible to everyone involved in the process, the first traditional stop on the brand research checklist. Many companies stop right there. Unless you really know how to run them and interpret the findings, often the skew falls precariously close to the opinions of the moderator, the alpha consumer, or the senior client behind the one-way mirror.

No matter how much you rely on them, love them, or find them useful (we particularly like them for collecting and capturing customer language), focus groups have an environment that is in no way similar to the environment of a department store or a living room. Humans behave very differently in each location. They tend to act and speak very differently when they know they are being watched (what psychologists call the Hawthorne effect).

Our company receives calls, e-mails, and letters each week from consumers who want to have their names placed on lists to be called—and paid for—attending focus groups. That alone has to get you thinking about who is sitting in the room. Add the fact that we're dealing with consumers who have more information about more things than ever before, and we're not dealing with naive or value-sharing consumers any more.

The normal limitations and complaints about focus groups and focus-group recruiting notwithstanding, this means that you are definitely going to have a more difficult time discerning between a real "target audience respondent" or someone who learned that focus groups are an easy way to pick up $50, or $100, maybe more for an hour's work.

Unlike focus groups, research tools that dip below the consumer's consciousness level can't be sent wandering down the wrong insight trail. That's because they ferret out underlying values and expectations through indirect questions and answers. Good customer loyalty research methods take into consideration people's love of performing and sometimes less-than-truthful reportage when it comes to their true behavior and feelings. No cause for blame, they're just human. Don't confuse anecdotes, stories, rationales, and exciting one-ups for steely trends or generalizable insights.

Optimize Your Focus Group

You can mitigate these problems and optimize your focus group by *overlaying the screening process and discussion guide design with some customer loyalty measures.* For example, we know that certain groups of consumers see the category or the brand differently than other consumer segments This is most accurately measured not by *asking,* but by *examining* the way different consumers rank the importance of the order of the category drivers. Here's where research methodology is everything.

It's true that you have to take respondents at their word when they tell you their ages or their levels of product usage, or the particular brand they most often use. But by making customer loyalty metrics part of the screening process, you can actually configure your groups with people *who really and truly view the category or brand in the same way.*

As with any questionnaire design, the order of importance of drivers creates a road map identifying the order in which focus group discussion questions will engender the most collective—and insightful—verbal interplay.

There are other ways to use the customer loyalty metrics to optimize your focus groups. Knowing the expectation levels of the category drivers provides additional insights that can be melded into the discussion guide.

Seeing how one group differs from another group in how they view the category opens up other areas of useful inquiry. Seeing how the group evaluates the brand (another question that can be included in the screening process) allows the moderator to raise specific issues that might otherwise have gone unnoticed and undiscussed.

You can get sophisticated and use customer loyalty measures in the screener to collect respondent self-assessments. You can be as inventive as your creative self-image and moderator allow. Optimizing the group sessions with loyalty-thought architecture provides you with new, predictive insights that can be infused directly into today's focus group discussions.

Online Interviewing

Interviewing respondents online has its advocates and opponents. On the one hand, it's relatively fast and cost-efficient. On the other hand, it often can turn out to be a research-by-the-ton generator. Brand Keys receives plenty of spam e-mails every day offering us the chance "to make money answering online questionnaires." In an average nine-hour day, I receive 10 to 15 e-mails asking me to participate in national surveys having to do with insurance, ice cream, cookies, Oreos as opposed to just cookies, soda, Coke versus Pepsi, computers, banks, or snacks, Home Depot as opposed to Lowe's, McDonald's versus Burger King, and so on. This approach lends a new meaning to the words security screener.

Oh, I do understand the need to recruit participants. Call me odd, but somehow I feel more confident in a telephone or central location interception interview where respondents are not earning their livings answering the questions asked.

While we recognize that no one interview technique is going to be perfect, the screening of respondents and the design of Internet interviews *could benefit from all of the previously cited customer loyalty applications.* The medium is new and fabulous. From a researcher's perspective, all it is is a different delivery mechanism. It's still people talking to people.

When the question is not one of strategic importance or brand necessity, it's fine. Polls are the perfect example. Do you think the president lied? Should there be more aid to Africa? What's your favorite color? They are after gross numbers of respondents, nothing more. When volume and study size with a huge sample group outweighs strategic import or brand necessity, it's perfect. It works best with the mostly harmless questions about preferences, flavors, and the like. Basic, rational attributes.

RESEARCH BY THE VIRTUAL POUND

Our company, Brand Keys, recently received an e-mailed—spammed—research questionnaire. This was not unusual; we receive many of them as I've mentioned. And, as is so often the case, the subject of this research request had absolutely nothing to do with what our company does or with any expertise that we might possess. This didn't seem to matter to those who sent the questionnaire. In their blind embrace of the cyber medium, all they wanted was answers to their questions—from anyone. The organization behind the questionnaire, like so many other research houses, was guilty of trying to bend the Internet to its will. What it wants, obviously, is to save time and money. At first glance, the Internet fits the bill: a cheap two-way delivery system connected to just about everyone.

This approach is not new.

The spammed-questionnaire type of problem has reared its head before. In the twentieth century, in the days before the Internet, there were people who thought it would be splendid to wire the world with interactive cable television. "Wow," they said. "We could question people in their own homes and tabulate results immediately!"

And so they did. What they discovered was that most of the time they were getting evaluations from folks who were mind-bogglingly outside the desired sample set. Children could (and did) respond to questions about beer with the click of a button, men—presumably with nothing better to do, or without any concept of feminine hygiene—responded about women's deodorant. And then there's my favorite story about a respondent outside the desired sample. One household responded to all questions all the time. When thanked for their enthusiastic participation, the perplexed family informed the researchers that no one had been home during daylight hours over the entire course of the study. No one except the family's golden retriever who, it was soon discovered, had taken to pawing the buttons as a way of filling his day! Nice doggie. Sit. Stay. Tabulate.

The twenty-first-century version of this situation is a TiVo that, for example, is left on, even when it's *not* actively recording a show it's been programmed to tape. The TiVo keeps registering that the household is watching the last channel viewed even though the television was turned off and the household had gone to bed. You want to be careful about that when ratings and demographics are reported.

Pets responding to questionnaires, random people with computers responding to questionnaires, and perpetual electronic signals create a good news/bad equation with electronic polling. The good news is that it's easy to get lots and lots of answers. The bad news is that it's very difficult to know from whom those answers are coming. (Sure, we can assign cookies, but even that doesn't tell us precisely which person with access to that particular computer has responded to our questions. There is a famous *New Yorker* cartoon pinned somewhere in virtually every office in the United States and captioned "On the

Internet, nobody knows you're a dog," unless the family fesses up.) If we applied such loose standards to our traditional—nonelectronic—research methodology, our clients would fire us. We'd deserve to be fired.

There are issues specific to electronic polling: How do you adjust for the fact that the opinions of those who ignore e-mail polls are underrepresented when it comes time to tabulate results? Do people respond differently to a computer than to a human interlocutor? How are responses affected when a respondent can answer a question, stop, make a sandwich, answer another question, and so on?

In an online environment, you can improve the questions by organizing the information along loyalty lines. You can't make the process any better. Before engaging in the study, you must be willing to sacrifice a certain degree of accuracy by being aware that you cannot be certain who is answering the questions. Face to face, at a mall, or on the phone it is obviously easier to judge.

CUSTOMER RELATIONSHIP MANAGEMENT

Were any of us truly surprised when the marketing world acknowledged the fact that it had gotten increasingly more difficult to market effectively and profitably to consumers using television, cable, and print? To address these continuing problems—and with tremendous fanfare—marketers just shifted their focus into a sector that allowed them to imply that they could talk to their consumers and understand their needs on a one-to-one, customized basis. The logic was that by being able to do this, one could more effectively manage the customer relationship to the benefit of the brand.

So, what marketers did was reach into an old trunk and pull out—*voila*—a database and a recommendation to do direct marketing. They dusted the databases off, gave them a new coat of paint, and renamed the combination with a high-tech term: customer relationship management (CRM).

Customer relationship management works for many things. Database marketing, direct marketing, and CRM are efficient ways to track behavior, manage inventories, and even communicate with customers. It's just not the Holy Grail of marketing. Ask any three professionals in the business what CRM is or does and you'll get three different descriptions. There were always limitations with databases and direct response approaches, and there are problems with this CRM positioning, tempting as it sounds. Think of CRM as the traditional 30 percent of the marketing input and you have a better perspective about its use as an antidote to brand lethargy. The reasons for this reside deep in the value of the databases.

Databases are fine, as long as the data included have any relevance to understanding how to manage marketing and communication activities that actually motivate customers. I am not talking about systems that automatically send a reminder that the recipient may want to consider ordering new ink cartridges. In that regard, what the base tells you is—much like satisfaction measures—what happened the past time a customer did something but not what is going to happen in the next quarter. It's not, for example, going to tell you that expectations for the "Price/Value" driver have increased to the point where another, lower-cost supplier is now far more appealing than the previous provider.

Regardless of your mailing list, unless you sell luxury goods, you never really market to an individual, no matter how sexy and promising that sounds. Ultimately, you end up marketing to groups.

KMART: LET THAT BE A LESSON TO US ALL

Remember the story I told you about Kmart?

"We maintain a database of eight million transactions a month. Our K-trends tell us everything we need to know about our customers and how to better serve them."

That's a direct quote from a senior marketing research person at Kmart. Under other circumstances, I might have thought that statement was, at worst, wishful thinking in the face of declining market share, reduced profits, and increasingly skeptical looks from Wall Street. It *wasn't* wishful thinking but a measured and confident statement, the grand finale to a conference call that had already been awash with such language. This brand of hubris leads directly to serious—often lethal—difficulties that so many companies of late face with increasing frequency.

This conversation happened some months before Kmart saw its stock plummet, just before it circled the wagons into chapter 11. Astonishingly, the arrogance continued despite marketplace realities. What is a mere marketplace compared to billions of bits of research data? Kmart seemed comforted (lulled might be a better word) by its trend data. It had tons of statistics to slice and dice to its heart's content.

The insights and findings it ended up with—and ultimately acted on—were statistically reliable, perhaps even excellent answers, but to meaningless questions. The past 30-day transactions data *might* have even been helpful in addressing inventory control issues, but it gave no clue at all as to what consumers really valued, what made them feel valued, or what would make them come back to the store. It would not help Kmart marketers understand how their customers actually shopped the category. It would not tell them how customers viewed the category, compared offerings, and, ultimately bought—and bought again. The data they based their decision making on could not predict the way the customers *were going to behave* in the near future.

They were missing the other 70 percent of the equation.

So knowing what your customers did last week isn't much help when what you really need to know is *what they are going to do two and three weeks from now.* Not only what, you have to know why. More often than not, multigigabyte databases offer only a highly accurate historic perspective of what they did, but not why.

To be successful, even CRM marketers need to plan for where consumers' values and expectations are headed, not where they were yesterday. Here's where customer loyalty metrics come into play.

You take *those* insights and overlay the data in your base. There's where a computer particularly comes in handy—for identifying the patterns of the combined what-they-did facts with the emotionally based needs and expectations. After that, the direct response copy will virtually write itself.

TACTICAL MANEUVERS

A few times a year, I get calls from reporters asking about some sort of new loyalty program one or another company has put into place. Most of the time these programs have very little to do with loyalty and more to do with maintaining a degree of continuity that, if it makes you feel better, *seems* like loyalty, but isn't.

Continuity programs create a false sense of security for marketers. You see, with virtual ubiquitous consumer penetration and use of loyalty cards (in all their varied forms), what was once consumer delight has turned into consumer expectation. "Yes, yet another point card in my wallet. What are you going to do for me now?" are the questions that providers face, even if not specifically articulated by the twenty-first-century bionic consumer.

Success in the form of more loyal customers will come to the provider that utilizes new technologies; that delivers better, more fluid consumer experiences; and that creates new value propositions and authentically communicate with consumers. If you build these core values into your programs, you end up with an actual loyalty program.

When it comes to card-based programs, for example, the most resonating we've identified is that of stored-value cards. Our strategic partner in this arena is the world leader, Stored Value Systems. They taught us that these virtual currencies are seen as being the same as (or better than) cash and are often more preferred to mere points. We showed them that leading-indicator values confirmed that stored value cards and loyalty cards will shortly merge to better meet—or exceed—consumer expectations. So, they're well ahead of the pack.

Current loyalty data predicts that hybrid stored value loyalty cards will emerge as the leading process for managing loyalty programs and engendering higher levels of consumer loyalty for those who institute them. This will be proven in terms of convenience, functionality, consumer preference, and both real and perceived levels of added value, which is much more than just plain, short-term continuity.

If expectations are met, consumers will be able to use these cards to pay for products and services in traditional retail channels as well as all the newer channels (like the Internet) and will accommodate the newest of the value propositions—convenience—by operating much in the same way as the Mobil Speedpass™ fob—another creation based on values identified via Brand Keys loyalty metrics.

On the basis of the consumer ideal, appropriately configured shared-value card programs could easily be integrated into inventory, pricing, and payment systems. Points could convert to cash or other currencies that could be used to pay for downloaded music, mobile phone minutes, video on demand, or even eBay transactions. If you do all that, you exceed customer expectations, and that makes it the most important—and likely most used—card in the consumer's wallet. That's a perfect example of what we mean by loyalty.

A REVIEW: WHY OPTIMIZE WITH CUSTOMER LOYALTY METRICS?

As I mentioned earlier, there aren't many research souls brave enough to discard their traditional measures, no matter how many nagging doubts they may have about them.

However, the key word that brand managers are now vocally acknowledging is *capitalization,* from both a financial and marketing perspective. To be able to acquire a financial value, the brand must be managed and measured in new and predictive ways. The reason the Brand Keys customer loyalty optimization approach *is* broadly used is that is allows each organization to be unique. For every brand, there are different objectives, and, therefore, different values placed on the brand and on brand communication programs.

A customer loyalty metrics approach can be adapted to fit almost any brand, marketing, or communications system, and it can be used in almost any form that allows for apples-to-apples comparison of results. From an Executive Suite point of view, this will have major advantages because comparisons can be made across initiatives and finite corporate resources can be allocated more efficiently. It doesn't hurt that you can provide a realistic return on investment (ROI) format either.

BRAND-TO-MEDIA ENGAGEMENT— HOW TO KNOW IF YOUR MARKETING IS ACTUALLY HURTING YOUR BRAND'S VALUE

So, you've supercharged your research and your agency has produced advertising, and now you've got to get it out there in front of your audience. Now, you need to remember what department store magnate John Wanamaker said 100 years ago, an observation that still haunts the advertising industry: "I know half my advertising budget is wasted—I just don't know *which* half."

In times gone by, this wasn't as much of a problem as it is today. Agencies shrugged, marketers paid, and everyone moved on. Today, executive suites and shareholders are looking to understand what they are getting for their investments—ROI in the form of engaged consumers. That's why most advertisers defected from *Martha Stewart Living*. They could actually see that they were getting fewer readers. They *knew* they were paying a higher rate for *Martha Stewart Living* than for a comparable audience in another print vehicle. But it's not always that easy or that clear cut.

Long after Wanamaker's lament, the situation is remarkably similar, only on a much more expensive scale. Why are connecting with, engaging consumers, optimizing media selection, and delivering advertising effectiveness more complex and prone to error than ever before? Because the media planner's job is more difficult now than ever before.

Where and how to find target audiences has gotten extraordinarily complex. Consumers are no longer glued to three television networks, and fewer than half of Americans subscribe to newspapers. Where once there was a single dominant sports magazine, there are well over 100, subdivided by special interests. People now spend 10 percent of their time online. You get the idea. Here's how we sum up some of the current brand connection conundrums:

- *Overchoice:* An unprecedented cluttered global media ecology makes it harder than ever to guarantee the most effective media plan. Strategizing is more complex and prone to errors and omissions than ever before.
- *More overchoice and consumer ad self-selection:* Media alternatives have mushroomed even in traditional channels, particularly television and print. Consumers have increasingly more power to self-select the ad messages to

which they are exposed. This is not even to mention zapping off commercials or zipping through channels.

- *Target fade:* Lines are increasingly blurred between the demographic and psychographic (lifestyle) profiles. This makes media differentiation far more difficult. The list of acceptable media options gets longer every day.
- *Audience attention deficit:* When the previous issues converge, compounded by consumers' busier-than-ever lives, there is substantially reduced attentiveness to and engagement with advertising messages.
- *The incredible disappearing dollar:* Flat or shrinking ad budgets leave advertisers with fewer arrows to shoot at consumer targets. There is less financial resilience, smaller tolerance for too much media spending and not enough return.
- *Your ad is nothing special:* To a media vehicle, an ad, is an ad, is an ad. It makes no special provisions for how your brand is perceived. Yet, media choices can have enormous impact on brand attributes and consumer engagement levels.

What *Should* Marketers Be Asking?

Q: Why can't the world's leading media planning organizations and advertising agencies achieve maximally effective media plans with their existing tools?

A: It's because traditional metrics do not—they cannot—address the very real, critically important issue that a brand's appearance in a particular media vehicle can either enhance or detract from a brand's level of advertising awareness and imagery.

BRAND-TO-MEDIA ENGAGEMENT

To provide these metrics, we adapted customer loyalty metrics and created the Brand-to-Media Engagement (B2ME) model. It is a quantitatively rigorous, empirical system that charts the precise effects on advertising awareness, brand image (or equity), and purchase behavior that are attributable to a brand's appearance in a particular media vehicle.

In the real world, *certain media properties can actually reduce attention levels, and damage the reputation, image, or equity of a brand,* while other properties can greatly enhance them. This is true no matter how seemingly appropriate the editorial environment is or the reported demographics are. In addition, our validation research proves that positive or negative effects on brand imagery based on media placement alone can have very direct, profound effects on the impact of the actual advertising for the brand.

To evaluate B2ME, we use the same approach that we have been discussing thus far in this book—employing a psychological assessment questionnaire that provides an indirect way of revealing loyalty drivers that are usually both rational and emotional in nature.

It is no easier for consumers to differentiate equivalent media types (e.g., *Time* versus *Newsweek*) than for media planners to choose the best option for a brand based on traditional planning techniques. So, we have to go undercover to see where the fault lines are in the brand-to-media engagement equation.

In loyalty terminology, a media vehicle is considered to be engaged when the advertised brand's equity or image is enhanced by the very act of its appearing in that media vehicle.

A TYPICAL SCENARIO (YOU ARE PROBABLY HERE)

Your company has invested countless dollars in developing and supporting your brand. You would feel better about how you were spending your money if there were some way to insert your brand's values into the media planning process; you want to go beyond standard reach-and-frequency thinking.

The concept of inserting a brand-values-to-audience match into the media plan has been talked about before, but until recently, the process has not been validated on a quantitative, statistically generalizable basis.

Media planners are not to be blamed directly. They haven't had the tools or knowledge to introduce meaningfully real-brand values into the planning process, so they do the best they can. We feel that this is no longer acceptable. Planning by reach and frequency alone is far too limited because the brand's values and the media vehicle's values may not be consonant—even when the editorial environment and reach-and-frequency numbers look and feel right. Loyalty metrics take the subjectivity out of the analysis.

It is an obvious (and industry-accepted axiom) that your brand will perform better in media environments that are *clearly* in sync with your products or services. For example, over-the-counter drugs are often placed on television news since news consumers tend to be older. But how can media planners find the fine consumer value profile line between, say, *NBC Nightly News, 60 Minutes,* and CNN? On one side of the line, your key brand attributes may be well received, while on the other side, they may not be. Mistakes can be costly. Better to know what you are getting, and going to get back, *before* you commit.

By inserting brand values into the media planning process, marketers can better assure they connect with—and communicate core brand values to—

their consumers. Aligning brand values with the values of the individual media vehicle in which you plan to advertise lets planners predict increased levels of brand awareness and positive brand imagery *before* you spend your money. Thus, you connect better with your target audience and maximize your brand's ad effectiveness, and have total brand-based control over your budget.

Loyalty metrics can be profitably extended to the complex process of media selection. It validates what we knew was true but did not know how to quantify. Nobody can deny that selecting media so that your target audience *thinks better of your brand, pays more attention to your marketing messaging, and has a greater chance of actually buying your product* is integral to increased advertising effectiveness.

THE LOYALTY FRAMEWORK FOR BRAND-TO-MEDIA ENGAGEMENT

The framework for inserting a brand into the media planning process relies on the same loyalty metrics we discussed in Chapter 3. In this case, however, loyalty metrics determine whether—and to what degree—a media vehicle helps or hurts a brand's equity or strength.

We've defined the Ideal and measured the brand's ability to meet or exceed customer expectations *not* in the context of any particular marketing or media vehicle. Using the same loyalty approach, we are going to now measure the brand advertised (for example) in *People* magazine, or the brand as sponsor of the Winter Olympics (see Figure 5.1). (You do need to make sure that your respondents are comfortably aware of the media or marketing vehicle to ensure that they have some sense of the values inherent in the particular media option, but it works for virtually anything you can show or tell a customer.)

We already have a weighted average of the brand's assessments (how it measures up to the customer's conception of an ideal) that is employed as a baseline measure for the brand as a stand-alone entity (not in the context of any marketing or media vehicle). The same assessments are conducted for the brand *in* the context of a variety of particular media vehicles or options.

Based on the scores, the vehicles are classified into one of three categories:

1. *High-Engagement Brand Enhancers:* Vehicles that enhance the brand's equity—and therefore its awareness, image, and desirability—by the very act of its appearance in that media vehicle.
2. *Negative-Engagement Brand Detractors:* Vehicles that actually hurt the brand's equity and reduce awareness, positive imagery, and preference.
3. *Neutral Engagement:* Marketing or media options that neither enhance nor detract from the brand's equity but can be utilized when achieving

Figure 5.1
Measurement of Brand Sponsorships

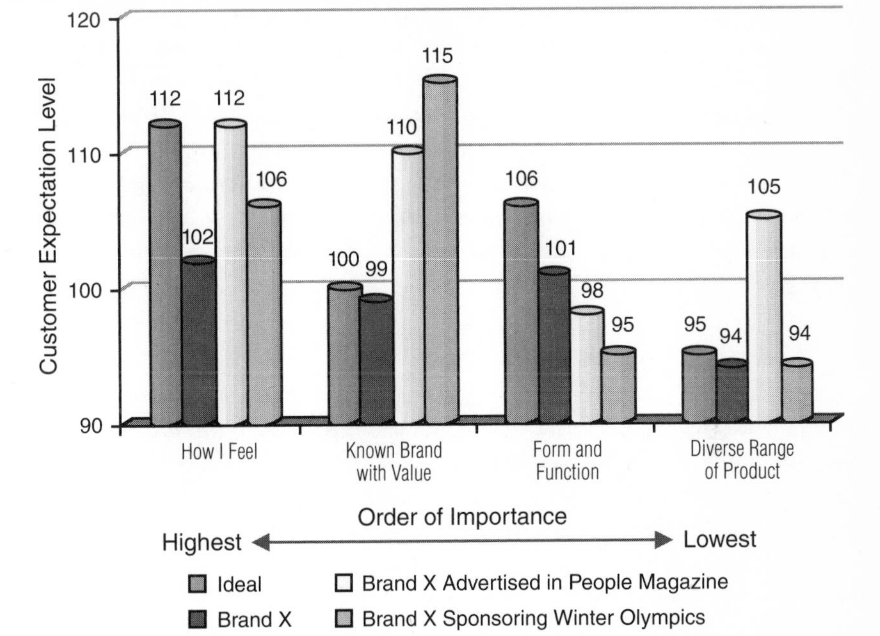

certain levels of audience reach, frequency, and awareness or just showing the brand logo is required.

So, the assessments for Brand X would look like this:

High Engagement:	In *People*	116
Neutral Engagement:	Sponsoring Winter Olympics	102
	Brand X	99

BRAND-TO-MEDIA ENGAGEMENT IN ACTION FOR YOUR BRAND: SO MANY MAGAZINES, SO FEW EFFECTS

A manufacturer of bathroom and kitchen fixtures wanted to know the degree
to which a publication in which an ad for its products might appear would either enhance or hurt its overall brand equity score. It also wanted to see what
the ad's subsequent performance via a traditional tip-in test on measures of
both *category-aided advertising awareness* and *direct image ratings for the brand* on
eight product imagery statements would be.

In the first phase of the research, respondents were asked to evaluate the brand as a stand-alone entity (i.e., not in the context of any particular media vehicle), and *in* the context of each of 20 print alternatives (10 magazines that were on their current roster, and 10 that were being considered for use).

Data were analyzed using the Brand Keys loyalty formula to identify the top four drivers of brand loyalty in the fixtures category, the brand's overall brand equity score based on its performance on those drivers independent of any specific media context (calculated to be 126), and the overall brand equity score in the context of each of the 20 print alternatives—its B2ME assessments.

Eight publications were selected for the validity test based on their effects on overall brand imagery. Some publications had enhanced the brand's overall brand equity score, while others worsened it—below 126 (see Table 5.1).

The same print ad was inserted in (tipped in) to the then-current issues of each publication and was tested among eight separate samples of target respondents. Respondents were given a copy of one of the magazines and were asked to look through it just as they would do if they were at home. A series of questions then elicited data in two areas:

1. Category-aided awareness of the ad
2. Ratings of the brand on eight category attribute statements on a seven-point rating scale (their average yielded an overall brand rating)

Table 5.2 shows the B2ME scores for the publications and the attendant ad awareness and attribute ratings.

Amazingly, there is an almost perfect correlation between the B2ME scores that each print option produced for the brand in the first part of the study and real-world consumer engagement (see Figure 5.2 on page 136).

Table 5.1
Current versus Proposed Magazines

Current Publications	Brand Equity Score	Proposed Publications	Brand Equity Score
Traditional Home	161	Vanity Fair	153
Martha Stewart Living	146	BusinessWeek	145
Sunset	126	InStyle	106
Southern Living	123	People	102

Table 5.2
B2ME Scores and Awareness and Attribute Ratings

	Phase 1	Phase 2	
	Brand Keys B2ME Score	Category-Aided Advertising Awareness (%)	Average Attribute Rating*
Current Publications			
Traditional Home	161	30	6.50
Martha Stewart Living	146	27	5.98
Sunset	126	21	5.31
Southern Living	123	20	5.16
Proposed Publications			
Vanity Fair	153	28	6.21
BusinessWeek	145	26	5.94
InStyle	106	18	4.50
People	102	17	4.38

* Average of eight items on 1 to 7 scale. The brand's Brand-to-Media Engagement score independent of an immediate media environment was 126.

Moreover, there was another almost perfect correlation between the B2ME scores and the mean brand attribute ratings it received in the actual publication (see Figure 5.3 on page 137).

DIAGNOSTICS: SHINING LIGHT INTO THE HEART OF MEDIA PLANNING DARKNESS

The loyalty-based B2ME model will also identify *which* of the top four drivers of brand loyalty are being most highly influenced by the media placement. For example, the brand that received an overall assessment of 126, received a 161 B2ME assessment score when placed in *Traditional Home*. When placed in *Vanity Fair,* the brand assessment was 153. Both high scores indicate that the ad would benefit by being placed in *either* of these media.

While that is true, however, the actual *strategic effects* (which of the category drivers were being positively influenced—and to what degree it *differed*) depended on the specific media choice. Figure 5.4 on page 138 indicates how and to what degree.

Figure 5.2
B2ME Scores and Consumer Engagement

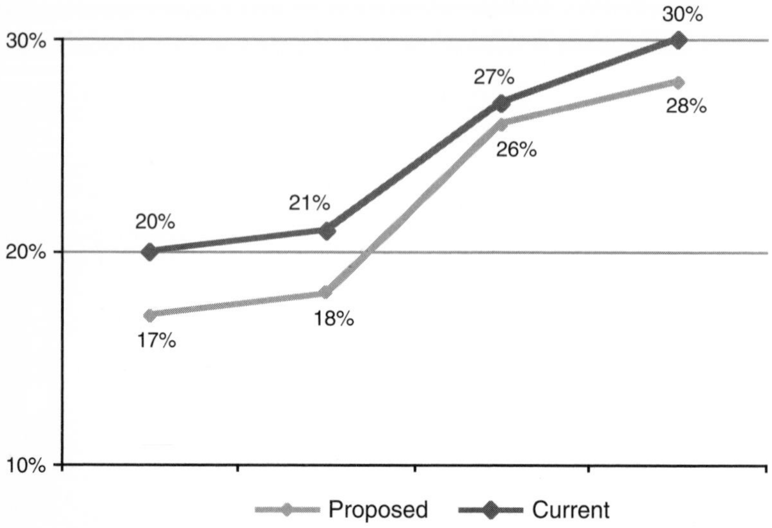

With these loyalty insights for each of the media alternatives being considered, it is even possible to select media for an ad campaign based on the option that was most highly consistent with—or better reinforced by—the brand's copy strategy objectives. That's how sensitive the loyalty metrics are.

This approach can be used to test the best fit for *any* media. It can tell you which of the following options will work hardest for your brand:

- Television channel
- Television show
- Cable network
- Magazine
- Newspaper
- Radio station
- Promotion
- Co-Branding opportunity
- Internet

Figure 5.3
B2ME Scores and Mean Brand Attribute Ratings

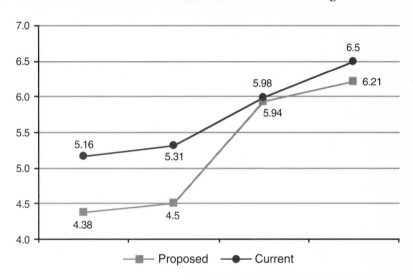

- Outdoor
- Branded entertainment
- Product placement

BRAND VALUATION AND THE LOYALTY BRAND MULTIPLE: FIGURING OUT WHAT YOU GOT

To paraphrase Orwell, "All brands are *equal,* some are just more *equal* than others." Make this statement and heads nod. But when you start the drill-down, confusion ensues. Do we want to slouch our way toward 2084, not knowing why some brands dominate and why others follow like sheep, while the unaware are carted off to the glue factory?

The confusion is hard to avoid given the quantity of brand chat in marketing circles these past few years, including brand image, brand awareness, brand equity, brand valuation, brand IQ, or brand everything.

Figure 5.4
Media Choices

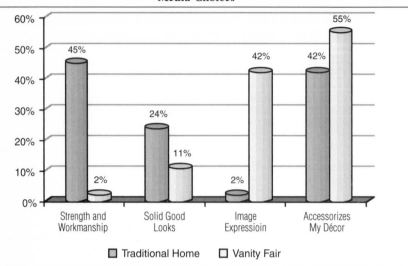

This analysis reveals a subtle but crucial distinction between brand equity and brand valuation and how to use "Equity" to predict whether your brand efforts will be a rousing success or fall flat. Unaware of (or maybe preferring to ignore) that distinction, many marketers use the phrases interchangeably. Here's where we find the telling difference:

- *Brand equity* describes the brand's strength compared to the category ideal, the category competitors, and *how* consumers view the brand as being able to meet or exceed the expectations they hold for the category generally. Think of it as brand strength.
- *Brand valuation,* however, must be viewed in the context of the business as a whole. Definitions based on brand equity or exclusively on financial measures lack either the financial or marketing components to provide a full assessment of the economic value of the brand. Real brand valuation begins with envisioning the brand as an asset capable of generating future profits. The degree to which it can generate those profits depends largely on your point of view, especially if your company is buying or selling the brand. It's like the stock market. Whoever sells a stock believes it will lose value.

There are several financially driven accounting methods for calculating brand value:

- *Comparables:* Arrive at the value of a brand on the basis of something comparable to it. But exactly what would compare? True comparability can thus be maddeningly difficult to ascertain.
- *Cost-based valuation:* Define brand value as the aggregate of all historic costs required to bring a brand to its current state—the sum of all development, marketing, advertising, and communication costs. This approach is weak since there is no direct correlation between the financial investment made and the value added by a brand.
- *Premium pricing:* Calculate value as the net present value of future price premiums that a branded product would command over an unbranded, generic equivalent. This sounds simple until you try to find a generic equivalent to use. Good luck! Some store brands are as strong as name brands today.
- *Economic use models:* Develop a multiple of a brand's strength by assessing a range of factors averaged over time to avoid any remarkable events in previous years. This technique combines brand equity and financial measures, and works on the marketing side, the theory being that the brand generates customer demand that translates into revenue. On the financial side, valuation relates to the net present value of *future* expected earnings.

The economic use concept is widely used in business, and has been championed by Interbrand, a Brand Consulting company. The technique is also widely publicized but it, too, suffers from gaps in knowledge, assessment, and often perspective and reality.

For example, private companies do not publish financial data, so by definition that information can't be included. There is also a lack of specificity about how different brands should be treated. Companies with multiple subbrands are treated as a single entity—yet are compared to single brands by exactly the same rules. Media conglomerates are often missing due to the inseparability problem. The approach still depends on a large number of subjective choices and viewpoints, perhaps acceptable by accounting standards, but still open to varying degrees of bias and error.

Consultant Russell Abrap has commented that the advantage of economic use is that it is widely accepted and it takes all aspects of branding into account. The major shortcoming is that it compares apples with oranges. For example, an international component should not be applied over local brand earnings; if a company wants to bring its international aspects into play, it must include potential international profits. Here two valuation bases are muddled; on the one hand, there is an in-use basis, and on the other hand, there is an open-market valuation.

We're not the only ones who have questions about this approach. David A. Aaker, author and Professor at University of California Berkley, in his book *Brand Leadership* (New York: Free Press, 2000) noted, "the Interbrand system does not consider the potential of the brand to support extensions into other product classes. Brand support may be ineffective; spending money on advertising does not necessarily indicate effective brand building. Trademark protection, although necessary, does not of itself create brand value."

My big complaint with the economic use approach is the fact that it relies so heavily on historical data. In 1997, Interbrand rated IBM as one of the top-five most valuable brands in the world. Yet, in the following year, when IBM lost money due to write-offs (in spite of all its satisfied customers) because it was unable to provide the PC consumers with what they wanted, it dropped IBM to the bottom of a list of 290 brands. For a system to insist that the actual value of the IBM brand had changed so dramatically was laughable.

In its most recent iteration (2005) of "Best Global Brands," Interbrand rated Coca-Cola as number one. But Coke's sales in the past 5 years have only been up 2.3 percent versus Pepsi's gain of 7.5 percent. Coke's quarterly profits have been down 2 percent and its stock price was down 13.5 percent over the past year (compared to Pepsi, which was up by 5.6 percent). It makes you wonder how it is number one on the list.

The brand valuation issue (both subject and list publication) generally gets raised once a year or when the information is necessary in an acquisition.

Some models play inside the "brand-equity-as-a-form-of-valuation" arena, when they really ought to be placed in the "brand-equity-as-brand-strength" corner.

David A. Aaker's model uses multiple criteria to value brand equity. His equation looks like this:

$$\text{Brand awareness} + \text{Brand associations} + \text{Perceived quality} + \text{Proprietary assets} + \text{Brand loyalty} = \text{Brand equity}$$

But this is not an equation—the ideas are not additive, so the assumption is that *if* each of the five variables is analyzed separately to provide a different perspective about a brand's strength in these areas, once you add them all together you have the total integrated value of a brand to a company.

Despite the semantic difficulties of deciding on which definition of brand associations or especially brand loyalty to adopt, it blurs the functions and initiatives and doesn't even begin to factor in the problems associated with cross-vertical department alignment, communication, and coordination of integrated marketing.

The advertising agency Young & Rubicam developed a multiple criteria method called the Brand Asset Valuator (BAV) to measure brand equity growth (and potential decline). It involves several brand criteria: relevance, differentiation, esteem, and familiarity, with the following assumed equations:

$$\text{Differentiation} + \text{Familiarity} = \text{Stature (potential for growth)}$$
$$\text{Esteem} + \text{Familiarity} = \text{Strength (present size)}$$

Critics have pointed out that while all are suitable criteria for evaluating brands, their range is unsurprising and generally subjective, and that equating stature as an actual leading indicator of real brand growth and profitability is both subjective and extraordinarily assumptive.

Everyone can agree that your brand will be better positioned for growth if you are relevant and differentiated rather than commoditized and irrelevant, but this doesn't guarantee growth. These days, we really need to use a relaxed definition or assessment to show real differentiation in most categories. Professor Kevin Keller, Professor of Marketing at the Tuck School of Business at Dartmouth University has also pointed out that this approach "trades product specificity for cross-category generality," which may be helpful in creating advertising, but has very little to do with how people actually behave in a category. People do not buy cars the same way they buy cola. No matter how much the agencies wish it were so.

So, you need to make sure that the parameters you set up for yourself are going to correlate with positive behavior. Loyalty is a leading indicator of profitability. If you have loyal customers, you can virtually bet the farm that your company will be profitable.

In January 2005, R. L. Polk presented its 10th Annual 2006 Automotive Loyalty Awards and announced that General Motors (GM) "outpaced the rest of the industry in manufacturer loyalty," winning for the sixth consecutive year in the "Overall Manufacturer" category.

A few days after that announcement, however, the New York Times reported: "G.M. Posts Worst Loss Since 1992: Deficit for 2005 is $8.6 Billion." Eight and a half billion! That's an eight with nine zeros following it. One of the reasons for this loss, noted the Times, was "G.M. sold 150,000 fewer large SUVs in 2005 than in 2004." I guess the Times didn't see the Polk press release. Don't those kind of non sequitur assessments make you wonder just how GM was able to "outpace the rest of the industry" and lose more money than the gross national product of some countries? They got the award because 63 percent of GM owners returning to market in 2005 opted for another new GM vehicle. Maybe that was 63 percent of only 100 (or 1,000) drivers. Maybe the GM Employee Discount wasn't such a good idea. However you do the math, it clearly wasn't enough to make GM profitable. That kind of math gives economics rigor, but alas, in this case, also mortis.

The fact that marketing and research managers are utilizing or recommending systems that measure communications and sponsorships—and marketing program results based on awareness and attitudinal change—or just collecting excellent answers to meaningless questions, does not provide any readout of *financial* returns to the organization as a result of the planned spending.

So, rather than adjusting or refining these increasingly futile processes, the time has come to move ahead to other measurements that correlate with actual, in-market sales and transactions: loyalty metrics.

And, as mentioned previously in this book, these loyalty measures can be configured to provide a brand multiple, the predictive version of a corporation's price/earnings (P/E) ratio—a return-on-equity (ROE):

$$\text{Return-on-equity} = \frac{\text{Increase in brand equity due to initiative}}{\text{In-going brand equity}}$$

For example, a program for clothing manufacturer/lifestyle guru Karen Neuburger could have been executed in one of three ways. The techniques aren't important for this example, but suffice to say that they could have been found in the toolbox of any modern brand.

The Neuburger brand equity—absent of any marketing, promotion, or communication program involvement—was a brand equity strength of 111.

Consumer assessments based on exposure to the three program options revealed that the Karen Neuburger brand's values were enhanced—or degraded—depending on the specific program, as follows:

Program A: 124
Program B: 114
Program C: 118

As these loyalty metrics correlate so highly with behavior, this allows for the calculation of the Brand Multiple and ROE of:

$$\text{Program A} = \frac{(124-111)}{111} = \frac{13}{111} = 0.117 \times 100 = 11.7 \text{ percent}$$

$$\text{Program B} = \frac{(114-111)}{111} = \frac{3}{111} = 0.027 \times 100 = 2.7 \text{ percent}$$

$$\text{Program C} = \frac{(118-111)}{111} = \frac{7}{111} = 0.063 \times 100 = 6.3 \text{ percent}$$

Which return would you want on your investment? Do the math.

This approach also helps cut through the haze created by trying to configure the annual financial accountability of a brand by linking it to marketing functions and long-term growth. It addresses the dynamics of real brand equity and provides yardsticks for both current *and* potential strength (and earning power) of a brand.

Recently an independent business equity valuation firm, *Aquetong Capital Advisors,* examined the correlation between *Brand Keys* loyalty metrics and company value. We didn't pay them. They did the study on their own.

They selected 10 of the 35 categories we include in the Brand Keys *Customer Loyalty Index* (their choice, not ours) and conducted correlations against our loyalty rankings. They did not include our full, indexed diagnostics, just the rankings of the brands from first, second, third, and so on.

The company value metrics they used in the analysis were Total Enterprise Value (TEV = market capitalization + outstanding debt), free cash flow, Earnings Before Interest, Taxes, Depreciation and Amortization (EBITDA), and revenue (Rev). These three metrics were converted to two ratios: TEV/EBITDA and TEV/Rev for comparison to the Brand Keys loyalty metrics.

The correlations between the *Customer Loyalty Index* performance and these measures ranged from a low of .830 to a high of .901. Let me repeat that: Correlations from a low of .830 up to .901.

We feel this independent assessment once more confirms the ability of a loyalty-based system—whether you call it ROI or ROE—to correlate with positive and profitable behavior toward the brand without having to trade product specificity for cross-category comparisons.

LOYALTY TALES FROM THE REAL WORLD

Should You Take Me Out to the Ball Game? Determining Which Sports Sponsorship Will Work Hardest for Your Brand

We recognize that it is redundant to state that the job of engaging with consumers to optimize brand marketing effectiveness is more complex and prone to waste than ever before. That you can reach your target consumers is a given. That you do so *in the most engaging and profitable way* is not.

Former Coca-Cola Chairman and CEO Roberto Goizueta had an interesting marketing philosophy that went something like, "if it moves, sponsor it and if doesn't, paint it red." We believe that it is safe to say that this is a marketing approach that has fallen into disuse. Over the past two decades, many companies, having relied primarily on above-the-line techniques, have now been devoting increasingly larger portions of their attention and their marketing budgets to the area of sponsorships.

These increased levels of attention and funding have given birth to an ever-increasing number of sponsorship opportunities. All attractive, all involving, and all seemingly appropriate for an ever-increasing number of brands seeking a below-the-line-sponsorship silver bullet, with marketers buying sponsorships that are ideal for their demographics and that have, one presumes, some reasonable connection to the category in which their brand competes.

Utilizing this loyalty approach, KeySpan Energy—one of the largest energy providers in the northeastern United States assessed seven possible sports sponsorships:

1. Yankees
2. Mets
3. Red Sox
4. Brooklyn Cyclones (Mets "A" League)
5. Rangers
6. Islanders
7. Knicks

KeySpan's brand equity strength based on the weighted average of the four category loyalty drivers was 112.

The sports team assessments were drawn from the Brand Keys *Sports Fan Index*®. This is an annual measure of all of the individual teams of the four major league sports franchises (Major League Baseball, National Football League, National Hockey League, and National Basketball Association) by self-identified fans. The participation in a sponsorship is based on the expectation that benefits *will* accrue to the sponsor. Knowing how strong one team is compared to another, or what the average game attendance is, reveals little on which to make a brand decision.

Utilizing the same assessment approach, the KeySpan brand was measured in the context of various sponsorship opportunities—KeySpan sponsoring the New York Yankees, KeySpan sponsoring the New York Mets, and so on, with the resultant assessments in Figure 5.5.

Using customer loyalty assessments we can statistically determine which sponsorship provides positive, neutral, or negative effects *on the brand values* (see Table 5.3 on page 146).

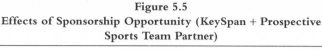

Figure 5.5
Effects of Sponsorship Opportunity (KeySpan + Prospective Sports Team Partner)

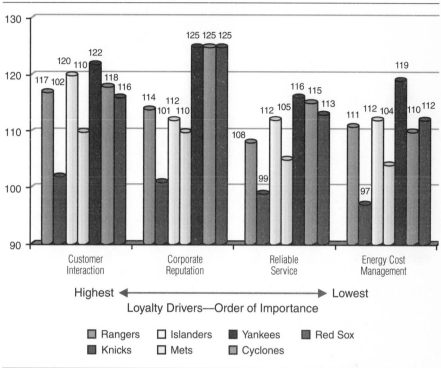

So, based on this assessment, we can confidently say that KeySpan should consider sponsoring baseball (but not the Mets) and should avoid basketball as a sponsorship venue. Table 5.3 shows that KeySpan's sponsoring of the New York Yankees, the Boston Red Sox, or the Brooklyn Cyclones will positively enhance the KeySpan brand. In doing so, the sponsorship will increase consumer engagement as well as the traditionally expected benefits of increased attention paid to the KeySpan brand, increase positive KeySpan brand imagery, and increase levels of purchase intent, in regard to KeySpan products and services.

But, as the saying goes, even sponsors have to write reality checks, so what we managed to do was to condense a list of perfectly acceptable, appropriate and available sports sponsorships down to a list in which we identified how the brand *could be* the beneficiary of the investment in the marketing exercise. Now actual decisions—and commitment of budgets—had to be made.

Reality plays a part in the ultimate sponsorship decision process. What do I get? How long do I get it and for how much? These are basic questions that,

Table 5.3
Assessment of Sponsorship Opportunites (+ KeySpan)

Team	Brand Keys Score
Positive Effects	
Yankees	120
Cyclones	116
Red Sox	116
Neutral Effects	
Islanders	114
KeySpan	·112
Rangers	111
Negative Effects	
Mets	108
Knicks	99

we hope, responsible marketers would have asked of any sponsorship. Corporate realities also play a part in the decision process. In KeySpan's case, its service area did not encompass the Bronx, making a sponsorship of the New York Yankees superfluous from a marketing point of view. KeySpan (prior to its acquisition of the Long Island Lighting Company) used to be Brooklyn Union Gas, so sponsoring the Brooklyn Cyclones—albeit a minor league, A-league team—would seem to be a marketing home run. A prospective sponsorship of the New York Mets indicated negative brand effects, but the borough of Queens, New York—the location of Shea Stadium, the Mets home field—*is* part of the KeySpan service area. If it didn't become a Mets sponsor, a competitor might. So, the decision was made to sponsor the Mets—via an enormous KeySpan sign (15 feet wide and 85 feet high) directly next to the scoreboard—and to sponsor the Brooklyn Cyclones—via the purchase of stadium naming rights, "KeySpan Park."

As energy providers are different from packaged goods, the process of selling additional products and services is more complex. An excellent barometer of any marketing campaign for this category is *how many product and service sales inquiry calls were generated by the effort?* By assessing the unaided sponsorship awareness of the callers, we were, therefore, able to extrapolate the market effects of the sponsorship. In the case at hand, the three-year results are shown in Table 5.4.

Based on the *Brand Keys'* sponsorship assessments and the resultant product and sales calls generated, we believe that it is fair to quote Yogi Berra regarding the findings when we say, "It's déjà vu all over again!" As Mr. Berra also

Table 5.4
Product/Sales Inquiry Calls Generated:
Percentage of Callers Citing
Awareness of Unaided Sponsorship

Year	Brooklyn Cyclones (%)	New York Mets (%)
2003	33	21
2004	35	19
2005	37	18

pointed out "you can observe a lot just by watching." But only if you watch in the right way.

Even lagging indicators—sponsorship awareness, brand imagery, traditional top-two box intent to purchase—reflect the predictive nature of the initial Brand Keys assessments. These measures are provided for respondents in both the service area and the sponsorship venue itself (see Table 5.5).

On the basis of these traditional measures, we can see that the predictive metrics allow marketers to optimize their sponsorship selection as well as virtually guaranteeing better consumer responses to the marketing initiative.

To stick with our sports metaphors, when we talk about engaging customers and leveraging loyalty metrics, winning isn't everything; it's the only thing. That it will get increasingly harder to justify sponsorships to clients will come as a cruel surprise to venues that are not proactive in their ability to

Table 5.5
Traditional Measures

| Indicators | Brooklyn Cyclones (116) | | New York Mets (108) | |
	Service Area	Sponsorship Venue	Service Area	Sponsorship Venue
Awareness	42%	51%	36%	40%
Brand Imagery*	5.82	6.05	4.96	5.06
Top-2 Box Purchase Intent	22%	28%	17%	19%

*On a 1 to 7 scale, average of 4 Driver Attribute Assessments (Total Audience Corporate Tracking Rating is 4.75).
Note: The numbers in parentheses are the Brand Keys Sponsorship Index.

provide predictive rationales beyond the traditional 3 A's: Acceptable, Available, and Appropriate.

By aligning your brand's values with a given sponsorship's values, you can better engage your target audience, maximize your brand's marketing effectiveness, and build loyalty. Whichever team you play for—client, agency, or sponsor—it's a win-win.

Q & A

Dan Hanover, *Event Marketer* **magazine:** *How long does loyalty last?*

Robert Passikoff: Loyalty lasts as long as your product or service maintains the strongest brand equity among your competitive set, with *brand equity* defined as the brand's ability to meet or exceed the expectations consumers hold for the category's loyalty drivers.

Product Placement—Truths and Wishful Thinking:

Thomas Mucha, *Business 2.0* **magazine:** *How effective is product placement on a television show or in a movie for driving consumer brand loyalty?*

Robert Passikoff: Product placement needs to provide something more specific than the sense that you are getting your brand more exposure via this below-the-line or nontraditional medium; you need to know its value in terms of reinforcing loyalty. Product placement is another way of getting the product out there. Anecdotally, it can work very well, often for a correspondingly very large price tag. More often than not, product placement can usually be seen as yet another act of brand differentiation desperation, with a lot of "throw it out there and hope" when you drill down into the logic and motivation for the spend.

Seinfeld and Snapple made product placement a success from a buzz and awareness perspective because the show scripts were written as complete, funny stories around the brand. Also, the Tom Hanks movie *Cast Away* starred Federal Express as the ultimate hero. You have no problem convincing us that virtually any car product placed into a James Bond movie, that is made a true focal point, and that is the hero of a 22-minute chase-and-kill-and-elude-the-villains scene is likely to engender—at the very least—attention paid to the product. It is very different from "cars provided by Ford" at the end of Efrem Zimbalist's *The FBI* back in the 1960s.

Are there product placement failures? We don't really know. There are no measurements in place, and most folks have the sense to realize that a Disney film is not a likely candidate for a Trojan condoms placement in a steamy love scene.

For most marketers, the PR leverage, buzz generation, and awareness hits that get tallied as the collective barometer for success of the campaign and spend. Today, that is enough for smart brands, but it shouldn't be. It's likely that if you have the money that product placement costs these days, you are a brand that is already well established in the consumers' memories.

Effectiveness, however, isn't defined by mere onscreen presence. The main factor is how much the presence of a brand on a television sitcom or in a movie reinforces the values your customers have about the brand. That is the only real indicator for driving loyalty. To know this, you test and measure the loyalty attributes for *both brand and medium*. Effectiveness for product placement can no longer be measured by reach-and-frequency estimates or by an assumed value of borrowed equity or association because of the profile of popular actors. Every component of the interaction has to be dipped in the loyalty litmus to see if there is consonance between brand and show.

So, the question becomes, are the brand values enhanced by the exposure? Keep in mind that not all placements are equal. Is your brand a new BMW coupe or a "Q's-special" Rolex in a Bond film, on screen with a very real role in the script for 20 minutes? Or is your brand a breakfast cereal or beer bottle, good for a five-second shot in the hand of television's latest star on a popular sitcom?

Is your brand like Coke, which screens a prefilm film by Coke for Coke starring Coke? The key is to quantify what the buy will be worth in terms of reinforcing brand loyalty *before* you make it. That will define your return on expectations and investment.

Theresa Howard, *USA Today*: *Does each medium provide a different level of loyalty response or reaction?*

Robert Passikoff: Yes. Your product is a brand with distinct values, and so is the individual television show, magazine, radio station, and so on.

Therefore, it is true that your brand will perform better in media environments that are clearly in sync with your products or services. By inserting brand values into the media planning process, marketers can better ensure they connect with consumers. Aligning brand values with the values of the individual medium on which you advertise enables you to predict increased levels of brand awareness and positive brand imagery before you spend your money. You connect better with your target audience and maximize your brand's ad effectiveness via more cost-effective, strategic media planning.

Theresa Howard: *Television and billboards are as different as apples and bananas. Can we develop a usable, meaningful way of comparing their effectiveness in engendering loyalty?*

Robert Passikoff: Media planners haven't been given the tools to deal with real consumer value shifts. Planning by reach and frequency alone is flawed: Even the same numbers—in two different ideal vehicles, say television and billboards—rarely produce the same results for the advertised brand. That's because the brand's values and the media vehicle's values may not be aligned with each other—even when the numbers look right. By right, I mean that the target may not feel the same way about the brand and the specific medium chosen to advertise that brand (example: using a low-tech medium to advertise a high-tech brand that could benefit from demonstration may be a complete disconnect, rendering the media impact almost worthless).

You can maximize advertising effectiveness and increase the likelihood of engaging your consumers by aligning your brand's values with each given media vehicle's values. It's not that difficult. Keep your target-audience and reach-and-frequency data. *Just add a step that accurately measures value dimensions typically left unexplored by traditional media research models.* You have nothing to lose: you gain a system that allows you to do an apples-to-apples comparison of effects, and you can factor in what you should pay for the exposure based on your return on value, engagement, and loyalty.

"*Next question: I believe that life is a constant striving for balance, requiring frequent tradeoffs between morality and necessity, within a cyclic pattern of joy and sadness, forging a trail of bittersweet memories until one slips, inevitably, into the jaws of death. Agree or disagree?*"

CHAPTER 6

THE FOUR PROVEN DRIVERS OF CUSTOMER LOYALTY: A CATEGORY-BY-CATEGORY EXPOSÉ

> The companies that are lasting are those that are authentic. If people believe they share values with a company, they will stay loyal to a brand.
>
> —*Howard Schultz, Chairman, Starbucks*

OPEN SOURCING LOYALTY METRICS

We have already demonstrated the extremely important finding that, across most product and service categories, consumers are becoming increasingly demanding. Do you need more proof?

The levels of consumer expectations for delivery of the key brand loyalty drivers have been steadily increasing over the life of our Brand Keys *Customer Loyalty Index* survey.

Our survey, conducted every year since 1998, has shown consistent and strong gains in consumer expectations for the vast majority of the product and service categories we cover. The gains continue through the most recent survey wave, fielded in 2006.

These trends have profound implications for marketers, especially since most brands have been unable to keep pace with what consumers expect. The gap between what consumers want or expect from their brands and what they believe they should receive from those brands continues to increase.

This growing gap between expectations and delivery is the very definition of consumer disengagement and consumer disloyalty. It makes logical sense that a consumer will shop around for another brand if she feels that her current brand is failing to provide what is expected. This potential disengagement (i.e., behavioral disloyalty) will occur even if a consumer has been a faithful user of a brand for many years. For example, most portable CD players are probably languishing in a drawer, as people rush out of their homes plugging in iPod earbuds.

The increasing gap between consumer expectations and perceived product or service delivery provided by the brands is just one source of turmoil for marketers. Further complicating the issue is that in many categories, the order of importance of the brand loyalty drivers is changing over time. And in some cases, the very nature or composition of the drivers themselves is changing.

Just when a brand manager, an executive, or a small business owner feels that he really understands what drives loyalty in the category, the top drivers shift in importance, in some instances moderately, but in other cases, profoundly.

To illustrate the shift in the order of importance of the loyalty drivers that is occurring in many product and service categories, we have open sourced the relative driver importance for 29 categories from the Brand Keys *Customer Loyalty Index* for two years—2004 compared to 2006—to show what can happen in just two years.

The importance of the category loyalty drivers is identified from the loyalty metrics themselves. The drivers reveal what people think and not what they say they think. These figures are *not* derived importance numbers or *stated* importance. Do not confuse these two ideas, because they are *not* the same. Devoting marketing resources to less important areas (areas in which the brand does not need bolstering), spending money on low expectation drivers, or—worse yet—depending only on what consumers tell you can burn a great deal of money quickly.

Some key observations:

• Over the two-year period (from 2004 to 2006), in 7 of the 29 product and service categories (24 percent) there were *no* changes in the order of importance of the top four loyalty drivers. In other words, there was at least some volatility in approximately three-fourths of the categories.

There appears to be no apparent consistency or pattern among the seven categories for which no changes were observed in the order of driver importance. Expectations are always increasing, but driver order is a different consumer engagement and loyalty indicator. These seven categories, illustrated in Figure 6.1, were:

Figure 6.1
Seven Categories for Which No Changes Were Observed

Regular Beer

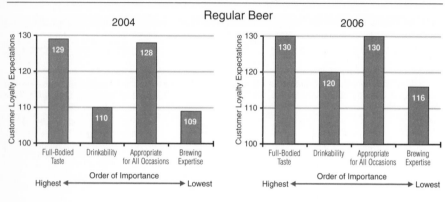

Regular Soft Drinks

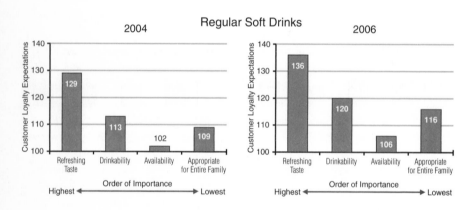

Banks

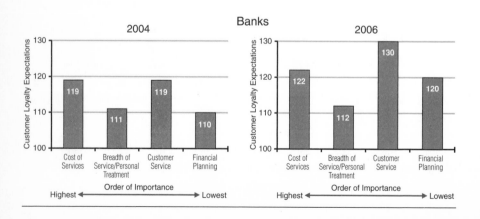

Figure 6.1 *(Continued)*

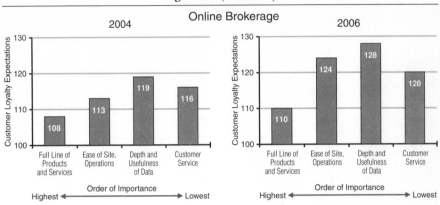

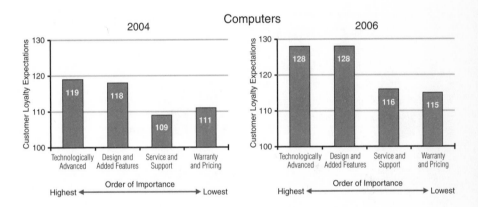

(continued)

Figure 6.1 *(Continued)*

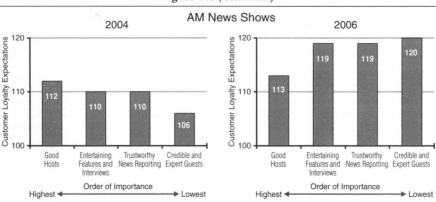

1. *Regular Beer:* Light Beer, however, did not remain static.
2. *Regular Soft Drinks:* Diet Soft Drinks, however, did not remain static.
3. *Banks.*
4. *Online Brokerages:* It has become increasingly difficult to differentiate online brokerages from banks.
5. *Personal Computers.*
6. *Retail Stores.*
7. *Morning News Shows.*

• In another seven instances, there was only one shift in the relative importance of the drivers, one specifically that occurred between the third and the fourth most important drivers: the two least important of the top four drivers (Figure 6.2). In these cases, the first and second most important drivers remained the same from 2004 to 2006; only the third and fourth most important drivers exchanged places with each other, although these kinds of shifts are generally harbingers to larger shifts down the road and may reflect consumer disappointment in marketing or process activities taken by the brands themselves.

These seven categories were:

1. *Airlines:* A shift in driver importance and increased expectations may present an opportunity for airlines who *do not* charge for a pillow, a soft drink, or an aisle seat.
2. *Athletic Footwear:* As shoes become more and more the same from a "Materials and Manufacturing" perspective, consumers want shoes with more/better imbued meanings that resonate with them.

Figure 6.2
Seven Categories That Showed Shifts in Drivers

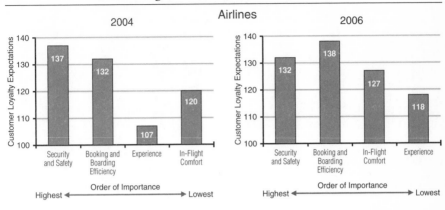

Airlines

2004

2006

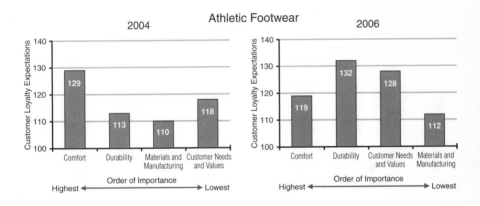

Athletic Footwear

2004

2006

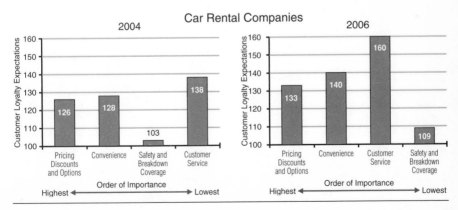

Car Rental Companies

2004

2006

(continued)

Figure 6.2 *(Continued)*

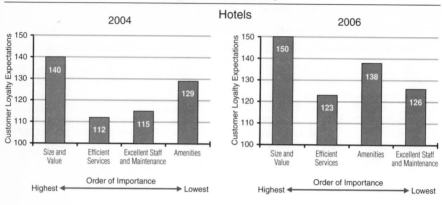

Hotels

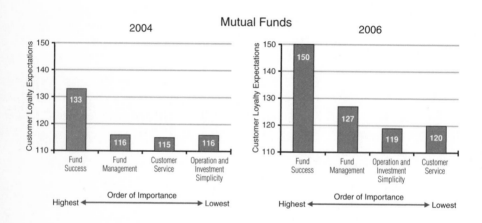

Mutual Funds

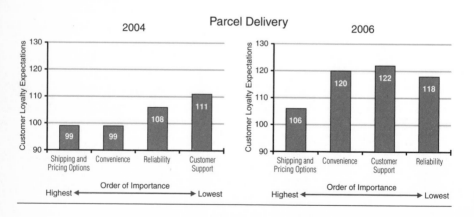

Parcel Delivery

Figure 6.2 *(Continued)*

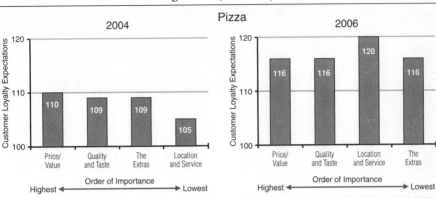

3. *Car Rental Companies:* The ubiquitous rental car may have "Price" and "Convenience" as its price of entry to the category, but smart marketers will speed ahead of the pack by providing exceptional levels of customer service.

4. *Hotels:* Providing exceptional customer service is important in this category, where process reengineering and Total Quality Management activities have virtually guaranteed "Excellent Staff and Maintenance." As delight turns to expectation, smart brands will offer more amenities and greater convenience to their customers.

5. *Mutual Funds:* As more and more consumers get comfortable managing their own investments, "Operations and Investment Simplicity" will continue to grow in importance.

6. *Parcel Delivery:* "Reliability" has been a given in the category for a long time. But higher levels of usage and more complex options have conspired to make customer service more important.

7. *Pizza:* As this category will compete more and more on price and added-values (like bread sticks), the brands who have wider distribution and can deliver faster will be the winners.

• In five product or service categories, there was a single flip-flop in the order of importance of adjacent drivers, which occurred between either the first and second most important drivers, or between the second and third most important (Figure 6.3). Since these switches involved drivers more important to brand loyalty than what was involved among the first group of categories, they should be considered occurrences of more significant shifts.

These five product and service categories are:

Figure 6.3
A Flip-Flop in the Order of Adjacent Drivers

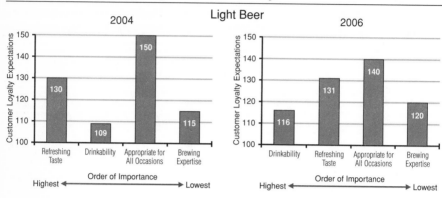

Light Beer

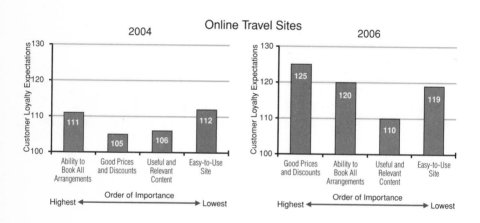

Online Travel Sites

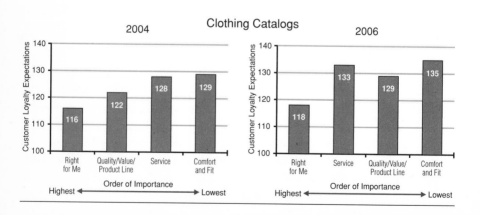

Clothing Catalogs

Figure 6.3 *(Continued)*

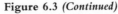

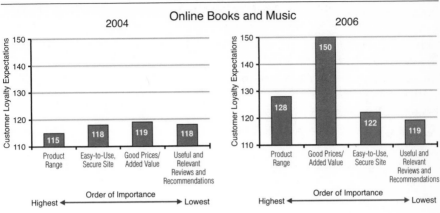

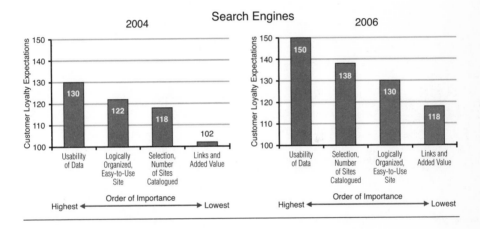

1. *Light Beer:* There were changes involving the first and second most important drivers where consumers apparently would like to quaff more beer more easily.

2. *Online Travel:* There were changes in the first and second most important drivers.

3. *Clothing Catalogs:* Drivers 2 and 3 changed with "Service" becoming a more important differentiator for a category fighting for differentiation.

4. *Online Books and Music:* Drivers 2 and 3 changed with "Good Prices and Added Value" becoming more important and having the highest expectations for a category fighting commoditization.

5. *Search Engines:* Drivers 2 and 3 changed with consumers expecting more from their searches.

Three of these five categories involve online services. Since online products and services, as well as consumer expectations regarding what those products and services should provide, are rapidly evolving, it probably should come as no surprise that fairly significant shifts in driver importance in online categories will often occur (Figure 6.4).

It's critical that marketers for brands that compete in these categories have early warning predictive metrics in place to alert them to such changes or risk being left behind by more prescient brands.

- In 8 of the 29 product or service categories (28 percent), a truly significant shift in the order of driver importance occurred from 2004 to 2006. In 7 of these cases, a driver's rank-order position shifted at least two places, for example, from third most important to first most important; in the eighth instance, two switches took place among adjacent drivers.

These eight categories, along with the driver whose importance shifted significantly, are:

1. *Coffee and Doughnuts:* "Variety" went from first to fourth; "Location" is now the most important driver as more and more consumers leave their homes to travel to preferred locations for morning coffee and doughnuts.

2. *Energy Providers/Utilities:* "Energy Cost Management" went from fourth to second likely in light of increased energy costs.

3. *Gasoline:* Two small shifts among adjacent drivers; as the result of one of the shifts, a price-oriented driver is now number 1.

4. *Insurance Companies:* "Premiums and Rates" went from fourth to second indicating that as the population ages, people are far more concerned about medical and health care costs.

5. *Mobile Phones:* "Unit Size" moved from first to third, as most brands offer most all sizes, but "Product Design" represents opportunities for real (and perceived) innovation.

6. *Office Copiers:* "Customer Support" moved from second to fourth as "Reliability" has increased and more and more consumers expect to be able to do more and more with their copiers.

7. *Quick-Serve Restaurants:* "Menu Variety" went from third to first as the consumers' competitive sets has expanded beyond the ubiquitous Hamburger and Family Restaurant sobriquets.

8. *Wireless Service Providers:* In addition to a small shift among adjacent drivers, "Technological Leadership" and "Equipment" went from fourth to second. "Customer Service" and "Calling Plans" are so twentieth century. Customers expect to make calls from anywhere with equipment that does everything.

Figure 6.4
Shifts in the Drivers for Online Services

Coffee and Doughnuts

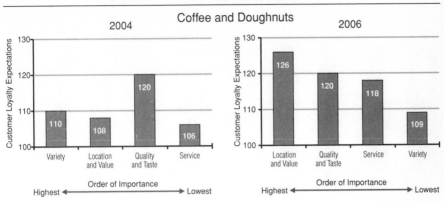

Energy Providers/Utilities

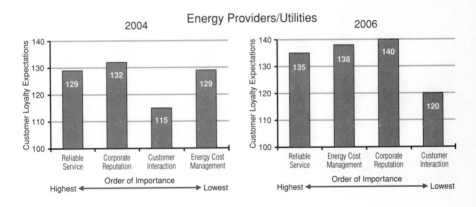

Gasoline

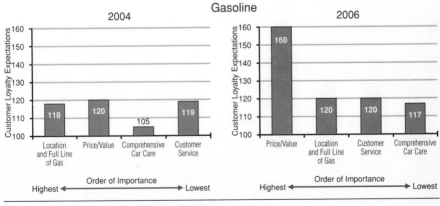

(continued)

Figure 6.4 *(Continued)*

Insurance Companies

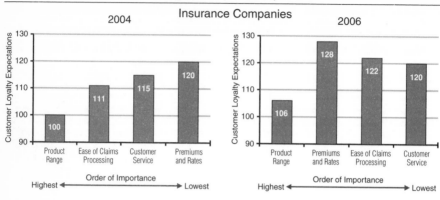

Mobile Telephones

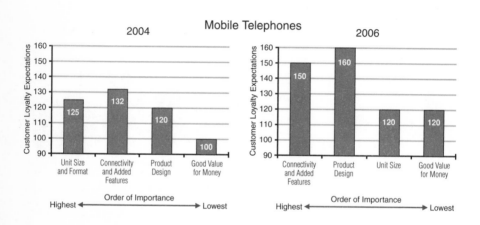

Office Copiers

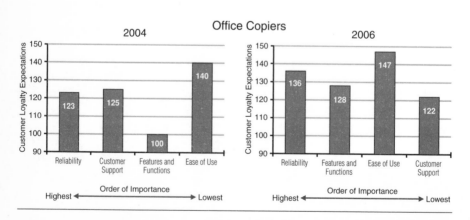

Figure 6.4 *(Continued)*

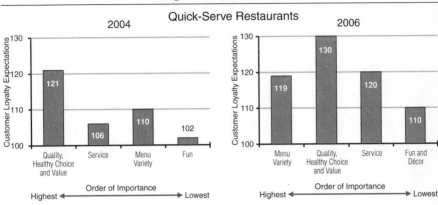

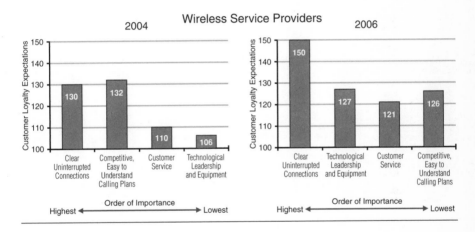

• In the remaining two product and service categories, changes in the dynamics of establishing and maintaining brand loyalty occurred to such an extent that a relabeling of at least one of the loyalty drivers was required (Figure 6.5). These categories are:

1. *Long Distance Providers:* In which a 2004 driver called "Billing Accuracy" disappeared and was replaced in 2006 with a driver called "Plan Options," which was fourth in importance.
2. *Credit Cards:* Fully three of the four loyalty drivers were reconstituted due to changing category and consumer values and expectations.

The only driver to have survived from 2004 to 2006 was "Ease and Speed of Interaction" (now second in importance).

Figure 6.5
Shifts Requiring Renaming of the Loyalty Drivers

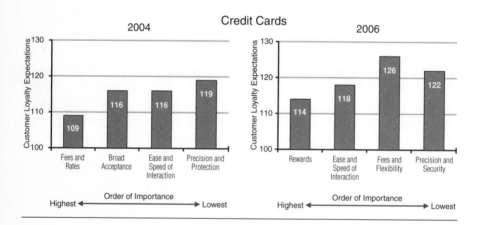

Among the three instances of relabeling, perhaps the most interesting involved "Precision and Protection" in 2004 becoming "Precision and *Security*" in 2006 (fourth in importance for both years), with the relabeling due to the recently increased threat of identity theft.

Another way of looking at these findings is that in 15 of the 29 product and service categories (52 percent), shifts occurred in the order of driver importance that involved either the first or the second most important of the drivers.

Thus, in just over half of the categories, a marketer who had not kept abreast of changing consumer wants and needs over the past two years would have been making decisions based on incorrect or out-of-date data—a fundamental misunderstanding of category dynamics. You cannot—you will not—engage customers if you make that mistake.

With respect to major themes that have been involved in the shifts in driver importance in recent years across the various categories that we study, most apparent has been the increased importance of factors pertaining to the price of the product or service. In five instances, a driver dealing with price has moved up in importance:

1. *Energy Providers/Utilities:* "Energy Cost Management" moved up two places to second.
2. *Gasoline:* A driver relating to "price" is now first in importance.

(Note that both of the above shifts are due to the recently experienced sharply higher cost of oil and gas.)

3. *Insurance Companies:* "Premiums and Rates" moved up two places to second.
4. *Online Travel:* "Good Prices" is now first.
5. *Online Books and Music:* "Good Prices" is now second.

A secondary theme is that in two of the fast-food categories (Coffee and Doughnuts; Pizza), the driver pertaining to "convenient location" has increased in importance. Not surprisingly, this reflects the increasingly time-pressured lifestyles of typical Americans, augmented by their increased desire for convenience generally.

LOYALTY TALES FROM THE REAL WORLD

Brand President

John Kennedy was the first U.S. president to become a brand. Although eminent *New York Times* columnist Theodore H. White may not have thought of it exactly that way when he wrote about JFK's media savvy in *The Making of the President* (New York: Atheneum, 1961), there is no doubt that Kennedy and his handlers thoroughly understood the power of the media and played to it with all the strategic finesse and tactical gusto of a new product launch. What they did not know—and what you are learning—is that the behavior of voters in that election, and indeed many subsequent elections, could have been more accurately predicted had they possessed the methods of values-based research that we are discussing in this book.

Values are values. A defined set of values exists for just about everything we deal with (e.g., furniture design or preferences for fish or chicken). Values-based loyalty research, therefore, can be used to measure, frame, and help predict almost anything. Frustrated as we were with the way the last election presented the candidates and issues, we took the liberty of applying marketing research methods to the political arena. We posed our own questions: Is a brand personality different from a presidential personality? How much of a voter's choice is based on what he or she thinks is really in the box, free prize (or tax breaks) notwithstanding? Or can what we think about a candidate and what influences how we vote be reduced to packaging via marketing?

The inevitable suppertime political pollster call comes, interrupting your meal. But instead of letting fly the usual "Who are you going to vote for in the presidential election?" the pollster queries: "Which of the presidential candidates do you feel is most like you?"

Answers to the first (unasked) typical question would reveal your deepest political convictions, or at least it would be interpreted that way. This answer could merely reflect your state of mind at that particular moment. You pause between bites to think, answer, hang up, and enjoy the rest of your dinner. Therein lies the imprecision of traditional polling: Consider the countless variables that can occur between our answers during dinner in August and the time when we are actually in the voting booth, pulling levers in November.

Responses to the second, less familiar question uncover some much more interesting *and* much more reliable results for predicting electoral outcomes. What is my Ideal President like? How much does he represent what I represent? How do either of these two guys measure up to that ideal? Here we've mined information that is much less likely to shift between when the question is asked and when the ballot is cast.

As with all market research that predicts future behavior, the value lies in both *how you ask the questions* and *how you interpret the answers*. We apply to political values, perception, and motivation the same methodology that is used for brand research that consistently correlates extraordinarily highly with actual sales behavior.

The loyalty approach uses a combination of psychological inquiry and statistical analyses to fuse emotional and rational elements (e.g., issues, imagery, positioning, or benefits) along three key dimensions: how voters view the presidency, compare candidates, and, ultimately, vote. The technique is more effective than traditional, direct polling because it measures what voters think, as opposed to what they *say* they think. It is more efficient than traditional quantitative techniques because it can project results based on a small sample (provided the sample isn't skewed toward a given group).

Consider why we vote for a particular political candidate. Do we compare his or her position on issues to our own and then vote for the nominee who comes closest to articulating our own views? Is our choice simply based on the numbers on the state of the economy, growth, jobs, and inflation? How much of our decision is rational and how much is visceral?

For decades, social scientists have noted that political candidates have been marketed pretty much like packaged goods and have relied on television advertising to get the message—and the image—out to the electorate. But how effective is that approach if the party plank is largely refined by focus groups and predictive mumbo jumbo?

By measuring the television advertising for each party, we can identify messaging that resonates with viewers or misses the mark. This strongly suggests that it is possible to gauge public reaction to candidates just as we gauge public reaction to new product launches (equivalent to political challengers) or new models of existing brands (incumbents) and measure the effects of the ad campaign created for each.

As with any category, the methodology determines the electorate's concept of an Ideal President. Next, each candidate's perceived qualities are measured against that ideal. The effects of the individual television ads are then measured, revealing significant changes in the perception of a candidate and an effective (or ineffective) television ad. At the end of the campaign trail, the candidate that best meets or exceeds the qualities of the ideal always wins.

The four drivers that define an Ideal President are:

1. *Perception:* Does the candidate have a deep understanding of the problems facing the country? (smarts)
2. *Resolve:* Does the candidate have the strength and leadership to guide the country? (guts)
3. *Action:* Does the candidate have a comprehensive, realistic, well-considered plan for solving the problems facing the country? (job skills)
4. *Compassion:* Does the candidate care about all the people? (love)

The drivers themselves apply equally to self-described Republicans, Democrats, or Independents. Voters claiming loyalty to each party rank the drivers differently in terms of importance to them, and differently for the expectations that they hold in judging candidates. Significant differences require a plus-five point change.

The three parties' ideal president is described in Figure 6.6.

How do the different parties describe an Ideal President? In the most recent election, Republicans wanted someone strong and with a concrete plan. They didn't mind if he or she wasn't a caring person. Democrats preferred someone empathetic and smart. Independents blend Republican and Democratic values, but since their top two drivers exactly match the Republicans' top two,

Figure 6.6
Applying Brand Keys Drivers to Presidential Candidates

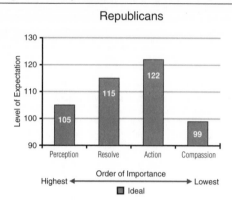

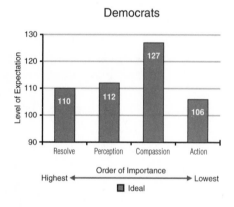

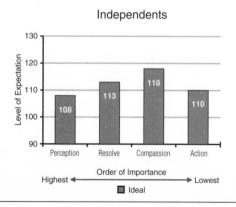

Independents were more likely to vote for Republicans than Democrats should they not find a suitable Independent candidate.

This loyalty-based information identifies what works, what needs improvement to be more time and cost effective, and what attracts the political equivalent of sales: votes.

Ironically, reported spending by both parties in the last presidential election came to over $250 million in advertising. The Brand Keys loyalty assessments revealed the electorate (on both sides) as *not* being influenced by TV messaging. Since the Brand Keys approach is as accurate a predictor of voting returns in a presidential election as it is of dollar returns for a brand, creating candidate brand equity becomes as understandable a process as creating equity for any other branded product or service. Our approach is a highly useful technique for measuring loyalty in a most volatile marketplace—the American voting constituency.

This also sets off a series of fascinating cultural questions about what shapes the public's presidential ideal. Martin Sheen, who played the role of President Jed Bartlet on the weekly series *The West Wing,* may represent or fulfill more of a presidential ideal in the public's mind than either Bush or Kerry could ever have hoped to do. Television powerfully shapes our attitudes, consciously and otherwise, and allows for weekly upgrades to character and plot, brand modification in situ, based on ratings, not the Congress, the Constitution, or the constituents. The character of Jed Bartlet resonates with us because he's not worried about reelection, only weekly ratings.

The television perception leaves the public in a tight spot, setting up viewers—a large percentage of the voting population—for a fall because of somewhat unrealistic expectations for presidential behavior. Does the electorate get the president it deserves? That we cannot answer. Does the public get the president it wants (and why)? That is one question that we can answer.

Q & A

On Losing and Stealing Customers

Dan Hanover, *Event Marketer* magazine: *What is the easiest way to lose a customer for life?*

Robert Passikoff: Fail to meet or exceed a person's expectations of your brand. As customers, we all have different expectation levels for different product categories. For example, when we rent a car, it had better not have a funny smell or dried spilt coffee on the console. We carry those expectations around with us to make sure they are met when we make purchases. We have expectations we are capable of articulating, and those we cannot; together, these expectations determine if we will purchase the brand again next time.

Each category has its own characteristics that make large contributions to loyalty. Some of these characteristics are what we call *table stakes:* Either you have the stake or you're not in the game. Customer loyalty metrics can help identify those characteristics that operate for (or against) you in your particular category. *In general, if the characteristics that make big contributions are missed, it virtually guarantees losing a customer for life.*

On a cross-category basis there are six general areas that you have to watch for, cleverly dubbed the *Six C's.* Their contributions vary slightly among categories, but the percentages attributed to each show why not delivering on these six makes it easy for a customer to move to one of your competitors:

1. *Customer Interaction* ("Service," "How quickly problems are resolved," or "One-call problem resolution"): 25 percent
2. *Credibility* ("Believing what the brand can deliver"): 21 percent
3. *Convenience* ("Location" and "Distribution"): 19 percent
4. *Corporate Reputation:* 17 percent
5. *Class* ("Image" and "Quality"): 11 percent
6. *Costs* ("Value" Perception): 7 percent

Dan Hanover: *How much more difficult is it to steal loyalty from a competitor than to steal market share?*

Robert Passikoff: Market share is vastly easier to steal. Tried-and-true (and quite rational) pricing, promotional, and added-value strategies and techniques can leverage consumer behavior to the benefit of your market share. This is sometimes called "producing maximum short-term volume." It is also known as "renting the customer," because while the promotional activities can help to increase share, *growth tends to evaporate when the promotional activity ends.*

Loyalty, however, is more emotionally based, anchored in understanding and managing the expectations that consumers hold for a category. *Do it right and you own the customer.* It's a long-term proposition with more substantial cost efficiencies and contributions to the bottom line.

The Alchemy of Premium Brands

Cheryl Hall, *Dallas Morning News***:** *Why are customers willing to pay a premium price for product or service quality?*

Robert Passikoff: The biggest problem that twenty-first-century brands face is their inability to differentiate themselves from competitors. Having gone through the satisfaction programs of the late 1970s, the Total Quality Management movement of the 1980s, and Process Reengineering in the 1990s, most companies are doing just fine, but their products and services are virtually indistinguishable. So, when there is an acknowledged difference in the quality of a product or service, it manifests itself, and that aspect of the offering will end up exceeding expectations. If brands exceed expectations, people are willing to pay for that advantage, which is why customer loyalty models correlate so highly with positive behavior and profitability. Besides, if price were truly as important to customers as they say, only the least expensive, generic style product or service would survive.

CHAPTER 7

The Power of Human and Celebrity-Based Brands: When It Works, When It's Wasted

It is awfully important to know what is and what is not your business

—Gertrude Stein

Brand marketing and popular culture have much in common. Both have—or should have—their roots in people's lives and people's values. Both should have meaning for people and consumers. Maybe that's why, when reviewing the results of the most recent Brand Keys *Customer Loyalty Leaders Index,* a portion of Ira Gershwin's great lyrics—somewhat altered—sprang to mind:

> Oh, my dear,
> My brand is here to stay.
> I need not fear value will go away.
>
> In time, the market may crumble,
> The Dow-Jones may tumble,
> That was so yesterday; but—
> My brand is here to stay.

So, it doesn't flow like Ira's version, but we *should* sing the praises of those brands that are doing it right by measuring the direction and velocity of customer values, capturing the values for which customers have the highest expectations, and then leveraging those values. Doing it right creates meaning for your brand.

Advertising, promotions, direct response, point of purchase, and process reengineering are all elements designed to stimulate customer loyalty. But they're all procedures, not *ideas*.

The category leaders all feature *ideas* that mean something to customers, that really resonate with customers' values defining their categories, as well as procedures and distribution systems. These companies recognized the differences between twentieth-century values and the values and expectations of the new century, and figured out how to make who they were, and what they did, mean something to consumers:

- Avis was ranked number 12 in 1999 and is now ranked number 2 out of a total 238 brands on our "Loyalty Leaders" list. It is likely that such levels of customer loyalty were arrived at by recognizing—and delivering—customer service that still tries harder.
- Sprint was number 91 in 1999 and has since risen to number 14. They've managed this by leveraging the expectations that customers have for high technology and have done so without the appearance of chintzy bargain-basement carping on low, lower, lowest cents per minute, although more recently they have leaned toward that strategy.
- Mobil gasoline always ranked well. It did it by capitalizing on customer expectations regarding speed—not of your car, but of getting you in and out of the station quickly. Its Speedpass is a benefit that offsets increased prices.
- Discover Card did it by meeting the expectations regarding added-value (beyond the ubiquitous air-mile continuity programs) with cash back for cash spent.
- New Balance did it by meeting the expectations of comfort and being made in the United States.

The biggest brand slippage has been in utilities. They're not concentrating on loyalty drivers. They're fast becoming the telecoms of the twenty-first century, relying mainly on cost savings and themes on keeping your home cool or warm enough to get new customers and keep old ones. Apparently, the signs over their doors, large enough so that even dairy animals can read them, spell out what all customers really think of utilities: C-O-M-M-O-D-I-T-Y. Moreover, the rising price of energy hasn't helped.

Once upon a time in brand history, delighting the customer used to be enough to differentiate the brand and increase chances of keeping that customer loyal. That worked until delight became expectation. Unless you can *always* meet or exceed expectations—or convey to consumers that you are *trying* to meet or exceed expectations—in ways that are deemed meaningful and engaging to the customer, you won't keep your customers loyal.

For a company to plan for real engagement—and attendant loyalty and profitability—it *must* be able to create marketing plans, communication programs, products, and services that consistently exceed customer expectations. To do that, it needs to understand which values will make customers feel valued, making and keeping customers loyal.

You want your brand to keep doing that for as long as possible. But couldn't everything be a brand?

Only products with enough values and meaning that resonate with and engage consumers are actually brands. It depends on who and what you are, and it depends on where you are on the Commodity-To-Human Brand Continuum—a flowchart that indicates the degree of meaning with which a product or service is imbued.

Since brand has become the convenient catchall for a product or service that someone wants to put his or her name on—think branding cattle—we have an identity conundrum. Just because a product is yours and you put your name on it does not automatically make this product a brand. Nor does having been around for a long time or having many people recognize your name make you a brand—in the twenty-first-century sense of the word.

Entertainers feel that (being a brand themselves) they have license to enter fields that are outside their area of expertise and add immediate positive impact. They seem to believe (and so do the companies that hire them as spokespeople) that their popularity currency translates magically into the currency of revenue.

But those values simply do not translate that seamlessly and usually do not stand up outside the entertainment arena—for example, Britney Spears and restaurants; Joe Namath and pantyhose; Michael Jackson and *anything* in the real world; rock stars asking if we "got milk?" Even in the twenty-first century, there's a difference between what's creative and what's productively believable.

Some people talk about designers as if they were a bankable brand. Calvin, Donna, Oscar, Ralph, P. Diddy, Tommy, and a few other brand demigods are noteworthy exceptions. Most designers, entertainers, or artists do not meet the mandate. Sure, everyone has heard the names, but awareness is not the issue. It's how much the designer represents values that have meaning and that reinforce loyalty, that create trust and connection, and that get people to buy. In many cases, outside the industry nobody knows the designer's name. The announcement that "Tom Ford is moving from designer to brand" is more likely to engender a "Who?" from consumers, and not a statement along the lines of "Wow! You can't imagine how long I've been waiting for that." However, certain designer celebrities would argue the point.

B. Smith, the famed restaurateur and lifestyle guru (but *not* a brand), was described by *Essence* magazine as "licensing B. Smith to front a line of classy must haves." Smith declared, "I am not just a 'front' . . . but am actively involved in their development and production." That may well be, but it still doesn't make her a brand.

At one end of the brand continuum, we have the commodity, what we all know as the stuff that provides some reasonable level of primacy of product or service. At the other end, we have the Human Brand, the occasional exceptional person who really is the brand: Wolfgang Puck, Colonel Sanders, Martha Stewart, Paul Newman, or Donald Trump.

But it is in the middle of the continuum where the arguments get heated. In one sense, the argument about brands and their human mascots comes down to one short statement: Show me the values, the meaning, the measurements for the association, and we can all agree that we do (or do not) have a brand.

Many companies (in the presence of great names, but in the absence of values that are meaningful to the consumer) are hard-pressed to be more than economic and category placeholders. The Gap seems to have had significant difficulty identifying a meaningful position for itself. Over the past few years, it has wanted to stand for something more than consumers were willing to believe about it, so the announcement that it ended its relationship with Sarah Jessica Parker didn't surprise us.

A celebrity spokesperson can be extraordinarily helpful to a brand, or he or she can be an expensive drain on the budget. Age, a hit television show, and all the press in the world shouldn't be the deciding factor when picking a representative for your brand. Success comes from finding someone who can better communicate the brand's basic values. Bridge the gap and you virtually guarantee better results. For example, what do you know about Michael Jordan? People know his name, and they know him via one particular arena: athletic excellence. He seems to be a nice, personable guy. No page-one court cases. But those are his only great values. It doesn't necessarily follow that they are great enough to be meaningful or important to the cologne, steak house, underwear, or airline categories.

What is one way to solve the continuum conundrum? Simple: Measure the affects of the association—person, magazine, or sponsorship—and run a test to show whether the value inherent in the spokesperson (or media vehicle, promotion, or sponsorship) will help build loyalty or hurt it. That way you establish a baseline for which people, actions, slogans, logos, or programs in which you place your product help your brand more than others do.

The issue needs to be framed differently before you start naming names because the problem is not if you can get someone famous. Most celebrities will shill for companies (even if they only do so in Japan, like Paul Newman or Woody Allen), and there are artists who will only deign to lend their voice to commercial ventures, like Sean Connery or Julia Roberts.

But what did you get? Did you increase loyalty, make more sales, or build higher profits? Will you settle for recognition? Many actors are netting huge $1 million-dollar-and-up paychecks just for lending their voices to commercial ventures. Can you match up the voice and the product in Table 7.1?

Thinking about those products, did the big name *mean* anything to you? Did a celebrity better engage you? What did the client get beyond some bragging rights and the chance to shake hands with a celebrity at the recording studio?

If you are okay with an answer that lacks mettle and costs a lot but feels good in terms of the way you are communicating your message, you have mostly harmless sponsorship.

What I invite you to do is to draw new correlations—before, during, and after the sponsorship plan. You never want to build a field of dreams without knowing what people are willing to pay for the price of admission. The marketing landscape of the late-twentieth and early-twenty-first centuries is littered with companies and products that built but no one came. So, before you do anything, measure it. Before you market—predict what is going to happen (see Figure 7.1).

Table 7.1
Do You Recognize This Voice? (Does It Matter?)

1. Jeff Bridges	A. Oppenheimer Funds
2. George Clooney	B. Honda
3. Sean Connery	C. Panasonic shavers
4. Richard Dreyfuss	D. Pizza Hut
5. Gene Hackman (does 2)	E. AOL
6. James Earl Jones	F. Budweiser
7. Queen Latifah	G. Duracell
8. Julia Roberts	H. Level 3 Communications
9. Christian Slater	I. Lowe's
	J. Verizon

Answers: 1I, 2G, 3H, 4B, 5A and F, 6J, 7D, 8E, 9C

Figure 7.1
Brand Keys Commodity-To-Human Brand Continuum

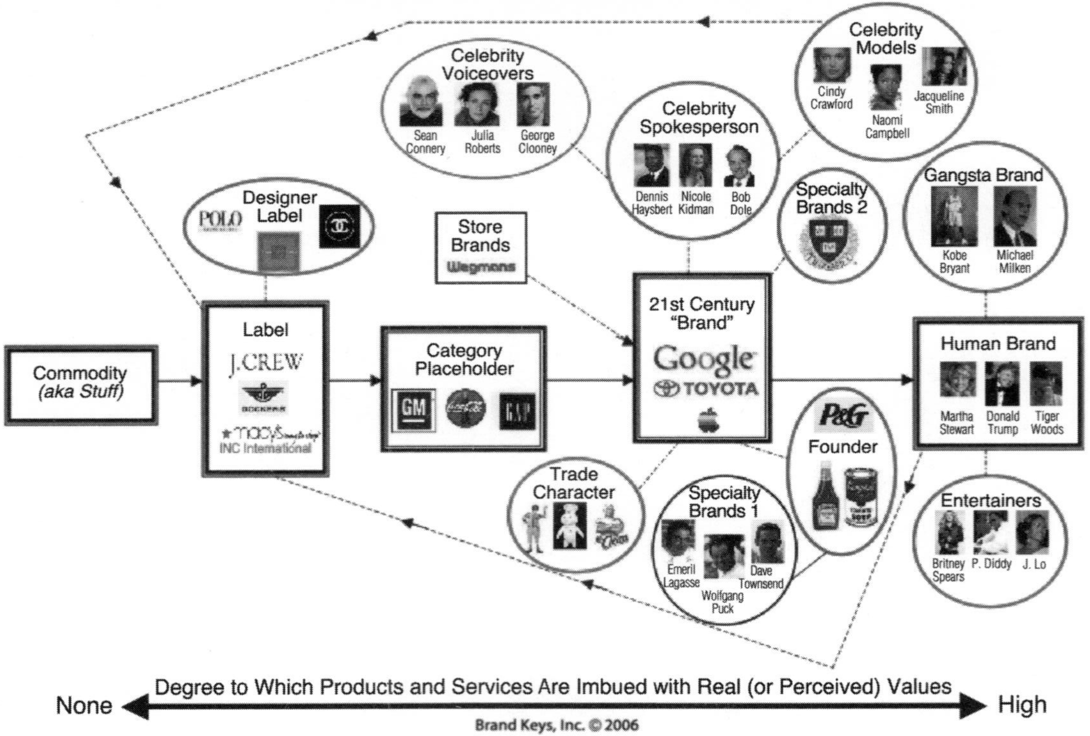

Commodity (aka Stuff)

Designer Label
POLO
CHANEL

Label
J.CREW
Bloomingdale's
MACY'S
INC International

Celebrity Voiceovers
Sean Connery
Julia Roberts
George Clooney

Celebrity Spokesperson
Dennis Haysbert
Nicole Kidman
Bob Dole

Celebrity Models
Cindy Crawford
Naomi Campbell
Jacqueline Smith

Gangsta Brand
Michael Milken
Kobe Bryant

Human Brand
Martha Stewart
Donald Trump
Tiger Woods

Entertainers
Britney Spears
P. Diddy
J. Lo

Specialty Brands 2

21st Century "Brand"
Google
TOYOTA

Founder
P&G

Specialty Brands 1
Emeril Lagasse
Dave Townsend
Wolfgang Puck

Store Brands
Wegmans

Category Placeholder
GM
Coca-Cola
GM

Trade Character

Degree to Which Products and Services Are Imbued with Real (or Perceived) Values

None ← → High

Brand Keys, Inc. © 2006

180

WHERE DOES YOUR PRODUCT OR SERVICE FALL?

Here are some brief definitions of where products and services might fall. The visual of the continuum provides some specific examples for each category with the degree of brandness escalating as you migrate from left to right:

- *Commodity:* Products and services so basic that they cannot be differentiated in the minds of the consumer. They are usually sold on price.
- *Label:* The name of a retail store or manufacturer selling clothing identifying the goods.
- *Designer Label:* Well-known or regarded name of person who has designed the clothing. Usually denoting or pretending to be highfashion. Note that it is possible—and often profitable—for human brands to migrate backward to create another leverageable consumer contact point.
- *Category Placeholder:* This is the new—and accurate—designation for products or services with strong awareness in the category in which they compete but with values so basic, and so absent of meaning, that they cannot be differentiated from the competition in the minds of the consumer.
- *Twenty-First-Century Brand:* Name, term, symbol, or a combination thereof that identifies the goods and services of one seller versus another that is so strongly imbued with values and articulated meaning as to be easily and strongly differentiated from the competition. The research identified five subsegments by which twenty-first-century brands are often represented:
  - *Celebrity Spokesperson:* Person with high awareness and moderate-to-high personal values that can be borrowed by the product or service the person represents. Advantage is attained via use of voice, face, or figure in two subgroups: (1) Celebrity Voiceovers and (2) Celebrity Models.
  - *Founder:* Name of the person who created the company.
  - *Trade Character:* Symbols, often cartoons, in the form of animals, people, or other animated characters that are used to represent or create an association with the product or service.
  - *Specialty Category Brand (1):* A half-way point between Founder and Human Brand, usually denoting a specialized category like chefs and cooking who, once they have reached this place on the Commodity-To-Human Brand Continuum are able to migrate back and introduce lines of labeled cooking-related products.

—*Specialty Brand (2):* A segment of brands where specialty products and services reside: colleges and universities, for example. To quote Thomas W. Bruce, Cornell's vice president of community and university relations, "branding should not be a dirty word in academia." Which is one reason why Beaver College in Philadelphia changed its name to Arcadia University.

- *Human Brand:* An actual human being, most often the company founder, who represents 100 percent of the values of the company. This designation represents the highest level of imbued meaning, values, and differentiation. (The dotted lines in Figure 7.1 indicate that after a while the values of the Human Brand can be profitably migrated back to be used as a label, for example, Michael Jordan.)
- *Gangsta Brand:* Human Brand in or just out of prison, where the notoriety has become viewed as positive value or a badge of honor, in the minds of some consumer segments.

Have you figured out where your product or service falls on the continuum? It was probably easy if you located yourself toward one end of the continuum or the other, but the middle of the range gives companies real problems.

Labels are not brands. Just ask Human Brand-wannabe Steve Madden, who served 42 months in prison for engaging in dozens of rigged trades in his company's own stock and nobody blinked an eye. When he was released from prison, his company tried to turn him into a Gangsta Brand, with ads that read, "A New Meaning for the Word Spring Time" and "Steve Returns. Spring 2005." The campaign was largely ignored because most consumers only knew him for his stylized advertising, the name on the label, and little else. As such, most consumers didn't get the joke, and Mr. Madden didn't get anywhere near the attention that Martha Stewart (the Queen of Human Brands) received. Martha's homecoming *meant* something to consumers. Meaning is everything. Real brands, like Google and Toyota, are imbued with real (or perceived) values and meaning that effectively differentiates them from their competitors and successfully engages consumers. But brands that are well known but possess no real values or meaning for customers are *not* brands. They are Category Placeholders, and as such are recognized in the category in which their product or service competes, but little else. Think General Motors, Coke, or The Gap.

The Sound a Dying Brand Makes

Here's a brand word-association test to determine whether your product or service is (or is not) a brand: Ask a consumer to tell you the first thing that comes to mind when you name a particular product or service. Something like this:

You: Mercedes Benz
Customer: Luxury
You: BMW
Customer: German engineering
You: Volvo
Customer: Safety
You: Pontiac
Customer: Uhh

That "uhh" is the sound of a brand turning into a Category Placeholder. If you have no values or meaning to leverage—much like GM—all you can do is resort to tactics like lowering your price or trumpeting your satisfaction levels. To give credit where it's due, the creative shell around the price drop—the GM Employee Discount—was just brilliant. A week later, Ford and Chrysler were doing it, too. But not Toyota. Makes you realize how important being a brand, a real brand, is.

Although, maybe that is not always true. Everyone talks about fashion brands, but they are becoming more and more alike. In the Brand Keys *Fashion Loyalty Index*® we've discovered that every year there has been an increase in the share of Americans who say that labels and logos for their apparel hold less significance than they did a few years ago.

In 2006, more than two-thirds of adults (69 percent) declared that fashion brands were less or much less important to them. This is up from 67 percent in 2005 and 64 percent in 2004. As with most products, there's been a leveling of quality, and there are fewer significant differences at various prices and channels. It's not a trend you'd want to compete with for long—not without the ability to track real values and imbue your clothing with real meaning.

HOW GOOD OR BAD IS SOMEONE FOR YOUR BRAND?

Andy Warhol may have said that eventually everyone will have his or her 15 minutes of fame, but he never even hinted that everyone will be a brand. And he never said whether that 15 minutes would end up selling or sapping the afterlife of the famous 15 minutes. Think about this in the context of intentional brands and the people who rep for them. There are many human brands out there who are marketed like so many boxes of detergent: politicians, musicians, sports figures, comedians, domestic divas, celebrities (often with no particular reason for being celebrated), and the like. Whether these people *are brands* themselves, such as Martha Stewart or Donald Trump, or are spokespeople for brands (think about any number of endorsers), their humanity brings a certain twist to the branding process, presenting challenges that can be addressed via values-based research.

Take this test: On the continuum of bad things a person could do, which would impact your brand the worst if he or she were a hired spokesperson—or for that matter, which would have the most dire consequences for his or her own human brand:

A. Taking drugs
B. Stealing
C. Beating up someone else
D. Gambling

Before you answer aloud, here's a bit more context: The stealing I'm talking about here is a white-collar crime (think Enron). Taking drugs is on the personal level, albeit to enhance public performance, not recreational consumption à la the dark-shaded, designer-clad Hollywood jet set. And beating up someone has nothing to do with protecting or pummeling a loved one. Fair is fair and context is, after all, everything. Think in terms of how your customers think. Would customers or management care? Would they be able to make the distinction among different types of bad behavior? Would your brand suffer for a while and then recover?

Let's look at a couple of specific examples that, as the Greek philosopher Sophocles (the author of *Oedipus Rex*) said about human history, are bound to repeat themselves.

Sports and Drugs Don't Mix

While youth-like energy or Ponce de Leon's quest for the eternal fountain of youth may be something most of us want for ourselves, right now the value meter says "just not for our athletes." Still we dream, "Ahh to be 36 (or is it 29?) once again."

Current values and reality indicate that it does not matter what we all want for ourselves. We hold athletes, as opposed to celebrities, to a higher, unadulterated standard. Hypocrisy, unfortunately, it not a value we can measure on this one—it's one of those things that people do not articulate easily or well. So, when athletes take performance-enhancing drugs, this behavior erodes trust—the bond that fans form with individual players—and, therefore, loyalty toward the players and their sports as human brands plus any brands they may be promoting. Indeed, you can measure the impact it will have.

Consider what happened to Jason Giambi, Gary Sheffield, or the legendary Barry Bonds who were all accused of taking steroids. Botox would have been one thing. People shifted their trust, loyalty, and, shortly thereafter, interest and dollars as a result of illegal drug use. Fans have a great deal of choice when there is a loss of trust in a human flagship for a sports brand, never mind the impact on loyalty to the team for which he might play. Baseball fans (customers) can and will turn to golf, watch another major league sport, or indulge their secret love of synchronized swimming—even spend their money on concerts, movies, and other activities and spectacles, all of which *are not* baseball. To brands, this means: any beer, soft drink, or potato chip that these bad boys or girls have been touting will be toast. Parenthetically, the sports figures are generally viewed as only one of the value components that make up the team.

Olympic Expectations

The same pattern of human trust toward particular individuals and brand loyalty erosion holds true with the Olympics, where we have the peccadilloes of athletes, ongoing Olympic committee scandals, and endless, shameless competition for Olympic hosting rights to darken our collective regard. How different each one of these phenomena are and how much they affect loyalty and trust (which in turn affects behavior and sales) is what needs to be measured to accurately understand the correlation to loyalty, behavior, and profit.

When the expectation in the category shifts; when the percentage of contribution to loyalty—to the players, the teams, the sports industry, and any brands unfortunate enough to be swept along—changes, you can see it only after the greatest untapped marketing opportunity has come and gone. It works that way in sports just as it does in business. Leaders and followers there will always be. The former are usually the more informed.

Brand Lance

Consider America's newfound love of competitive biking tours. We love Lance Armstrong. He's done for competitive biking what Pelé did for soccer a few decades ago—bringing competitive biking into mainstream America. We love what Lance does, but even more we love what Lance represents. He fulfills more of our expectations: He is a champion athlete in a sport in which the United States never had much presence and a cancer survivor who defied the odds (or, in customer loyalty terms, exceeded expectations). We buy, give, and wear his lifesaver wristbands because he is a survivor and a champion with a comeback story better than Hollywood could ever concoct.

So far, Armstrong's amazingly victorious personal brand is untainted by any of the currently common athlete drug or behavior scandals. He's the most poked, prodded, calibrated, and medically researched athlete in sports history. Scientists know that his heart is at least 20 percent larger than a normal person's; Lance produces one-third less lactic acid than do other top cyclists, and he delivers oxygen to his legs at a rate higher than all but maybe 100 of his fellow earthlings. None of that is held against him.

Timing helps. With not much perception of cooperation between the United States and European allies on the ongoing Iraqi war, America loves to kick European butt, especially when it is French. Armstrong was the conduit for the Tour de France, tour de *anywhere* for that matter, having generated a huge percentage of American interest. Even interest in velodrome racing is up in the United States, for those of us who like to watch tall people on weird-looking bikes race around what looks very much like an elevated roller-skating rink.

If Lance were found to be a juicer, secretly on steroids, regardless of the collective love and allegiance to Lance the human brand, an undisclosed percentage of this loyalty and value would be quickly and irrevocably eroded. Positive customer behaviors would shift over to another human, or brand, even another sports category, as a direct result. How much and how fast is always a function of how the negative revelation is handled and what the public was willing to believe before its loyalty to him—and all the brands he represented—was affected. That is why we measure, in good times and otherwise.

Loyalty is not finite, but it is constant and behaves in predictable ways. Loyalty (as subject) waxes and wanes in relation to brands (as objects), whatever they may be. More often than not, loyalty shifts from one brand to another or switches categories based on preference changes all together. Humans are, more so perhaps than most other mammals, defined by their loyalty.

Loyalty to the expectations of physically pristine athletes will shift. In the future, anabolic enhancements will be as commonplace in the competitive sports category as Viagra has become for male personal performance in more indoor, nonspectator sports. Do you hear people talk about life-extension or beauty enhancement products with any shame or fear? For the most part, values shift independently of reason.

Violence Begets a Number of Things—Brand Erosion in Sports Is Not One of Them

Violence, unlike steroids, is not exactly a new human behavioral trait. How much can it degrade a brand's value? When discussing sports and violence, not all that much. Violent or other aggressive comportments in the category of sports does not really matter to people. In some cases, it actually strengthens the loyalty through delivering on fans' violent expectations, as in football or hockey. Translation to marketing terms: In-game violence does not erode any of the brand strength or shift the driver needles in terms of percentage of contribution to loyalty. At worst, it's just something that people are going to "tsk-tsk" at while they watch the videotape replays over and over again. Violence outside the game may be another matter (think about the fallout that has beset certain athletes who have roughed up wives and girlfriends or shot firearms in residential neighborhoods). In-game overzealousness is almost part of why we watch football or hockey. Basketball has gotten particularly interesting, with Latrell Sprewell strangling the coach—the negative effect on the sport was just over 3 percent. Ron Artest's leap into the stands resulted in about the same decrease—so, no real worries there.

Phil Donahue taking a swing at Geraldo Rivera, however, has a very different human brand effect. Audiences, especially men, certainly do want to see violence in sports, but only in certain environments. Fans at violence-prone events sit back far enough to avoid being hit—or worse yet, spilling their drinks.

The National Football League (NFL) has done well by expanding their consideration set and successfully evolving the franchise (while engaging more consumers) from sports to sports/entertainment. Wise business people tend to diversify their investments to lower the risk. NFL teams now market like crazy, offering fans full spectrum entertainment, from season kick-off to Super Bowl. And they offer the whole package: pregame analysis to half-time shows that are more rock concert (or striptease, depending on the "wardrobe malfunction"), as well as marching bands, waving celebrities, postgame analyses, and value-added goodies until your beer runs out or you fall happily asleep, whichever comes first.

Brands That Just Say No to Drugs Do Better

So, the worst brand offenders are people who take drugs. Why? Because the perception of *unadulterated skill* in sports makes a larger percentage of contribution to loyalty or the major league sports than personal violence. Even bigger than the percentage of contribution that trust and honesty make to a retail brand (à la Martha Stewart), and both of those values make a contribution that is nearly 10 to 12 times what punching a fan turns out to be.

Taking a Chance with Your Brand

What about gambling on sports? Does bad behavior trade at a discount or a premium? In 2005, right after the Congressional steroid hearings, the *Wall Street Journal* examined the effects the scandal had on memorabilia prices.

In 1985, Pete Rose broke baseball's 57-year-old career-hits record and by 1988, his 1963 rookie card was worth $600. In that same year, Pete was banned from baseball for life. The value of the card went up as high as $1,000, valued more than Nolan Ryan's (another record-holder career strikeout leader) whose rookie card was only worth half the value of Rose's.

Not surprisingly, loyalty metrics confirm that being able to hit or having a great jump shot makes a larger percent of contribution to loyalty and value than gambling or violence.

Some brands are more immune to bad behavior than others. Take mutual funds. They just change their names in the old mutual fund shell game. It works. Change the name and move on. Flexible, faceless, and everyone forgets after a brief interval, and the same people often continue to do the same no-no's, just in a different uniform, under a new logo.

What about a sex discrimination suit against Wal-Mart? Does a sex discrimination case degrade the brand to the point that it affects sales?

In a word, no. Why? Because the percentage of contribution that being "an equal opportunity employer" makes is a fraction of 1 percent. Gender bias does not drive loyalty, as unfortunate as it sounds.

Should people act badly and get away with it? No. But that's a moral argument. The publicity aspect of all this is a reflection of moral indignation, *not market indignation*. Does it hurt your brand? It might, and you need to know. Managing public relations in this environment is different from managing your brand, regardless of how it's reported in the news or talked about over coffee. As brand steward, use this kind of information to manage both.

When Good Brands Do Bad Things

What happens when a well-known brand, a brand people like, and a brand many people buy finds itself in a precarious and uncertain situation because of the behavior of a human spokesperson? Despite a galaxy of publicity spin doctors and lawyers galore, the situation can devastate brand equity and brand profitability.

Death is an unavoidable, self-evident eventuality for any brand. But it's even more ghastly, public, pronounced, and potentially detrimental when the brand is invested principally in a human being. We see how impermanent these brands can be, or how dependent on different degrees of public whim they turn out to be. Any sudden change in public perception of that human brand has an immediate and potentially devastating effect on the brand's equity, and soon after, its profitability.

What's more important to know is that effects differ depending on the degree to which the brand is invested in the human being. Looking back at nearly 10 years of misbehaving brands, four general patterns of public response reveal themselves (see Table 7.2):

1. A brand that is heavily invested in an actual human being (think Martha Stewart) will suffer more devastating negative effects during bad times.
2. Brands that have a human being's name on the label (like Steve Madden) but *do not* have their entire brand equity and image invested in that individual alone will see less damage to the brand during bad times.
3. The public tends to be more forgiving about human brands invested in men than they do to similar brands invested in women.
4. A brand that has *no* human association at all (like Nike), but finds itself assailed by similar negative publicity and public accusations (like those launched against Kathy Lee Gifford) will see about half the negative brand effects felt by the human brand.

But when it comes to spokespeople, even very famous spokespeople need to be more than just famous. Their association with the brand they're touting

Table 7.2
When Good Brands Do Bad Things

Brand	Equity Brand	Post-Event Equity	Loss to Brand Equity (%)
Kathy Lee Gifford	108	80	−26
Tommy Hilfiger	105	90	−14
Nike	109	96	−12
Sean Combs	108	100	−7
Steve Madden	102	100	−2
Calvin Klein	107	107	0
Martha Stewart	120	79	−34
Ralph Lauren (control)	110	111	+1

must first reinforce the brand's values. If not, the connection may do nothing or actually harm the brand. Neither of which are outcomes that most marketers actually expect to pay for.

What's more, more executives are asking more often, "What did we get for all that money we gave [insert famous name here]?" Happily, customer loyalty metrics allow marketers to evaluate the brand-to-spokesperson value—before they sign the contract. Because to be profitable today, a brand must stand for something in the consumer's mind besides being the product standing next to someone famous.

CELEBRITY BRAND ENDORSEMENTS

Henry Kissinger once mused, "the nice thing about being a celebrity is that when you bore people, they think it's their fault." Today, even no-fault boredom won't help a brand that has shelled out a large amount of money for a celebrity spokesperson who doesn't actually help the brand.

Celebrities—whether known for their entertainment or sporting skills, how they look in (or out of) haute couture, or just for their eccentricities—are increasingly known mainly for being well known. Unlike decades ago, when it was considered a no-no for respectable celebrities to soil themselves doing commercials, today virtually any famous person is willing to represent one product or another. Options are mostly limited by how much money you have to put on the table.

Borrowed versus Built Celebrity Equity

There are two basic ways celebrity brand participation or endorsement can affect a brand. The first is by creating what we all refer to as *borrowed equity*. The second results in an actual increase in brand equity.

Borrowed equity happens when the celebrity causes more attention to be paid to the brand than otherwise would be the case. This is a tactic generally relied on for generating initial or higher levels of awareness for a brand. We've found it to have limited use for well-known brands, and that there is almost no way to connect the impact of the endorsement to profitability.

Increasing a brand's equity is the result of understanding whether or not the values inherent in the celebrity reinforce (or degrade) the brand's values. This has a direct correlation to profitability, so we prefer to rely on it (especially given that the number of well-known personalities willing increases every day), and it provides a better return on the investment decision process for selection of spokespersons.

Here are two of my favorites: Nicole Kidman and Tiger Woods.

Chanel No. 5 is rated in its category at a brand strength index of 114. With Ms. Kidman, the brand is significantly reinforced, coming in at 122 (see Figure 7.2).

Buick is rated in its category at a brand strength index of 107. With Tiger Woods, the brand is measured by consumers at 115 (see Figure 7.3).

Keep in mind that the index ranges vary from category to category, but the benchmark is always 100. Straight statistical analyses show that both of these brands benefit from their celebrity associations at a significant level.

Okay, so you know that something positive is going on. Today, that's not enough. Ms. Kidman reinforces all the values that consumers use to select—and remain loyal to—a perfume. This is true as well of Tiger Woods as spokes-golfer for Buick.

Given the scads of celebrities out there willing to endorse anything for the right fee, you have many from whom to choose. So, don't rush to join the Celebrity-Flavor-of-the-Month Club.

Neither willingness nor creative ideas are good enough reasons to hire someone to front for your brand. Take a look at P. Diddy (formerly Puff Daddy) and Diet Pepsi (see Figure 7.4).

Figure 7.2
Nicole Kidman and Chanel No. 5

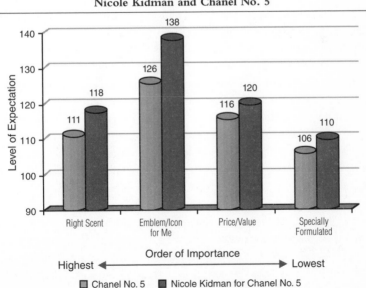

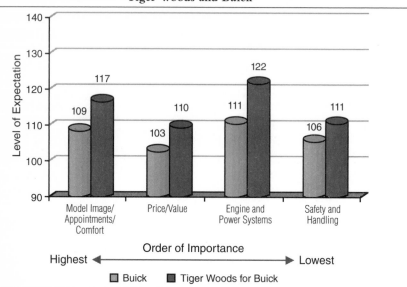

Figure 7.3
Tiger Woods and Buick

The commercial that appeared in Super Bowl XXXIX (2005) showed P. Diddy having to cadge a lift to an awards ceremony in a Pepsi truck and then having celebrities follow his lead, and it was extraordinarily amusing. His association did nothing to reinforce the brand values. It garnered awareness, but little else. You expect—or should expect—more from your investment.

This is particularly true of products launched from the "boy-are-we-lucky-we've-got-a-celebrity" value perspective, with the following unassailable logic and boundless optimism that earned the Donner party their place in history: We have a product. We have some money. We have production and distribution capability. Now all we need is some celebrity to front for us, so we can leverage his or her fame (or even notoriety) to imbue the product with instant recognition and irresistibility—and thereby guarantee success.

Among the more egregious examples of this strategic brilliance are companies that attempt to launch celebrity-branded fragrances. The celebrities don't actually design the aroma (or even the bottle). Celebrities' only real connection to the product comes when they attend the launch conference, do an advertisement or two, and maybe make a couple of high-profile personal appearances. What do the celebrities even have in common with the perfume or lotion they're pushing? Wherein lies their credibility, their "brand-to-celebrity consonance?"

Figure 7.4
P. Diddy and Diet Pepsi

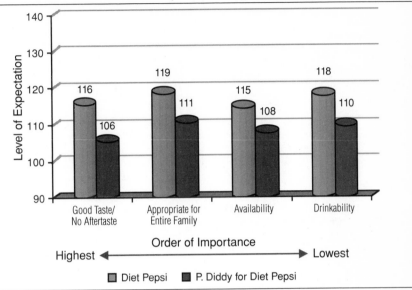

So, here's a little test to show what we mean. Table 7.3 is a list of celebrities. See if you can match them up with their signature fragrances—maybe not as easy as "Donald Trump, The Fragrance" (as opposed to "Donald Trump, The Shirt and Tie," or "Donald Trump, The Wristwatch," "Donald Trump, The University") or Paris Hilton's "Paris Hilton," but pretty easy. Fair is fair, after all. It's a real marketplace out there.

You should take your time to assess who will be better for your brand overall, but also make your selection based on the brand strategy. For example, *if* Chanel No. 5 wanted to concentrate on the driver "Emblem/Icon for Me," look at *how much* Kidman reinforces that particular category driver.

From a pure ad measurement point of view, when a brand's values are enhanced, the consumer was better engaged, paid more attention to the ad and brand, gave the brand higher positive imagery ratings, and expressed a higher propensity to purchase. When brand values are degraded, the opposite occurs. A neat fusion of attitudinal and behavioral outcomes begins to emerge.

Advertisers talk about brand and being strategic, but appraisals of this kind allow you to *insert* brand values into the assessment process and understand from a diagnostic point of view to what degree, if at all, a celebrity is helping the brand achieve strategic goals.

Table 7.3
Celebrity Fragrances

1. Andre Agassi	A. *Always With You*
2. Antonio Banderas	B. *One and Two*
3. Britney Spears	C. *Listen*
4. Cindy Adams	D. *Still*
5. Debbie Gibson	E. *Spirit*
6. Elizabeth Taylor	F. *White Diamonds*
7. Herb Alpert	G. *CK*
8. Jennifer Lopez	H. *Life*
9. Mikhail Baryshnikov	I. *Foreman*
10. Olsen Twins	J. *Full Throttle*
11. Paul Teutul	K. *Curious*
12. Priscilla Presley	L. *Gossip*
13. Ralph Lauren	M. *The Fragrance*
14. Boston Rob Mariano	N. *Electric Youth*
15. Vera Wang	O. *Misha*
16. Calvin Klein	P. *Experiences*
17. Jessica McClintock	Q. *Blue*

Answers: 1H, 2E, 3K, 4L, 5N, 6F, 7C, 8D, 9O, 10B, 11J, 12P, 13Q, 14I, 15M, 16G, 17A

The Trials and Tribulations of Martha Stewart, Queen of the Human Brands

Looking at Martha's ups and downs through the loyalty lens, what is there to learn about how to proactively manage a boss/brand spokesperson and brand behavior?

Omnimedia's mistake was that it did not measure the drivers for brand loyalty in advance. The effect of the scandal had little or nothing to do with the woman, her elegance, creativity, or business prowess. None of those perceptions changed significantly. She still had products that people wanted. All that held constant. But in that category, everything has to do with trust. And trust eroded at the rate of 30 percent. That was *the* major bomb.

Consider Bill Clinton's moral fallibility as a good parallel. Everyone cares about sex scandals because sex changes the whole equation, but you can still measure (and control) the impact so that you can decide which risk you want to assume and how much. The worst thing Clinton's handlers could have done was to let him prevaricate, parse words, dissemble, and (as it turned out) outright lie to the public—and then lie about his lying. Like Martha, Bill should have taken the hit up front, thereby defusing the whole impeachment business.

What if Martha had said, "Whoops, I made a mistake. Sorry."? Right or wrong, no one cared about the financial issue. They cared that she lied, that they may no longer be able to trust her. Our data was correct throughout the whole Martha debacle, and the phone rang off the hook with media analysts and reporters calling for predictions on where the brand and the stock was headed. If Martha had simply said she was sorry and paid the fine, the trial would probably have been avoided, and it all would have all gone away.

The biggest trick is then to (1) test to determine if the brand can sustain the hit and manage for it, and (2) get the human elements to behave accordingly. The first step can be the tougher of the two by far.

Martha, to Date.   Figure 7.5 shows where we have traveled with Martha, and what there is to learn to date. First she, prior to the scandal, Martha, the human brand (measured in loyalty toward the actual brand) was extremely strong, as were profits. She was one of the strongest brands we had ever measured. Then she, brand and profits, were down. From a loyalty perspective, we're talking lower than Enron down. Why? Because it's easier to hate a real human being than it is to hate a relatively faceless corporation. (Quick, who was the CEO for Worldcom?) Do you see what I mean?

Here's our short list of lessons learned, applicable still to Martha and to future human brand debacles worldwide. Our recommendations are based on what she needed to do to improve profitability as measured in sales based on perceptions of loyalty and trust:

- *Closure:* When it starts to drag on, go directly to jail or come clean. Put an early cap on the ongoing human drama that beat the life out of the brand. (Every time there was silence in Martha world, sales, profits, and perceptions of the brand went up.) Close down or contain the bad news. Give closure to the consumers and create an environment where loyalty has the chance to be regained.
- *Apologize:* Then there is the contrition portion of our program, the attitudinal image side of things. Check your ego at the office door. Say you are sorry soon, and say it often. Even though we are a guilt-based, not a shame-based society, public acts of humility and apologetics go a long way in keeping the loyalty bond strong. In reality, Martha's handlers successfully altered her public perception from villainess to victim. This is a tried-and-true process to re-create trust (a big category driver for Martha Stewart the brand) that will work to make people feel better about the brand and the human. From a publicity perspective, the representatives

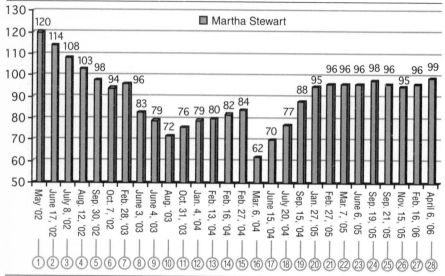

Figure 7.5
Martha Stewart Brand Equity History

1. Martha Stewart Brand: Indexed to measure Customer Value.
2. Martha Steward accused of selling ImClone shares before FDA rejection.
3. Stewart image and Martha Stewart Omnimedia (MSO) take battering. Stewart's broker's cell-phone records provided to Congress.
4. Martha Stewart stock continues to drop. Questions continue in insider trading charges.
5. MSO seeks Chief to succeed Martha Stewart. MSO shares fall on talk of plea deal.
6. Douglas Faneuil pleads guilty. Stewart quits as director of the Board. Stewart accused of making comments excusing questionable trade to keep own stock high.
7. Brand Update 2003: Brand Keys *Customer Loyalty Index* Wave 1.
8. Martha Stewart expecting federal indictment on criminal charges.
9. Martha Stewart indicted on multiple federal criminal charges.
10. Quarterly losses reported.
11. Brand Update 2003: Brand Keys *Customer Loyalty Index* Wave 2.
12. Brand Update 2004: Brand Keys *Customer Loyalty Index* Wave 1.
13. Trial questions raised in Faneuil testimony.
14. Trial: Week 1.
15. Judge throws out fraud charges.
16. Martha Stewart guilty on all counts.
17. Presentencing brand update.
18. Martha Stewart sentenced to 5 months in prison and 5 months home confinement and $30,000 fine.
19. Martha Stewart announces that she is ready to surrender to the Bureau of Prisons.
20. Brand Update 2005: Brand Keys *Customer Loyalty Index* Wave 1.
21. Week before Martha Stewart's release from prison.
22. Post 24/7 coverage of homecoming.
23. Brand update second quarter 2005.
24. 1 week after daytime television *Martha* airs.
25. *The Apprentice* premiers.
26. NBC cancels *The Apprentice*.
27. Brand update 2006: Brand Keys *Customer Loyalty Index* Wave 1.
28. Martha Stewart announces deal with Federated Stores.

are giving it an attitudinal spin. From a behavioral point of view, when people feel enough loyalty and trust to start once again buying pillows, plants, and paint, this path takes a long time.

For a company that has not been profitable in 16 quarters (and counting), the question remains, can it wait that long?

Any press is, well, just that: press. Profits come from loyalty and loyalty comes from, among other things, trust. Martha Stewart's release from federal prison generated a whirlwind of positive publicity in the general media. In the background, analysts who track Martha Stewart Omnimedia cautioned that the gush of good press does not necessarily portend a quick turnaround in the company's revenues. Pam McNeely, senior vice president and media director at Dailey & Associates of West Hollywood, put it bluntly: "We advertise in *Everyday Food* [the notably non–Martha-branded-title]. We didn't have any client resistance at all. We continue to have client resistance for the mother ship [*Martha Stewart Living,* the company's flagship magazine and cash cow that accounted for 32 percent of corporate revenue in 2004]."

Public relations hype from the practical reality of bookings and a balanced profit and loss sheet are two very different matters. Ms. Stewart's company has had a heck of a time luring back the advertisers who are still resisting a renewed association with a magazine whose figurehead is an ex-convict. But that's not all of the story. Companies advertise to sell their products and services. They don't (usually) buy advertising because of the relationship their CEO has with the magazine's CEO. They buy based on circulation and calculated Cost-Per-Thousands (CPMs). Keeping in mind that *Martha Stewart Living* lost nearly a third of its readers, it isn't a surprise that advertisers went elsewhere.

The Martha Difference: Blessed or Cursed Brand.   The difference in this brand-becomes-culture epic was for one primary reason: Martha had blessed the brand. This was the main differentiator and, because of their inseparability, their twin downfall. Even without the figures in front of you, there are a finite number of towels and sheets needed at any given time in domestic human history. Martha's ability will have to regain the blessed status (which is all about trust and loyalty) and pull Martha Stewart Omnimedia sales out of the muck and back into eveningwear black.

From where we sit now, we predict that it will be 12 to 18 months until you see profitability for Omnimedia. Not much else out there is going to change loyalty and sales significantly. Consumers were disappointed, went elsewhere, found out everything was okay in their world sans Martha. Now,

Martha must go through the Herculean task of wooing and retrieving them with her credibility, reengaging them if you will. She has to leverage them away from the Chris Maddens and Karen Neuburgers of the category. Following her house arrest in March 2005, ad revenues were up 42 percent at *Martha Stewart Living,* but still off by more than half compared with the period just prior to the scandal. Closure and contrition only go so far. The ongoing publicity problem will be that Stewart will be under a relentless and unforgiving public microscope. There will be zero margin for error in terms of loyalty lost and regained. Every negative action will be compounded, creating pressure on a woman who needs to be perceived as being kinder and gentler for many personal appearances and TV shows. Such appearances are about viewership and a curiosity factor, but they do not significantly correlate to loyalty and profitability. Martha and her handlers made a business and strategy decision to put *her* front and center, not a brand. Not only is there no guarantee of boosts to Stewart the human or the brand, there is great potential for further damage if she cannot keep up the image that people want and need to see to keep their loyalty (and faith) in all things Martha. Having a platform for product placement only goes so far, especially in the face of some *Martha: The Apprentice* contender openly weeping at the results of the Martha Stewart Jailhouse Chili Cook-Off.

A premature epilogue to the ongoing saga must be considered: Did Martha really see herself as one and the same with the brand from early on? Maybe she didn't get it or want it to be that way. That would explain much about how she comported herself in the early part of the trial—the discrepancy between being a human being (e.g., fallible, mean spirited, or put upon) and someone whose behavior is intrinsically linked to a brand, and, therefore, worthy of being managed more like a business than a personal crisis. Stewart's claim from early on was "I'm not the brand, I'm the CEO, and this is purely a personal matter." Perhaps that was her Achilles heel, focusing more about being right, or not guilty, rather than being President. Maybe Martha did not see that there would be brand effects to the degree there were. After all, every hero's tragic arc originates in a blind spot or a lack of vision, be it from bad information, hubris, or both. We can predict the effects of both, but only control for one.

According to Brand Keys loyalty measures, the Martha brand is still far below where it needs to be on a loyalty index to be profitable. And the loyalty numbers do not lie. We can't predict stock—too many variables—but we measure profitability based on loyalty and engagement. What we recommended back in October 2002 still applies: Wind the whole debacle down and get back to brand business. Consider even distancing Stewart slowly from the brand, migrating her left on the brand continuum toward label. Getting out of prison didn't hurt Steve Madden, who, no matter how much he aspires to being a gangsta brand, is really a designer label. For Martha, her personal life should remain low profile until the brand regains its former vitality—based on more diverse aspects, not vested in one individual.

Too Much Too Little Too Late?   Sharon Patrick, then-titular head of Martha Stewart Omnimedia, made the right decisions from a loyalty and strategy perspective, only she did them, for whatever reasons, nine months too late. Now, we'll see what her successor, Susan Lyne, can do with Martha's fingers back in the pie. The question remains, can Lyne do what needs to be done to the image of Omnimedia if her strategy and plan runs contrary to Stewart's?

Sixteen quarters in a row without profitability is not the place to take chances with long-term, image-based loyalty strategies. The Stewart/Omnimedia epic demonstrates perfectly a brand's fragility in being 100 percent invested in a human being. Look at the situation as a study in adding and taking out factors to see what changes in a living business model. Behavior and perception of the human brand—Stewart—is the only variable that changed significantly. The ads and media, the products on the shelf, and the distribution remained constant. Previously purchased linens and wallpaper were not disintegrating and artificial Christmas trees were not self-combusting in people's homes, creating instant and spiked demands for other brands. Stewart and the inseparable loyalty between her and the brand were what changed. We measure and track that change through a loyalty equation that is a highly accurate predictor of what actual sales are going to be and where profitability is heading—as long as everyone behaves.

Don't get me wrong, if anyone can keep pulling this hat trick comeback success off, it will be a human brand like Martha Stewart.

She ended what she called her "hideous" house arrest at her New York estate and appeared in *The Apprentice: Martha Stewart* and a daily how-to show, *Martha,* and she published a business book, so perhaps the worst is over. I just hope they are proactively watching the real loyalty indicators of what will change perception and, by positive association, profit once again. This is just a short though exceptionally prominent link in a long series of changes, hyperdramatic and highly televised, in a very competitive landscape. The queen was in the castle, now she's in the moat. There is always someone occupying both of these positions, albeit none so visibly.

Recently, one of the popular business magazines named Stewart as one of the top 20 entrepreneurs we love who "took one for the team." Perhaps.

Maybe the best hit would have been to take herself out of the game for a few innings before the rest of the team had to actually take a hit. What we do know is that it will be a slippery slope to climb in terms of recasting the image of this very human brand as the basis for regaining loyalty.

Has a new queen emerged? Who are the real pretenders to the throne of the home/all things domestic and comfy? No one is commanding the category from the high castle chambers at the writing of these prognostications. I do not see anyone even in the high garrisons. Most brands are on the field of battle, and it's pretty much a level playing field now.

LOYALTY TALES FROM THE REAL WORLD

What Happens to Reader Loyalty When the *New York Times* Lies?

The *New York Times,* a newspaper published in New York City by Arthur O. Sulzberger Jr., and distributed in the United States and many other nations worldwide, is nicknamed the "Gray Lady" and is often referred to as "the newspaper of record" in the United States, because of its high journalistic standards.

Much of the loyalty engendered by newspapers relies on what are arguably the most important assets of mass media; very high expectations revolving around the values of "trustworthy reporting," "accuracy," "truthfulness," and not being involved in "journalistic scandals," including practices like plagiarism, fabrication of quotes, facts, or other report details; staging or altering the event being putatively recorded; or anything else that may call into question the integrity of a piece of journalism. All newsreaders are familiar with newspapers publishing corrections even for minor errors soon after a story appears.

In early May 2003, *New York Times* reporter Jayson Blair resigned after being confronted with evidence that he fabricated quotes and details in at least 36 articles. It was discovered that he had faked entire interviews, plagiarized from other newspapers, and submitted false expense records to deceive the paper about his whereabouts.

All of this was bound to affect the brand equity of the *New York Times.* One could reasonably assume that this was going to impact the loyalty or readership of the paper. Or advertisers were going to question whether they wanted to have their products and services associated with a paper that had been involved in a journalistic scandal. As part of the Brand Keys *Customer Loyalty Index,* we had twice-a-year reader assessments of the *New York Times.* To judge the impact of the scandal, we took a custom measure one month after the fraud went public (see Figure 7.6).

Figure 7.6 shows there were effects to the *New York Times* brand. The question was could the brand do enough to come back to meet or exceed the expectations that readers had for journalistic integrity?

In May 2003, the paper asked "readers with information about other articles by Jayson Blair that may be false wholly or in part" to e-mail the *Times.* They ran articles correcting the record. In June, executive editor Howell Raines and managing editor Gerald Boyd resigned because of this scandal, and Joseph Lelyveld temporarily rejoined the staff as interim executive editor. In September, the *Times* named the first Editor for Standards.

Was all this enough to manage loyalty and reader values and expectations? The results are shown in Figure 7.7.

It took time, but the *New York Times* was able to rebuild its equity and was, after a time, able to retain its claim of "newspaper of record."

Douglas Adams once wrote, "nothing travels faster than the speed of light with the possible exception of bad news, which obeys its own

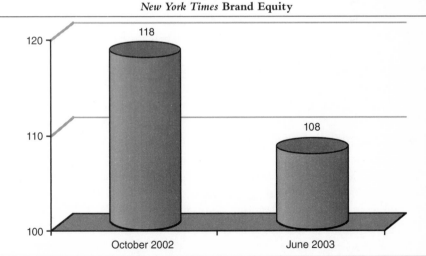

Figure 7.6
New York Times **Brand Equity**

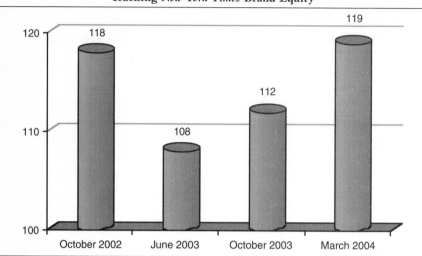

Figure 7.7
Tracking *New York Times* Brand Equity

special laws." It is well to note that customer loyalty has its own special laws too.

Q & A

Brand Actions and Loyalty Reactions

Farnoosh Torabi, NY-1 news: *When Oscar de la Renta designed a gown for Laura Bush for the inaugural ball, did that hurt his brand loyalty among die-hard Democrats?*

Robert Passikoff: To assess how an activity by one entity impacts loyalty toward another, loosely affiliated entity, you need to consider the effects on brand loyalty from dual points of view: in this case from the viewpoints of politics and designer clothing. And for this particular question, the answer is: not significantly in either case.

The component "behavior and values of the First Lady" makes a 5 percent contribution to a President's overall loyalty rating, and resides in the "compassion" driver. This is true whether she be Democrat, Republican, or Independent, but we've never factored in the "First Lady's designer" as a value. Even if the entire 5 percent was lost based on a designer's association with one political party or another, I do not expect that there would be a significant political backlash from die-hard Democrats because Oscar de la Renta designed the inaugural gown.

From the clothing design point of view, this finding is reinforced by measures from the Brand Keys *Fashion Index*. We can extrapolate percent-of-contribution items like "designs clothing worn by famous people" (at a 3 percent contribution), and "designs clothes for prominent celebrities" (also a 3 percent contribution), and make a reasoned judgment that any negative loyalty effect would be relatively minor—at least for the next four years.

Repolishing Tarnished Loyalty

James Madore, *Newsday* magazine: *How can a company or individual involved in a controversy that has tarnished their brand regain loyalty and trust?*

Robert Passikoff: In the past decade, we've seen that any sudden change in public perception of a corporation and its representatives can have an immediate—and potentially devastating—effect on the corporate brand's equity and, soon thereafter, its profitability. Think Martha Stewart.

That's because brands are based on inherent customer values. Invariably, the important, lasting values turn out not to be image items, which is why a good apology doesn't help to regain loyalty. The important issues are customer loyalty values that built the brand's success. More often than not, these values are not sexy: the really meaningful values always turn out to be ones like trust and confidence.

Look at what's happened to lifestyle brand values like "maintaining ethical business standards." Back in 1997, ethical business standards contributed only about 8 percent to loyalty. In recent months, the figure has more than doubled to a 20 percent contribution. "A brand I Trust"—a perennial favorite—always hovered around 5 percent contribution to loyalty (and therefore, profitability). That's now up to an 11 percent contribution. "Integrity" is up from 2 percent to 6 percent. Once a company or its executives remove those values from the brand equation, relatively less important items like "is really cool" or "has elegant advertising" or "is available in a variety of flavors or a full pallet of autumnal colors" have a lot of shoring up to do! By replacing those missing integrity values, the company is on its way to regaining loyalty.

Spokespeople and Brands

Valerie Seckler, *Women's Wear Daily*: *Is it necessary for a spokesperson to be the same age as the target audience to engender attention and reinforce loyalty? Is this more or less true for Baby Boomers?*

Robert Passikoff: When it comes to selecting a celebrity from an acceptable list, age is less important than the values personified by the spokesperson. Making that decision depends on both the brand in question and the target audience.

We're assuming that whatever age, the celebrity in question is appropriate for the category. Kate Moss may not have matured enough to speak for Cracker Barrel yet, and P. Diddy may not be the best representative for life insurance to follow the Art Linkletter/Ed MacMahon set. Common sense and creative sensibility do play a part in the decision of signing a spokesperson for your brand. Tiger Woods and Buick make a great fit to reinforce brand values, based on the high contribution of familiarity and trust both human and auto brand carry. Woods would work with many like brands for this reason, as long as he doesn't do too many. Robert De Niro representing American Express, however, requires different considerations of what is appropriate for the brand's values and target group: De Niro's brand values are more specific, and therefore limited, because of his public perception.

In the fashion set, appearing youthful has generally been a high percentage of contributed value to loyalty. But it is the brand's values that need—or need not—to be reinforced by elements of youth, especially when it comes to selecting a celebrity spokesperson. Ralph Lauren or Brooks Brothers won't require as much youth reinforcement as Versace or Hilfiger because of how the brand is perceived by the consumer. As such, they have a wider range of age-appropriate celebrity options open to them.

This paradigm is equally true for Gen X, Gen XBoxers, or Baby Boomers. The most appropriate spokesperson depends on the values that a brand is specifically targeting for a particular age cohort, not the age of a celebrity spokesperson. The values of the audience, and whether the spokesperson best represents them, reinforce or confirm the value of the brand.

Baby Boomers don't have to have been born between 1946 and 1964 to be an effective spokesperson or to stimulate product awareness and loyalty among Baby Boomers. Baby Boomers do have to embody the values that reinforce those of the brand to as great a degree as possible. Customer loyalty metrics provide those insights, and make the decision of a celebrity spokesperson clearer and, ultimately, more effective and profitable.

"Folks, I endorse Scrunchies because I eat Scrunchies. As God is my witness, I don't just say I eat them, I really and truly do eat them. In fact, folks, I never eat anything but. And if you don't believe me, I can supply documentation from my personal physician."

CHAPTER 8

THE FUTURE OF BRANDING

The future ain't what it used to be.

—*Yogi Berra*

FUTURE OF BRANDS: INSIGHT, INTEGRATION, IRONY, AND SOME SCENARIOS

Peer over the precipice of the next few quarters, into the horizon where expectations for future markets and earnings are already starting to poke through the pavement. A sharp eye can see that the blossoming consumer-led economy invades every niche of how businesses look at themselves and their customers. Remember, most managers are in the early stages of understanding what's next in terms of the evolution of customer listening and engagement strategies *and* where their products and services reside on the Commodity-To-Human Brand Continuum. The first step is understanding that it is possible to uncover concrete loyalty and engagement drivers that can impact existing and new brands alike.

Going forward, more reliable and specific customer loyalty and expectations research will increasingly inform every stage of modern brand creation, development, and management, from product inception all the way through to the package that sits on the shelf to the advertising that shows up on your cell phone or iPod. Each stage (product development models, differentiated archetypes, brand strategy plans, modern media planning, every possible manifestation of marketing campaigns, or calculating return on equity for a specific brand or program) can have continuity provided by specific leading indicators of value, loyalty, and engagement to guide its development and direction.

The key to maintaining a customer-savvy edge is to know what inquiry methods work for your brand; which questions to ask; how to apply the information you harvest; and how to measure the return on your marketing investment. Commit to continually using research that keeps up with shifts in customer values and loyalty and expectations and that can tie into behavior and, therefore, profits. Regularly revisit your information sources to check the steadiness, reliability, and accuracy of your customer loyalty feedback.

Finally, you should be aware that there may be an expiration date on your inquiry or research methods, contributing to a critical knowledge gap. Missing part of the customer expectations picture undermines the strength and longevity of a brand's ability to connect, and stay connected, to customers' lifestyles. More problematic, inaccurate, or overly general insights about underlying loyalty, expectation, or value changes can leave a brand team confused and frustrated while they watch their brand spin its wheels noisily but go nowhere. Coca-Cola Zero was far more than a failure to communicate.

GET A BETTER, NEWER CUSTOMER LOYALTY RESEARCH TOOL BELT

Every trade has its own version of a tool belt, from lab researchers to particle physicists to plumbers or electricians. The most successful workers update their tools to correspond with new challenges that they need to fix. What we seek to measure, explore, or build must, by definition, change because the customer and the brand landscape changes all the time. Marketers and brand managers who wish to stay in stride with future changes, must maintain their fluency with customer values. If more marketers at every level paid less lip service to flavor-of-the-week research crazes (like galvanic skin response and brain wave measures) and invested more intellectual or monetary capital in wisely upgrading their customer research gear, as an ongoing brand capital-improvement investment, we would see quite a different competitive brand set emerge in almost every product category.

It needn't be an expensive upgrade, despite the price tags some research groups hang on their work. Updating brand, category insights, and ongoing customer loyalty data typically require less than 0.1 percent of most companies' total marketing budgets. Considering the brands you can build, the customer loyalty you can strengthen, the customers you can engage with these new tools and the profits to be made, that's quite the bargain.

More companies are waking up to this despite the historic paucity of reliable, comprehensible research methods and accurate predictive customer insight information. Quantity has often trumped quality, so brand and customer research today is still largely an industry that prospers by selling big ideas and immaculately crafted opinions that may (or may not) reflect consumer values, and thereafter are doomed to deliver weak results.

Asking the right questions, if you haven't invested time to figure out what's going on, can be hard. You can ask the questions, but most of the answers don't predict anything close to reality. Research methods and interpretation vary widely across the industry. Few brand-side people have time to learn what questions to ask in research designs, let alone question the execution or conclusions. Let's raise the accountability and accuracy benchmarks and commit to good tools and market plans that are based on quantified customer expectations—hard evidence and predictive insights about customer engagement, loyalty trends, and brand opportunities.

We need to create a robust union of emotion, psychology, and free market forces. This is sophisticated stuff, but the results pay off when you play the game strategically. The methods of leading-indicator research can be likened to counting cards in a very large blackjack game: You know what card is likely to show up next before it hits the table face up. In the market, you know what brand attributes, media vehicles, or marketing activities are going to work to change behavior and sell stuff before anyone else. You stack the odds in your favor for meeting consumer expectations, the synonym for success. With true brand loyalty measures, the odds for a win are very high while the risk is relatively low.

ACCURACY WILL BE EVERYTHING

Accuracy in customer research and predictive forecasting will increasingly allow traditional R&D folks to break out of the test kitchen/laboratory mentality as research models become defined more by the preferences of the consumer, and less by what the factories or labs are able to produce. Brands that have the research tools to remain well calibrated to market preferences will remain high in the new order of brand leaders.

INTEGRATION: THE FUTURE OF MARKETING

I was speaking at the Brand Power 2005 conference, and the presenter prior to me made a statement about how "perception was reality." I corrected her, politely I hope, by pointing out that today perception is, well, perception, and *profitability is reality*. In order for companies to engage customers and drive profitability and shareholder value, they need to make substantive changes in the way they determine the true measure of their categories and customers.

We've made the point that to optimize success, companies need to identify and leverage the things that make the largest percentage of contribution to loyalty. But unfortunately the "things" you'll need to leverage most often aren't located in a single, corporate silo, no matter now much Marketing, Planning, or Research Departments insist that's the case.

This places extra stress on a structure that marketers have been discovering wasn't up to code in the first place. Integrated Marketing guru and legendary professor Don Schultz of Northwestern University has pointed out that success in this new marketplace—even one optimized by customer loyalty metrics—demands the integration of the firm's entire set of capabilities into a seamless system. He envisions a marketing machine capable of providing a totally integrated offer of what consumers value—Integrated Marketing (IM).

To offer twenty-first-century, bionic consumers the values they desire, corporations will be forced to view the marketing function in the broader context of integrated efforts to truly engage customers and engender loyalty. The way marketing planning and marketing activities must be conducted will be radically different from the way they have been historically performed. Jim Stengel, the often-quoted Procter & Gamble Global Marketing Officer, said, "without the right measurement, we really don't know how well our efforts work. We don't know if we are in touch with our consumers. We cannot continue to apply traditional thinking to the new world of technology and marketing channels available to us today." To do this successfully, we must demand higher degrees of precision in:

- Identifying and measuring customer values
- Managing these predictive insights with great skill
- Creating more strategic alignment and coordination

When we speak of IM we mean something more than taking 30 percent of your TV budget and allocating 15 percent to Internet activities and 15 percent to product placement on this week's must-see reality show. Integrated Marketing will force companies to reach out across the silo boundaries that have traditionally formed the corporate organization chart, and draw on all the resources and capabilities a company can muster to guarantee success—strategic alignment. So, you need something to help attain alignment.

How do four people with different silo perspectives, partial data, very different interpretations, and much at stake form a common view?

The view does depend on which mountain (department silo) you're standing. The alignment comes from getting behind the consumer-driven output for the category. It is not what the department thinks but what the consumer thinks. You integrate by getting behind the directions the customers provide to you.

Don Schultz has identified five barriers as to why IM efforts have generally failed. Happily, it is possible to offset some of these implementational challenges by integrating customer loyalty metrics into the management strategic dashboard. Briefly outlined, the barriers (and loyalty solutions) are:

IM Barrier 1: The attitudinal measurement model generally being used is difficult to connect to behavioral change or, ultimately, to organizational financial return.

Loyalty Solution 1: Loyalty metrics correlate with positive behaviors and— when properly configured—correlate with profitability and sales. Measuring corporate efforts in terms of *how* those efforts affect/support/alter brand equity provides a *leading indicator measure of profitability.*

IM Barrier 2: There is often no cohesion or agreement inside the various functional units and even less between them.

Loyalty Solution 2: Utilize the customer-derived order of importance of the category drivers as the foundation from which to manage process and strategic alignment. This allows you to expose employees to how the customers see the category and functional units to align themselves (or to be taught *how* to align themselves) with these values on a functional and cross-functional unit basis.

By revealing the customer attribute, benefit, value (ABVs), and expectation set for all the components that make the company, product, or service what it is, employees can clearly understand the percentage of contribution that *each* of the ABVs brings to loyalty and, ultimately, profitability. They may not agree, but it provides the foundation for understanding how customers and employees see the category and how areas of responsibility can be most effectively allocated (see Figure 8.1).

IM Barrier 3: IM implementation resides at the middle levels.

Loyalty Solution 3: Clearly this is not ideal, but it is usually where it shakes out. Most generally it is employees who have all of the responsibilities but none of the authority and must implement the IM process. Using the assessments from "Loyalty Solutions" 1 and 2, integration of the customer loyalty metrics provides a more process-driven-attribute-based identification of *where* responsibility most/best lies, and that helps settle "turf" issues.

Figure 8.1
How Constituencies "See" the Category

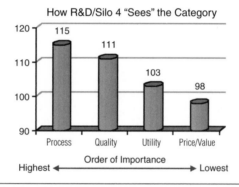

IM Barrier 4: No connection between employees and internal and external customers exists. It is often difficult for employees to understand that the work they perform, the activities they conduct, and the responsibilities they have are related to customer satisfaction and customer loyalty.

Loyalty Solution 4: Reorganizing the customer loyalty output so that you have a functional unit-specific process map will identify not only where the connections exist but also *how* specific process items make specific contributions to loyalty and profitability. For example, on a simple loyalty driver basis, acknowledgments or responsibilities might look like Figure 8.2.

IM Barrier 5: The greatest difficulty in developing and implementing IM programs is the lack of strategic management calculus or planning systems that can be used at the senior management level.

Loyalty Solution 5: The integrated loyalty metrics provide the benchmark for creating a program or employee-activity return on investment (ROI) mechanism. See "Loyalty Solution" 1.

Figure 8.2
Marketing Silos and How they Contribute to Loyalty

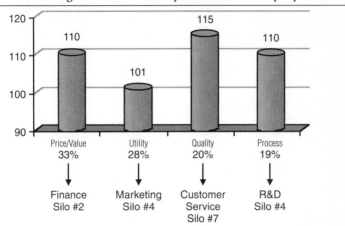

Again, as we are able to measure a corporation's financial position by its price/earnings ratio, the same reasoning can be applied by calculating a value called a *brand multiple:*

$$\text{Brand Multiple} = \frac{\text{Increase in brand equity due to initiative}}{\text{In-going brand equity}}$$

The integration of the loyalty methodology allows for the incorporation of customer-driven need, value, and expectation data that can be easily integrated into the IM management strategic dashboard.

Customer loyalty output correlates highly with positive behavior and engagement, allowing for realignment of internal activities and strategic perspectives. Integrated Marketing identifies the customer perspective regarding process and allocates responsibilities based on individual processes and the percentage of contribution various activities make. Perhaps most important, it provides senior management with benchmark measures from which return on equity (ROE) calculations can easily and reliably be configured and communicated.

It is clear that to be successful, IM requires a reverse-engineering mentality; start with customer loyalty and work back to see what must be done for the corporation to deliver better value. Identify which part of the company is most capable of delivering against those values and you're half-way to integration. Manage to align within the company, and you're home free.

Keeping corporate culture open, inspired, informed, and innovative is a requisite for authentic connections—engagement—to your target audience. No matter how well a company can predict or anticipate customer trends, the people who comprise a business must reflect the values of the customer just as much as the product or service itself does. Retailers and banks are just beginning to learn this lesson.

What mergers and acquisitions were to the 1990s, engagement and conversations based on customer knowledge are to the twenty-first century: They are keys to growth. Businesses have to compete for and earn loyalty and trust, and those who can identify customer expectations far out on the radar screen, and have the agility and process in place to meet or exceed them, will be several steps ahead of the competition in engaging customers.

Customers expect their brands and the companies that make the brands to know who they are and what they like. This is a tall order, but it can be filled if a business integrates both internally and externally so that it is singing the same tune regardless of where or how it intercepts its customers. A seamless program of brand offerings and communications must ring true at every touch point, from ad campaign to web site to customer-service call center.

And the lovely thing about real integration is that it breeds highly engaged, true believers both inside and outside a company: The more people who are brought on board, the more others will be brought on board through word of mouth and that marvelous thing called *brand advocacy*.

TRENDS AND WATCHES

Brand Keys loyalty metrics are an early warning system for shifts in values. Waiting for shifts to manifest as a cultural phenomenon (i.e., tipping points), be it Hush Puppies or Harleys, means that it's often too late to take advantage of them from a marketing standpoint.

Even when trend watchers are right, you do not know on which aspect of the trend to focus, or if you are focusing too late. A good example of this is people who are increasingly concerned with health. The health trend is up among almost all aspects of this category. Some, like yoga, will go up farther. Some, like Atkins, will go away, or go the way of the soon-to-be-created nutritional generics.

The details are in the drivers.

Only specific leading-indicator measurements in each subcategory of health will tell you whether to invest in themed spas and fitness clubs, in healthy snack food, in Suzanne Sommer's ab machine, or in Christie Turlington's guide to complete holistic fitness for women. Only the drivers for loyalty know. Until you do, you are making a very educated, informed prediction—a smart guess.

You can't rely on the theme of the moment like mean-spirited or shock-based reality TV shows or any of the low-life afternoon "bleeper specials," where vile people admit to humiliating or obscene behavior, confront other vile people, and keep lunging at them, only to be semi-restrained by "Security," to provide vehicles to advertise, promote, or place products.

At some point, the base category drivers that build loyalty for these shows will actually reach a saturation point. In light of the way expectations have been growing, viewers may become immune to the current levels of shock and scandal and move on. It's not as if this hasn't happened before. Disengagement isn't a new phenomenon.

Leading-indicator loyalty research can determine just how far audiences are willing to go, when the floodgates are likely to open, and whether this is a suitable media environment for a brand.

THE POWER, AND FUTURE, OF CHOICE

Here's the lay of the brand landscape.

Consumer expectations are up on average 28 percent. Brands, however, are only keeping up with those expectations by about 6 to 8 percent. Brand differentiation—the key to fueling brand equity and customer loyalty—is on life support. What's a brand to do? We offer the following question and answer:

Question: As you can't or don't know how to substantively change the product or service to meaningfully meet or exceed consumer expectations that will give you a differentiating advantage, what do you do?

Answer: Let the consumers contribute values that go into actually developing the configuration or appearance of the product or service so that it *is* differentiating.

Results from the most recent Brand Keys *Customer Loyalty Index* show that "customization/personalization" makes a 30 percent contribution to brand differentiation and, therefore, to loyalty and profitability (see Figure 8.3).

Personalization and customization don't *have* to be what might be regarded as significant aspects of the purchase. Not everyone is going to let you build an athletic shoe virtually from scratch. When it comes to brand differentiation, small things count, too. Ten categories that the *Customer Loyalty Index* has identified where personalization and customization are making themselves most felt are:

Figure 8.3
Customization and Personalization

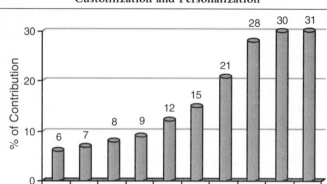

1. *Airlines:* Food (type and time served), entertainment choices
2. *Automotive:* Virtually all aspects of available models
3. *Backpacks and Bags:* Design, color, and interior compartments
4. *Clothing:* Design, fonts, color, and text
5. *Computers:* Look, desktop, sounds, and mouse
6. *E-tail/Web Sites:* Personalized recommendations
7. *Fragrances:* Customized
8. *Health/Diet:* Programs, diets, equipment, bicycles, and skateboards
9. *Mobile Phones:* Wallpaper, rings (selection and composition), games, and applications
10. *Shoes:* Design, base/mesh/accent/lining colors, logo, and plate/heel

In light of the increase in contribution that these values are making, companies have discovered that customization isn't a "nice to have" anymore but a "need to have." Not only are consumers actively seeking such opportunities, they are even willing to pay for them.

Computers and web sites have made enormous strides in allowing consumers to more easily interact with brands. From a process engineering point of view they've made it infinitely easier for brands to allow for personalization and customization—beyond your initials on clothing or a logo on a golf ball—that create a differentiating sense about the brand. Create differentiation, and you create higher levels of brand equity, brand bonding, loyalty, and profit. These days, that's a need to have, too.

The trend toward customization is really just having its surface scratched. In this movement, the power does not lie in the hands of the corporations. The direction and velocity of customization, and hence brand success, is being determined by consumers. Large or small, successful companies will be listening and following before they differentiate so that they can rise as high as possible on the expectations scale. Many twentieth-century brands, even the really well-known demibrands, will further morph into Category Placeholders because they do not stand for anything exceptional, differentiated, or meaningful. They just stand there. These Category Placeholders will be regarded more as shelf SKU numbers by retailers than as truly distinct products that are sought after for specific reasons by customers.

WHAT'S EXPECTED OF THE FUTURE: WHAT DO WE KNOW AND WHERE ARE TRENDS GOING?

From a *007, Blade Runner,* or *Dick Tracy* point of view, mini televisions still sound cool. They have been around for years and are even on watches and phones. But keep in mind that differentiation via technology and style is effective as a *possibility.* But neither the R&D folks nor the design department are defining or pushing expectations like they used to, whether we are speaking of plasma screens (invented over 80 years ago) or mini skirts (first introduced in the swinging 1960s). Staying laser focused on customer expectations builds a predictable loyalty response into the development process, where customers increasingly choose the direction.

Today, we are in the realm of pervasive, real-time information access for almost anything, if we're willing to pay for it. *The greatest market effect of individual and mass information access is the accelerated rate of change in expectations and brand preferences.* As online brand conversations and information sharing increase, there is a corresponding increase in how those exchanges affect expectations, increase or erode loyalty, and define value. This expedited communication environment ratchets up the means through which people develop alternate sets of expectations and values. Mind control or persuasion via the tube or the Web is a distant runner-up to word of mouth (or mouse) among the growing ranks of the hyperinformed consumers.

Information flow and access is making it harder for marketers to use traditional methods and measurement or traditional branding strategy to gauge customer behavior or preferences.

Marketer's Note to Self: This trend is going to get larger, and my job harder, unless I know where and how to access customer preferences for guidance and direction of my brand. Investigate Customer Loyalty assessments. Let's look at the future of a few categories as examples.

Gambling and Vacation (as in Vegas)

Are Disney and Vegas oil and water? Perhaps, but they may just represent a bipolar continuum that indicates people are looking for a recombinant vacation experience that meets or exceeds their expectations.

The aspect here is much the same way that McDonald's thinks that Burger King is its only major competitor, or Major League Baseball thinks the other three major American sports are the only competition it has to really worry about: Similar to almost every category found where the sun shines on modern markets, the consideration set has vastly expanded. It's no longer as black and white as the days of choosing between Florida and the Poconos, Whopper or Big Mac, Florida or Vegas. There are overlapping sets of values that all need to be fulfilled way beyond price.

Why does Vegas keep peaking? Because it can at least claim to provide almost all of the expectation clusters in one package destination.

Artificiality on and off the strip is the intentional rule instead of the exception. Disney wants to fool you, Vegas wants to excite you.

What are the differences? "What goes on in Vegas stays in Vegas" is not a position that works really well when you substitute Disney World for Vegas. Some day we may see more commingling of even those expectations. Yes, Vegas is becoming a family destination.

Here are eight things you probably think of when you think Vegas:

1. Desert.
2. Rat Pack.
3. Gambling.
4. Brothel.
5. Don't have to behave the way I do at home.
6. I can rely on the shows I want to see.
7. Shady gangster heritage like the Godfather movies.
8. Very much like Europe without the travel hassles and Europeans.

When most folks are looking for a domestic family vacation, they think Universal Studios, Disney, or the Grand Canyon. These places meet their expectations. That's tough to do in destination travel. These three are ahead of the other brand curve in terms of this and other categories. There is permission *to believe,* and there is also a unique, proprietary tacit approval that does not resonate in other brands.

The Blurring of Reality and Imagination

Welcome to cyberlife purposeful. Entertainment and information have become one and the same—competitive sets joined at the hip.

Angelina Jolie, enhancement notwithstanding, does not look like a video character for nothing. Reality is reality (and profitability). It reformats itself all the time. Most of the live culture in LA is still in the yogurt. Basing your movies on video games is not very original, but it's getting into our collective conscience very effectively. I personally do not want my kids to develop loyalty to Grand Theft Auto. But until expectations change, or profits fall, such trends will increase as long as there are values and dollars to support them.

Music Distribution

Retailers will have to keep up with expectations for what makes brick-and-mortar purchasing exciting and entertaining. Popular culture, with its rabid consumption of music and technology, may be the first to show us how to follow what the people want. Ironically, one manifestation may be the resurrection of vinyl on the shelves. It may be plugging in (or popping out) your wireless device, downloading, and paying for exactly the songs you want. Customer-driven, easy-to-use customization will be king.

Moving forward, lifestyle elements, listening devices, music-related paraphernalia like T-shirts, posters, and other artist-related merchandise may cater to what people want in a retail music environment.

Some futurists speculate that nightclubs and music stores may merge into a nearly 24-hour commercial music entity. Who knows what it will be called. Naming the trend is not nearly as valuable as predicting and capitalizing on it. Look at what *Virgin, Tower Records, Borders,* and *Barnes & Noble* keep trying as evidence of what resonates and what flops vis-à-vis what people expect and believe in when it comes to their never-ending thirst for music.

It is interesting to note how a wealth of virtual music services like iTunes are making themselves felt in slaking the thirst of music lovers. Recently, a number of oldies, songs that had not been hits for nearly a quarter of a century, are making a comeback on the digital charts. Since fans can now download a favorite single, that's what they've been doing.

But the ability for fans to cherry-pick a single, favorite song is causing problems for the music business that relies on the "Greatest Hits of [fill-in-the-blank performer]" to provide huge profits to its bottom line. Now, fans only have to buy one song (at a substantially lower price) instead of a compilation CD to get the song that they wanted in the first place.

One hope is that will all balance out. With so many more songs digitally available, and with downloading of music becoming as easy as going online, one view is that more fans will buy more music, since iPods and MP3 players provide virtually unlimited shelf space to store music. But so far the increase in sales of digital singles hasn't been large enough to offset the drop in CD sales over the past few years.

Is it loyalty to song, performer, store (virtual or bricks and mortar), or system? One thing is for certain: Fulfilling people's expectations and identifying the most valuable elements of the experience of collecting music or anything else for that matter will be what keeps them coming out of their houses and into the stores. What works for youth engaged in online buying, swapping, napstering, ripping, burning, mixing, iTuning their heads off will be an entirely different set of expectations and definitions of value than what the industry is used to. Music vendors will need to continually tap into, meet and, ideally, exceed those expectations if loyalty and brand survival are to be assured.

Nanotechnology

For most of us, the efficacy of a brand is ultimately determined by how we use something in real life. To remain competitive, manufacturers and their technologies must get in step with customer expectations for goods and services that have certain attributes that both work and demonstrate value. The typical time to market between a discovery or development of a technology and a ready-to-sell brand in the past century was anywhere from 10 to 40 years, depending on the category. Time to market, especially when a feature, design, or function provides clear competitive advantage, is getting smaller by the year.

That brands can now test what customers value and believe in *before* they go down one or more lines of development is quite a boon for brand design and R&D efficiency.

Consider the little things we may not even know to ask for by brand name. People's expectations for the function and promise of devices will increase much in the same way that Teflon became a requisite for making surfaces slippery or cameras and video recorders made telephones more desirable. The difference between what becomes a branded, value-add element and what becomes an *expected performance-enhancing ingredient* included without mention is a function of how the customer views that feature/driver in that particular category. Think of it like the sticker with "Intel Inside" printed on it that appeared on PCs for so many years, assuring customers that the machines had the best ingredients.

A mixture of wee molecules that keep your glasses, windshield, or even bathroom mirror from fogging up is going to be the new must have if it fills a large enough expectations gap.

Ionic or silver-based antibacterial coatings on kitchen sinks, counters, or fridges will thrive or die because people's expectations for a germ-free life change with perceptions of what reduces germ risks and promotes personal, family, or communal hygiene. Brands that correctly predict, partner with, or incorporate these technological add-ons based on highly specific customer preference and leading expectation studies will effectively engage consumers and will capture the lion's share of loyalty when they arrive in the market. Customer loyalty metrics can predict the success—or failure—of such brand efforts.

The truth is, until the customer votes, *we just don't know.*

Q & A
Loyalty and Corporate Responsibility

Lenore Skenazy, *New York Daily News*: *We've been told that in the future we'll see more companies linking their brands to social issues. Does loyalty increase in appreciation of corporate responsibility, like Kraft pulling its junk-food ads from kids' TV or McDonald's no longer supersizing its meals?*

Robert Passikoff: Most of what we see from large corporations is a slow-motion knee-jerk reaction to the market, to media, and to any public outcry. Perhaps some of these companies are responding to a higher calling, *but most are reacting to consumer value shifts that are attacking profitability.* They react because often they don't have systems in place that provide advance threat warnings. McDonald's radar was not sensitive enough to see that notions of health and nutrition were going to come up and affect consumer behavior. The cold, hard business facts are that companies do what they need to do when they are forced to do it— when the bottom line starts to move south. The question is: If they knew what the brand loyalty effects were going to be ahead of time, *would they get proactive and turn that knowledge into a loyalty differentiator* for market share and revenue opportunity?

Whether loyalty increases due to a change in brand behavior depends both on the emotional value of the issue and how a company anticipates or reacts to it. Anita Roddick's *The Body Shop* was, and still is, such a success because it established itself in critical value areas ahead of the tipping points of the trends turned requirements in the exploding beauty products industry: fair trade, local sustainable production, natural ingredients, and so on. Certainly, if you wait too long, the negative values become too entrenched.

If you could see problems that were coming at you a year or more before they showed up on the public's radar screen, it would be a possible, wise, and profitable business decision to get a step ahead of the situation so that you look like a champion of proactive change and preventative policies.

Given our nontraditional approach to brand equity and customer loyalty research, healthy debate ensues. Folks like you tend to engage us in very strategic discussions regarding the how's and why's of opting for *leading-indicator* brand or customer insights compared to data derived from whatever research methodology you have in place. Much of the discussion is spent clarifying the critical differences that predictive brand and loyalty metrics provide.

Q & A

In an attempt to let all of you benefit from our many discussions, we have assembled a collection of the most common questions asked by Fortune 500 CMOs and brand managers.

Question: *How do the Customer Loyalty Metrics that you describe as achievable really differ from other futurist systems?*

Robert Passikoff: Did you ever experience a situation where all of your research pointed to a particular brand position, everyone executed flawlessly, and the product bombed? Our friends at Coca-Cola who were responsible for C2 can relate. That was a classic (no pun) case of the difference between knowing what customers *say* they are thinking (via focus groups or direct inquiry) and what they are *really* thinking (addition of emotional/psychological *indirect* inquiry).

The key is how the measures are captured. The customer loyalty metrics system we propose combines two types of questioning, one to capture the emotional/psychological side of the consumer, and one to capture the rational side. Traditional research methods tend to use just one or the other, creating a strong bias to the data that inhibits brand differentiation and growth.

The customer loyalty metrics we propose identify which brand attributes will drive future customer purchases 12 to 18 months before those attributes show up in focus groups or on traditional research radar screens.

This method overcomes the limits of direct inquiry by revealing the underlying, largely unrecognized, difficult-to-articulate emotions and values that fuel loyalty to a category or brand in the first place. Such indirect methods are designed to capture unarticulated values, real expectations, and what consumers are willing to believe about your brand—things that might otherwise never come to the surface using standard research but that are the motives behind consumers' actual buying decisions. Thus, the need for psychology: We cannot always (or do not always want to) articulate what we are really feeling.

Question: *How is it possible to measure and produce leading indicators of future purchases?*

Robert Passikoff: I recently asked the Global VP of Marketing for a leading cell phone manufacturer if there was anything he still wished he knew about their consumers. He answered, "Yes, what they want next."

Measuring what will drive future purchase is simply a function of being able to determine what brand attributes will meet or exceed consumer expectations. Again, it takes a combined indirect/direct inquiry approach to do it. For example, cell phones that take pictures exceeded consumer expectations of cell phones, thus generating pull and moving the business forward.

The how is where so many metrics systems talk the talk, but cannot deliver due to the limitations of their methodology and analysis. Discovering what it will take to exceed consumer expectations happens via our ability to capture and combine the rational and emotional factors that drive human attitudes and behavior.

The outputs are absolutely accurate descriptions of how customers view (and will continue to view) the category, how they compare brands, and, because those outputs correlate so highly with sales, how they will buy. Measures of real expectations allow us to identify ABVs that consumers will use to make their future purchases—and their loyalty decisions.

The proof is in the fact that you can correlate well-crafted metrics with positive market behavior, share, and profits. For example, in first quarter 2003, when the entire world was riding the Krispy Kreme stock price up, our customer loyalty metrics system accurately predicted that the brand was heading for a fall due to unmet consumer needs/expectations. By third quarter 2003, "new store sales were below expectations" according to the Home Office; and by second quarter 2004, the average weekly retail customer counts had dropped severely, leading to a stock price decline of nearly 60 percent.

Question: *If these methods can predict future purchases, why can't they predict sales?*

Robert Passikoff: Loyalty metrics have been shown to correlate closely with sales. If your brand is positioned in line with those attributes that meet or exceed consumer expectations, consumers will behave positively toward your brand in the marketplace: They will buy; sales will increase, or vice versa (like Krispy Kreme). Once you measure the impact your marketing efforts are making on consumers' future behavior toward the brand (predictive loyalty metrics), these metrics will correlate with sales. That's as close as we can get to outright sales predictions, short of building a market model that allows for all the variables affecting sales since sales and profitability are the result of many functions in an organization, in addition to many external factors.

You have two main choices to get predictive sales information: Build an econometric model that is very, very sophisticated, or do as we do—identify future sales behavior via predictive attitudinal and behavioral means.

Question: *How can putting customer loyalty metrics in place enable me to demonstrate marketing ROI?*

Robert Passikoff: Simple. By putting true, predictive loyalty metrics in place, you will be able to quantify the elusive gap between marketing spend and fiscal ROI/sales. How do you do this? By quantifying the impact your initiatives made and will make on brand equity. Here's an equation you can use as a marketing performance model to demonstrate your ROI:

$$\text{Brand equity} \xrightarrow{\text{drives}} \text{Customer loyalty} \xrightarrow{\text{drives}} \text{Profitability}$$

So, when you are challenged by the fiscal side of the company to show the ROI, take responsibility for measuring what you are capable of influencing:

- The return on your brand's equity (defined as consumers' overall perception of your brand *not* a fiscal valuation)
- Whether your efforts are positively driving future purchase and loyalty, which *will* drive the company's bottom line

Question: *How do you measure whether your campaign tactics are positively driving future purchases and loyalty?*

Robert Passikoff: Keep the marketing performance model equation in mind.

First, put the measures in place and establish leading-indicator benchmarks for your brand equity and customer loyalty. Because this method is capable of evaluating what *will* impact consumer behavior toward your brand, it can by definition evaluate which marketing or media initiatives *will* impact consumer behavior. We call this our *Brand-to-Media Engagement* (B2ME) application. It lets you prequalify and optimize any and all initiatives in advance of the spend to make sure that the media channels and other program elements are aligned (i.e., consonant) with the expectations of your consumers.

You would, for example, have the ability to assess various advertising options right next to experiential marketing opportunities right next to product placement opportunities to find out which ones best match what consumers feel about the brand and the vehicles available for carrying the brand message. This approach redefines leveling the playing field.

Question: *So, how is a B2ME application different than all the other marketing-mix models out there?*

Robert Passikoff: Traditional marketing-mix models require existing brand data (i.e., transaction data) against which to model. They rely heavily on marketing costs as a key variable. Besides other impediments, an obvious flaw is that they *omit the brand's values and the consumer's emotions.* The B2ME application is the exact opposite: It measures how well each individual media vehicle or marketing initiative reinforces (or degrades) the brand's equity because only a reinforcing initiative can positively drive future purchase and loyalty. Those initiatives are the marketing spends you would want to make.

Question: *We tend to avoid black-box research methods. How would you incorporate your method into ours without having to reinvent our process?*

Robert Passikoff: The beauty of predictive customer loyalty metrics is that they can be used as overlays to existing measures. A major credit card company came to us unable to pinpoint a truly differentiating brand position for a large Asian market. This company had 77 different brand metric points being measured monthly in many markets around the world. Our system took the same 77 brand assessment areas, and, by using the combination of psychological and rational inquiry, was able to clearly identify which ones would provide the optimum positioning, thereby cutting research costs and time by focusing on roughly 30 percent of the points that made 85 percent of the difference in the outcome.

We can add a unit of Brand Keys measures to your standard tracking survey to make the results more relevant, predictive, and actionable. We call this *optimization*. Optimizing your current research approach by using this type of methodology will result in getting much closer to the truth—in a far more cost- and time-efficient manner—of what's going on and what's going to go on in your marketplace.

"It may be a figment of my imagination, Herb, but I thought I just felt another shock wave go through the business community."

CONCLUSION

The only thing to do with good advice is pass it on. It is never any use to oneself.

—*Oscar Wilde*

Nowhere is the recent phenomenon of overchoice more blatant than in the field of ideas. Bookshelves grunt under the tonnage of millions of papers purporting to guarantee success in your strategic planning, advertising, branding efforts, engagement, profit generation, equity building, shareholder value—or [*insert buzz word of the month*].

Weep for all those dead trees. With such great wisdom available, we can only ask, *"So, how come 85 percent of all new product launches fail? Why do so many confident brands shrivel?"* In a world where the bionic consumer rules, where profitability is more difficult to obtain, and where mind-numbing sameness is more likely to occur than meaningful differentiation, companies, products, and services that used to be real brands have now morphed into well-known, but virtually indistinguishable, Category Placeholders. Engaging the consumer is exponentially more difficult.

You can quibble over the degree to which they have lost their brandness. You can differ with us regarding specific vocabulary, but the situation becomes increasingly more difficult for companies to overlook.

Something odd is about. *Predicting Market Success* was written to address that oddity, and suggest ways to turn it to your advantage.

Savants point out the zany acceleration of change, the convergence of—and conflict among—many aspects of modern life. In this chaos, of particular interest to marketers, is the Brownian Motion of consumer values. Where are those values going, how fast, in which categories, and how will that affect your planning and your ability to engage customers?

When considering changes of this magnitude, both in market and in measurement, it helps to be open-minded, not tied to conventional ways of thinking about brands, customers, and assessments. It helps to be able to face the challenges of differentiation, return on investment (ROI), and profitability without having to mumble incoherently toward the floor—with no good reason or answer for "what was it?"—when such questions and issues come up, as they will more and more frequently. It helps not to rely entirely on research relics of the past century—before all those bionic consumers were suddenly sprung full-blown, Internet-wired, TiVo'd, and iPod-carrying, from the economic/brand primordial—actually postmordial—ooze.

The passion in what we've written about, our philosophy and practice regarding predictive metrics and engagement and customer loyalty, our conviction and commitment to the subject is probably not where doubts and fears may still linger, even those tweaked by my occasional outburst of frustration slipping through our "trying-to-be-balanced" filter.

Call us *leading-edge, avant-garde* or *pie-in-the-sky wishful thinkers.* Call us anything you like, but the success of predictive customer loyalty metrics cannot be denied.

The anecdotal evidence and the correlations provided by an independent business equity valuation firm prove the direct link between Brand Keys loyalty metrics and company value and profitability.

So, what are we to make of all this?

It helps to understand that relying on your past experience is no longer synonymous with strategic thinking. You can rely on experience only so much. With everything, including consumers, changing so fast and in so many ways, what good is experience? If you've spent 30 years analyzing markets, what guarantee is there you haven't been digging yourself into a 30-year rut? Could you have been doing the same thinking for one year, 30 times in a row? Although the basics of human nature remain eternal, what causes a consumer to meaningfully bond with a brand in a particular category, unfortunately, does not.

It also helps to avoid creating and using strategic maps that lead you into "what-if-we world." You know the place. What if we move our entire budget from TV to Internet? What if we work only with agencies that win lots of creative awards? What if we focus group all our ideas before we implement? What if we rely on online panels and buy research by the ton? What if we measure all the consumer touch points involved in awareness and consideration and purchase and advertise every place? What if we sponsor only reality shows? What if we product place in only really, really big summer blockbusters? More and more, what-if-we world is becoming the place where brand and desperation meet.

If you have read this book, you understand why that is a very bad place to be.

So, how do you avoid ending up in what-if-we world? We're not suggesting you jettison all your traditional tools or your accumulated market and research expertise. But please keep an open mind about the twenty-first-century alternatives. With customer loyalty metrics, you can optimize the effectiveness of your traditional tools. You can use them to help you design more insightful, more time- and cost-effective questionnaires that give you the data that lead to precise indicated actions. Loyalty metrics let you optimize the effectiveness of your media plan for virtually any advertising, public relations, Internet, sponsorship, or product-placement effort. They help you to engage consumers in your marketing efforts. They provide the basis for reliable ROI predictability.

What *is* clear is that the ever-expanding world of brands needs an informed action plan that makes sense to people on the brand side of the equation, *and* accurately tracks what people on the consumer side actually feel and actually do with their loyalty and their dollars. The current brand strategy conundrum is ubiquitous and gaining momentum for struggling start-ups and Fortune 500s alike.

This crisis is the result of one factor beyond any other market force: the failures of business to measure, understand, and predict loyalty—the preferences and expectations, now and moving forward, of the very modern, twenty-first-century, bionic consumers.

There's no time for bickering over blame. Suddenly, it's all about the edgiest, quarter-to-quarter business survival in our lifetime, if not anyone's. Data-mine your traditional lagging-indicator research all you want. But keep in mind that most people think in the box, bright people think outside the box, and those who will truly be successful will walk (or run) as far away from the twentieth-century box as possible and start thinking from another perspective, whatever its shape.

Today, that perspective is predictive customer loyalty.

"Somewhere out there, Patrick, is the key to increased sales. I want you to find that key, Patrick, and bring it to me."

EPILOGUE

When at some future date the high court of history sits in judgment on each one of us we will be measured by the answers to four questions: Were we truly men of courage? Were we truly men of judgment? Were we truly men of integrity? Were we truly men of dedication?

—*President John F. Kennedy*

THE LIGHT AT THE END OF THE TUNNEL

Compared to Introductions, Epilogues are tough. In an Introduction, you can focus on what is to come, create some interest in what is new, exciting, and innovative. Give the reader something to look forward to in the coming pages.

In an Epilogue, there's none of that forward-looking excitement. You've read the book, turned down the corners of some pages, and decided what's valuable, useful, and insightful to you and your business. And now, you're likely ready to move on and put your newfound knowledge to work.

So, this Epilogue's job is to remind you of what you have read, to point out areas you may have glossed over, summarize the views of Robert Passikoff, and relate them to what can make a difference in your world.

Fortunately, the Epilogue for this book is easier to write than many. The text provides answers to many of the questions I have been asking about marketing, communication, brands, and branding over the past 30 or so years. Questions about consumers, measurement, planning, forecasting, and all the other things that have become so important to brand marketers and senior managers alike.

Brands and branding have always been beset with one major problem: Their value exists in the future. (Unless, of course, you're going to sell the brand this afternoon.) Thus, true brand value is what revenue or value it can or will generate in the coming months and years. As Tim Ambler so aptly put it, "The value of the brand is the unrealized future revenue for the stakeholders."

The problem, of course, is that most of our research techniques are focused on calculating historical returns—what happened last month or last year or during a comparable decade. Interesting, but of relatively little value in terms of deciding how much to invest in a brand or what returns might be expected in the future. And let's face it, the value of all marketing and branding is based on tomorrow, not yesterday.

The difficulty in predicting the future is that we know so little about the variables, particularly customers and prospects. Thus, many organizations focus their efforts on the "outputs" of their branding programs, that is, the advertising, logos, packaging, and the like, because that's what they know the most about. They make the assumption that by tweaking those elements, they can influence customers and prospects. In very few instances, do marketers ever focus first on customers: understanding them, learning about them, and building programs and activities that customers want, not what the marketing people want. That's just too hard.

The major problem in learning about customers is the tools being used. They're simply out of date and don't provide the information the marketer wants and needs. Anyone who has even glanced through an article on the brain, neuroscience systems and processes, and the like in the past five years has to consider that most of our traditional concepts of how the brain works are diametrically opposed to how advertising, marketing, and, yes, branding are conducted. So, marketers rely on myths, old wives' tales, hopes, and dreams, not on scientific knowledge. Much of that is because the research techniques, many of which were developed more than 50 years ago, simply can't provide answers marketers and branders need today. Cognitive psychology, on which Robert's Brand Keys are based, is really the only current way to get underneath the conscious, top-of-mind answers that most research techniques generate. So, since we don't know customers, we guess. Sometimes right. Too often wrong.

As Robert so clearly points out, marketing success in the twenty-first century will be based on three key elements:

1. Research techniques that provide true consumer and customer knowledge and understanding.
2. A proven methodology that allows the marketer to relate those research learnings to actions and activities that are practical and possible for the marketer to employ.
3. A metric that enables the marketer to accurately estimate future consumer behaviors that can come as a result of branding efforts.

Those are the things I learned from reading *Predicting Market Success.*

Those are the tools I have acquired in understanding Robert's methodologies and approaches. Most of all, those are the answers I have been seeking for the past quarter century.

In this book, Robert Passikoff has finally connected the dots for marketers and branders. He's identified what makes consumers tick. He's developed a process to accurately predict what they will likely do in the future. He has provided a metric system that answers most of the questions senior managers have about the "dark and mysterious" world of brand and branding investments and measurement. But most of all, he has developed a method of connecting consumers to brands and brands to markets and markets to business success.

That's what I just read. I hope you got the same message.

DON E. SCHULTZ, PhD
Professor Emeritus-in-Service

Northwestern University
Spring 2006

INDEX

Aaker, David A. (Brand Leadership), 140
Abrap, Russell, 139
Absolut vodka, 1–2
Adams, Douglas, 201–202
Advertising:
  Brand-to-Media Engagement (B2ME)
    model, 12, 129–137, 225
  celebrities and, 190–193, 194
  DAGMAR (Defining Advertising Goals
    For Measured Advertising Results),
    65
  liking for an ad, and engagement and
    brand loyalty, 26
  Martha Stewart Living, defections from,
    129, 197
  Super Bowl, 187, 192
Advertising Research Foundation (ARF),
  Copy Research Validity Project, 31–32,
  66, 71, 105
Age, brands and, 50–53, 55, 204–205
AIDA (Attention, Interest, Desire, Action),
  65, 66
Airlines, 69, 99, 157, 216
Allen, Woody, 179
Amazon.com, 33–34, 35, 36, 86
Ambler, Tim, 234
American Express, 51, 115, 204, 226
American Girl Store, 49
Antibacterial coatings, 221
AOL, celebrity voice of, 179
Apologizing, 195
Apple Computer, 5, 29, 43, 47, 95
  iPods, 153, 220, 230
Apple record label, 47
Apprentice, The, Martha Stewart's, 17, 199

Aquetong Capital Advisors, 143
Arcadia University, 182
Armstrong, Lance, 185–186
Athletes, and drugs, 184–185
Atkins Nutritionals, Inc., 96–97, 214
AT&T, 23, 31, 56, 77
Attachments, Jung's theory of interpersonal,
  69–70
Attention deficit, audience, 130
Attributes, benefits, values (ABVs), 33–34,
  86, 211, 223
Avis, 100, 176

B2ME. *See* Brand-to-Media Engagement
  (B2ME) model
Baby Boomers, 38, 59, 204–205
Bad behavior, 183–190
Barbie dolls, 47–49
Bar charts, 17–18
Barnes & Noble, 33–37, 219
Baseball, 114–115, 185, 188, 218
Bernbach, Bill, 88, 91
Berra, Yogi, 146–147
Blair, Jayson, 200–201
BMW, 149, 183
Body Shop, The, 221
Bonding, 28, 32, 37–38, 70
Bonds, Barry, 185
Boyd, Gerald, 201
Brand:
  accountability, 25
  actions, and loyalty reactions, 202–203
  aging of, 55–56
  assessment questions, 11–12, 63, 67
  assets, 30

Brand *(Continued)*
  bonding, 70
  celebrities and, 179, 183–190
  connection conundrums, 129–130
  continuum, 177, 178, 180–183, 207
  crisis, 8–9
  culturing, 38
  DNA, 30, 38, 88–89
  equity, 9, 17, 30–31, 68, 86, 138
  image, 30, 86
  IQ, 38
  landscape, 215
  liking, 70
  logo, 44–47
  loyalty *(see* Loyalty; Loyalty metrics)
  multiple, 137–143, 213
  personality, 30
  portals for, 80–81
  premium, 173
  roots, 55
  valuation, 137–143, 233–234
  vision, and customer vision, 92
Brand Asset Valuator (BAV), 141
Branding:
  customer loyalty research tools,
     208–209
  emotional, 90–91
  future of, 207–226
  integrated marketing, 209–214
  postmodern, 90
Brand-to-Media Engagement (B2ME)
     model, 12, 129–137, 225
Brand-Scape, 38
Brooks Brothers, 204
Bruce, Thomas W., 182
Budget car rental, 100
Budweiser, celebrity voice of, 179
Buick, 191, 192, 204
Burger King, 123, 218

C(s):
  Six, 172
  Three, 2–4
Capitalization, 128
Card-based programs, 127–128
Car rental industry, 100, 157
Cast Away, 148

Categories:
  advertising awareness and, 133
  convenience as brand differentiator,
     99–100
  expectations gap increases in, 41–42
  loyalty drivers, category-by-category
     exposé, 152–167 *(see also* Loyalty
     drivers)
Category Ideal, 30, 70, 72–73, 113
Category Placeholders, 9, 42, 50, 181, 182,
     183, 217, 229
Causal-path analysis, 74
Celebrity(ies):
  borrowed versus built equity, 190–193
  brand endorsements, 190
  fragrances, 194
  Spokesperson, on continuum, 181
Central location tests (CLT), 113–114
Chanel No. 5, 191, 193
Children's books, 102–105
Chozick, Amy, 107
Chrysler, 10, 183
Class, in Six C's model, 172
Clinton, Bill, 194
Closure, 195
Coca-Cola, 20, 77, 123, 140, 143, 149, 182,
     222
Coffee and Doughnuts category, 8, 18,
     103–105, 224
Colley DAGMAR (Defining Advertising
     Goals For Measured Advertising
     Results), 65
Combs, Sean (P. Diddy/Puff Daddy), 177,
     189, 191, 192, 193, 204
Commodity-To-Human Brand Continuum,
     177, 178, 180–183, 207
Communication theory, 117–118
Commuters, and personal errands, 105
Company size, 62
Comparables, 139
Computers/web sites, and customization,
     216
Conjoint analysis, 74–75
Connery, Sean, 179
Continuity programs, 127–128
Continuum. *See* Commodity-To-Human
     Brand Continuum

Convenience, 39, 98–102, 128, 172
Copy Research Validity Project, 31–32, 71
Corporate reputation, in Six C's model, 172
Corporate responsibility and loyalty, 221
Cost-based valuation, 139
Costs, in Six C's model, 172
Creativity, 78–80
Credibility, in Six C's model, 172
Credit cards, 51–53, 115, 176, 204, 226
Customer/consumer(s):
  bonding, 28
  experience, and brand loyalty, 105–106
  listening to, 64–65
  losing/stealing, 171–172
  ratings, 86, 120, 133–134
  relevance, 94–96
  shifting values (*see* Value shifts)
  Three C's, 2–4
  vision, and brand vision, 92
Customer loyalty metrics. *See* Loyalty metrics
Customer relationship management (CRM),
  125–126
Customer service:
  silo perspective, 213
  in Six C's model, 172
Customization/personalization, 215–216

DAGMAR (Defining Advertising Goals For
  Measured Advertising Results), 65
Darwinism, 64, 88–89
Death, brand, 182–183, 189
Delight turning to expectation, 40, 43,
  176–177
De Niro, Robert, 204
Department of Transportation (DOT), 105
Designer celebrities, 177–178
Designer Label, on continuum, 181
Desk research, 73
Diesel jeans, 43, 90–91
Differentiation, 78, 92–96, 98–102
Discount Retailer category, 6–7
Discover Card, 176
Disengagement, 215
Disney World, 218
Domino's, 42
Donahue, Phil, 187
Drivers. *See* Loyalty drivers

Drucker, Peter, 15
Drugs, 187–188
Dunkin' Donuts, 8, 103–105
Duracell, celebrity voice of, 179

"Earning a Place at the Table," 16
Ebenkamp, Becky, 85, 86
E-commerce, value drivers, 34–36
Economic Darwinism, 64, 88–89
Economic use model, 139–140
Electronic polling, 123–125
E-mail research questionnaires, 123–125
Emotional bonding. *See* Bonding
Emotional Brand Asset Identifier (EBAI),
  38
Emotional branding, 90–91
Emotional measures, 36–38
Endorsers, 184
Engagement, customer, 3–4
Enron, 119, 184, 194
Enterprise car rental, 100
Entertainers, 177
Entertainment:
  information and, 219
  value shifts in, 39
Ethnographic research, 23–24
Expectations:
  age-based, 50–53
  changing, 49–50
  delight turning to, 40, 43, 176–177
  experiential, 43–44
  gap between delivery and, 40–43,
    152–153
  increase in, 215
  Three C's, 2–4
  tracking/measuring, 76, 96–98

Factor analysis, 74
Fads, 96–98
Fahrenheit 9/11, 83–85
Failure rate, new product launches, 28, 229
Failures of research (specific products), 31,
  77, 81–82
Fashion brands, 177–178, 183, 203
Federal Express, 148
Finance silo perspective, 213
Fine, Jon, 13

First Ladies, 202–203
Fixtures, bathroom/kitchen,
    133–135
Focus groups, 121–123
Fogging prevention, 221
Food shopping, convenience, 99
Ford, 10, 149, 183
Ford, Tom, 177
Founder, on continuum, 181
Four P's, 1–9, 59
Fragrances, celebrity-branded, 192, 193
Frost, Robert, 98, 100

Gaffney, John, 105
Gambling, 188, 218
Gangsta Brand, 182
Gap, The, 178, 182
Gender bias, 188, 189
General Motors, 9–12, 63, 65, 141–142,
    182, 183
Gen Xers/XBoxers, 59, 204
Giambi, Jason, 185
Gifford, Kathy Lee, 189
Gillette, 95
Gladwell, Malcolm (*The Tipping Point* and
    Blink), 8
Glaser, Garrett, 106
Gobé, Marc, 91
Goizueta, Roberto, 143
Good Morning America, 42
Google, 4, 71, 182
"Got milk?," 177
Groups and brands, 107–108

Hanover, Dan, 148
Harry Potter series, 102–105
Hawthorne effect, 121
Health value shifts, 39, 214
Hierarchy-of-effects hypothesis (Lavidge
    and Steiner), 65
Hilfiger, Tommy, 177, 189, 204
Hilton, Paris, 193
Hispanic marketing, 93–94
Honda, celebrity voice of, 179
Hotels:
    chocolates on pillow, 40
    convenience, 99

Howard, Theresa, 26, 149, 150
Human Brands, 178, 180, 182, 184,
    194–200

IBM, 118–119, 140
Ideal, Category, 30, 70, 72–73, 113
Ideal President, 169
Ideas, versus procedures, 176
Image, value shifts in, 39
Information access, real-time, 217
Innovation, 80, 89–90, 95
Integrated Marketing (IM), 209–214
Intel Inside, 220
Interbrand, 139, 140
Internet:
    blogs, 66
    e-commerce value drivers, 34–36, 99
    New Yorker cartoon about, 124–125
    online interviewing, 123
    spam e-mail research, 123–125
    web sites, and customization, 216
iPods, 153, 220, 230

Jackson, Michael, 177
JCPenney, 6
Jolie, Angelina, 219
Jordan, Michael, 178, 182
Jung, Carl, 69–70

Keller, Kevin, 141
Kennedy, John F., 167–171, 233
KeySpan Energy, 144–146
Kia, 89
Kidman, Nicole, 191, 193
Kissinger, Henry, 190
Klein, Calvin, 177, 189, 194
Kmart, 6, 7, 126–127
Kraft, 96
Krispy Kreme, 18, 103, 224

Labels, 181, 182, 183
Lambertville Trading Company, 5, 11
Las Vegas, 218
Latinos, 93–94
Launches:
    failure rate, 28, 229
    finding fit prior to, 29–30

Lauren, Ralph, 189, 194, 204
Lay, Kenneth L., 119
Lelyveld, Joseph, 201
Level 3 Communications, celebrity voice of, 179
Levi's, 91
Life, customers for, 92–96, 172
Life cereal, 93
Locks/keys, 69–70
Logos, 44–47, 183
Low-carbohydrate craze, 95, 96–98, 214
Lowe's, celebrity voice of, 179
Loyalty:
    brand versus store, 108–109
    crisis, 8–9
    defining, 13, 62
    evolution of, 86
    length of, 148
    repolishing tarnished, 203–204
Loyalty cards/programs, 127–128
Loyalty drivers:
    in bar charts, 17–18, 26
    category-by-category 2004/2006
        comparisons, 152–167
    e-commerce, 34–36
    saturation points, 215
    shifting, 117, 152–167
    weighted average, 17–18
Loyalty metrics:
    basics, 25–26, 67, 112–113
    Brand Keys approach, 21, 69–77, 90, 91
    creating category and customer attributes,
        benefits, and values (ABVs), 73–77
    Customer Loyalty Index, 34–36, 40, 93, 143
    identifying Category Ideal, 72–73
    measuring campaign effectiveness, 225
    methodological framework, 72–77
    optimizing with, 128–129
    versus other futurist systems, 222–223
    overlaying on other measures, 112
    overview/introduction to, 1–13
    politics of brand expansion and, 77–80
    predictive research, 6, 9, 15–26, 79,
        91–92, 223–224
    questionnaire, 32, 70–71, 113–117, 122
    theoretical framework, 69–71

versus traditional marketing research, 6,
    12–13, 15–18, 20–22, 231
what to measure, 65–66

Madden, Chris, 198
Madden, Steve, 182, 189
Madore, James, 203
Marketing research:
    branding efforts, 80–82
    Brand Keys approach (see Loyalty metrics)
    creativity and, 78–80
    meaningless questions, 63
    measurement and tracking systems, 65–66
    nontransactional behavior, 66–69
    politics of brand expansion and, 77–80
    secondary, 73
    traditional, 6, 12–13, 15–18, 20–22, 231
Marketing ROI, 224–225
Martha Stewart Omnimedia. See Stewart,
    Martha
Maslow, Abraham, 23
McDonald's:
    Arch Deluxe, 31, 77, 78, 79, 81
    competition, 123, 218
    employee uniforms, 53–54
    health/nutrition, 221
McNeely, Pam, 197
Media:
    aligning brand values with, 149–150
    Brand-to-Media Engagement (B2ME)
        model, 12, 129–137, 225
    ecology, value shifts in, 39
Mercedes Benz, 183
Message versus product, 100–101
Metrics. See Loyalty metrics
Miller Brewing Company, 18–19
Millward Brown, 102
Mobile phone providers, 41–42, 69
Mobil Speedpass, 128, 176
Moore, Michael, 83–85
Moss, Kate, 204
Movie industry:
    Fahrenheit 9/11, 83–84
    product placement, 148–149
MPG example, 76
Mucha, Thomas, 148
Music distribution, 219–220

Namath, Joe, 177
Nanotechnology, 220–221
National Football League (NFL), 187
Neuburger, Karen, 142–143, 198
New Balance, 176
Newman, Paul, 178, 179
New Yorker cartoon, 124–125
New York Times scandals, 200–202
Nike, 189
9/11 terrorist attacks, 82–83
Nontransactional behavior, 66–69
Notoriety, 182

Older brands and trust, 55–56
Olympics, 132–133, 185
Omnimedia. See Stewart, Martha
Open sourcing loyalty metrics, 152–167
Oppenheimer Funds, celebrity voice of,
    179
Optimization, 122–123, 128–129, 226,
    231
Order of questions, 117–118
Oreo Cookies, 56
Ostroff, Jim, 108, 109
Overchoice, 229

P(s), Four, 1–9, 59
Panasonic shavers, celebrity voice of, 179
Papa John's, 42
Parker, Sarah Jessica, 178
Patrick, Sharon, 199
P. Diddy. See Combs, Sean (P. Diddy/
    Puff Daddy)
Pepsi, 20, 96, 123, 140, 191, 192, 193
Personal space, value shifts in, 39
Pets.com, 17
Pizza category, 42
Pizza Hut, celebrity voice of, 179
Plummer, Joe, 66
Point programs, 127–128
Political candidates/parties, 168–171
Polk (R. L.) press release, 141
Polling, 113–116, 123
Pontiac, 183
Positioning, 92–96
Potter series, 102–105
Premium brands, alchemy of, 173

Premium pricing, 139
Presidents:
    drivers, 169–171
    First Ladies, 202–203
    Kennedy as brand, 167–171
Price/pricing, 7, 17, 62, 66–67, 102,
    139
Process Re-Engineering, 3
Product:
    features, 74
    innovation, 80, 89–90, 95
    placement on TV shows or movies,
        148–149
Psychological questionnaire. See
    Questionnaire design
Puck, Wolfgang, 178

Questioning consumers:
    asking right questions, 58–60
    asking right way, 60–64, 115–116
    order of questions, 117–118
    pitfalls of relying on direct Q&A, 70
Questionnaire design, 32, 70–71, 113–117,
    122

Raines, Howell, 201
Ratings, consumer, 86, 120, 133–134
Razors, 95, 179
R&D silo perspective, 212, 213
Relevance, importance of, 94–96
Research. See Loyalty metrics; Marketing
    research
Restaurants, convenience, 99
Retailers:
    convenience, 99
    Top 10 Rules for, 109
Retrofitting for the future, 43
Return on equity (ROE) and brand equity,
    68, 142, 225
Return on investment (ROI), marketing,
    224–225
Rivera, Geraldo, 187
Roberts, Julia, 179
Roberts, Roxanne, 86
Roddick, Anita, 221
Rogers, Will, 111
Rose, Pete, 188

Rove, Karl, 84
Ryan, Nolan, 188

Safety, value shifts in, 39
Sales, predicting, 224
Sanyo, 28–29
Satisfaction surveys, 118–121
Saturation point, 215
Schick, 95
Schultz, Don, 210, 211, 235
Schultz, Howard, 152
Sears, 100
Secondary research, 73
Security, value shifts in, 39
Segmentation, 37
Seinfeld, 148
Sex discrimination suit against Wal-Mart, 188
Sheffield, Gary, 185
Silo perspectives, 210, 212
Six C's, 172
Size, company, 62
Skenazy, Lenore, 55, 221
Smith, B., 178
Snapple, 148
Social interaction, value shifts in, 39
Social responsibility and customer loyalty, 106–107
Sole proprietors, 74
Sommers, Suzanne, 214
Spam e-mail questionnaires, 123–125
Specialty Brand, 182
Specialty Category Brand, 181
Speedpass, Mobil, 128, 176
Spokespeople, 184, 188–190, 204–205
Sports:
    drugs and, 184–185
    economic competition in, 218
    gambling on, 188
    National Football League (NFL), 187
    sponsorships, 143–148
    Yankee Stadium signage, 114–115
Sprewell, Latrel, 187
Sprint, 176
Starbucks, 4, 42, 103–105, 152
Stealing loyalty, 172
Steib, Michael, 97
Stein, Gertrude, 175

Stengel, Jim, 210
Steroids, 185, 187
Stewart, Martha, 194–200
    advertiser/reader defections, *Martha Stewart Living,* 129, 197
    Apprentice, The, 17, 199
    brand equity history, 195–197
    as Human Brand, 178, 180, 182, 184, 194–200
    lessons learned, 195–196
    loyalty metrics and, 20, 22, 197–198
    negative perceptions, impact of, 188, 189, 194–200, 203
Stored Value Systems, 127–128
Strategic alignment, 112
Sulzberger, Arthur O., Jr., 200
Super Bowl, 187, 192

Target discount store, 6, 7
Tarnished loyalty, repolishing, 203–204
Technology:
    customization and, 216
    differentiation and, 217
    nanotechnology, 220–221
    value shifts in, 39
Teflon, 220
Telecommunication services, 16–17
Television:
    Apprentice, The, Martha Stewart's, 17, 199
    mini/wristwatch, 95, 217
    morning news/entertainment shows, 42
    product placement, 148–149
    TiVo, 64, 123, 230
    West Wing, The, 171
    Yes, Prime Minister, 60–61
Terrorism, 82–83
Time to market, 220
Tipping points, 8, 214
Torabi, Farnoosh, 202
Total Enterprise Value (TEV), 143
Total Quality Management (TQM), 3, 66
Tour de France, 186
Toyota, 4, 67, 71, 182, 183
Trade Character, on continuum, 181
Trademark protection, 140
Trends/trend watchers, 24, 214–215
Trout, Jack, 78, 100

Trump, Donald, 178, 184, 193
Trust, value shifts in, 39
Turlington, Christie, 214
Twenty-First-Century Brand, on continuum, 181

Unilever, 96
UPS, 42
Utilities, as commodity, 176

Vacations, family, 218
Valuation, cost-based, 139
Value drivers. *See* Loyalty drivers
Value infusion/added-value, 40
Value language of customers, 64–65
Value shifts:
  category-by-category 2004/2006 comparisons, 152–167
  early warning system for, 214
  pace of, 117, 229–230
  then-and-now comparisons, specific products, 39
Verizon, celebrity voice of, 179
Versace, 204
Vetner, Craig, 89

Viagra, 186
Violence, in-game, 187
Voices of celebrities, brands associated with, 179
Volvo, 183

Wal-Mart, 6, 7, 100, 188
Wanamaker, John, 129
Warhol, Andy, 183
"Warp-o-matic" illustration, 38
Web sites, and customization, 216
West Wing, The, 171
What-ifs, 230–231
White, Roderick, 25
White, Theodore H. (*The Making of the President*), 167
Woods, Tiger, 191, 192, 204
Word of Mouth, 217

Yankee Stadium, signage in, 114–115
Yardstick, Category Ideal, 30, 70, 72–73, 113
Yes, Prime Minister, 60–61
Young & Rubicam, 141
Youth brands, 55